W9-DAT-694

INTEGRATED HEALTH CARE:

Reorganizing the Physician, Hospital and Health Plan Relationship

by

Dean C. Coddington, Keith D. Moore and Elizabeth A. Fischer

Center for Research in Ambulatory Health Care Administration
Englewood, Colorado

Center for Research in Ambulatory Health Care Administration (CRAHCA) publications are intended to provide current and accurate information and are designed to assist readers in becoming more familiar with the subject matter covered. CRAHCA published *Integrated Health Care: Reorganizing the Physician, Hospital and Health Plan Relationship* for a general audience. Such publications are distributed with the understanding that CRAHCA does not render any legal, accounting or other professional advice that may be construed as specifically applicable to individual situations. No representations or warranties are made concerning the application of legal or other principles discussed by the authors to any specific fact situation, nor is any prediction made concerning how any particular judge, government official or other person who will interpret or apply such principles. Specific factual situations should be discussed with professional advisers.

ISBN 1-56829-003-9

In Memoriam

John Hershberger, John Oswald and Larry Meierotto

Three good friends, each of whom passed away in 1993, and each of whom showed a stubborn adherence to quality, objectivity and innovation — the kind of commitment required to foster real change.

TABLE OF CONTENTS

ACKNOWLEDGEMENTS

The preparation of this book was truly a team effort. Experiences and insights from the 10 organizations that participated in the case study research process were invaluable. Members of our advisory committee made numerous worthy contributions, from commenting on specific chapters in their early stages to providing data to reviewing the entire manuscript. The staff at Medical Group Management Association (MGMA) and the Center for Research in Ambulatory Health Care Administration (CRAHCA) were tremendously helpful. Other individuals helped by reacting to our ideas and research findings. Meanwhile, our own support staff and colleagues at Browne, Bortz & Coddington, Inc. (BBC) worked diligently to make this book possible.

Case Study Organizations and Key Persons

Key individuals within each of the 10 case study organizations are identified below. We are indebted to each of these persons, whom we now view as friends, for their willingness to participate in this process and for their whole-hearted support.

(1) Presbyterian Healthcare Services, Albuquerque, New Mexico

Andrew Horvath, MD, Chairman Presbyterian Network

(2) Fargo Clinic/St. Luke's Hospital, Fargo, North Dakota

Lloyd Smith, President and CEO, St. Luke's, and John Paulsen, FACMPE, Executive Administrator, Fargo Clinic

(3) Marshfield Clinic/St. Joseph's Hospital, Marshfield, Wisconsin

Fritz Wenzel, FACMPE, Advisor to the President, Marshfield Clinic

(4) Carle Clinic/Carle Foundation Hospital, Urbana, Illinois

Kenneth Bash, FACMPE, CEO, Carle Clinic Association, P.C.

(5) Sutter Health, Sacramento, Cal. (including Sac Sierra)

Gary Susnara, Senior Vice President, Systems Development

(6) UniHealth America, Los Angeles, Cal.

Ben Snyder, FACMPE, Executive Vice President

(7) Oregon Medical Group/Sacred   Jim Schwering, CEO,
    Heart Health System, Eugene, OR Oregon Medical Group

(8) Geisinger System,   F. Kenneth Ackerman, Jr.,
    Danville, Pennsylvania   FACMPE, Senior Vice President
                                    Operations, Central Region

(9) Kaiser Permanente/Saint Joseph Chris Binkley, Vice President
    Hospital, Denver, Colorado   and Regional Manager, Kaiser
                                    Permanente, and Sister Mari-
                                    anna Bauder, CEO, Saint Joseph
                                    Hospital

(10) Montana Associated Physicians, Larry McGovern, Executive
     Inc./Saint Vincent Hospital,   Director, MAPI, and James
     Billings, Montana   Paquette, President and
                                    CEO, Saint Vincent Hospital

(Case studies have been published in a separate volume, *Integrated Health Care: Case Studies*, available through CRAHCA.)

In addition to these individuals, we are especially appreciative of the numerous persons within each case study organization who provided data or participated in interviews. It is no overstatement to say that this book would not have been possible without the cooperation of the more than 100 physicians, administrators, board members and others who participated in this research process.

Advisory Committee

In our prior research efforts leading to the publication of two previous books, we have relied on a number of individuals to help us understand health care industry trends, and who have acted as a sounding board for our ideas and research findings. Members of the advisory committee and their special contributions were:

- *Monte Dube, JD.* Monte is a health care attorney with the Chicago office of McDermott, Will & Emery. He has served as legal adviser to hospitals and physician groups developing integrated systems. He speaks and writes often on the topic of physician-hospital integration.

- *Richard Hoerl, PhD.* Dick is a partner in Hoerl & Associates, management consultants and a frequent speaker and facilitator with medical group practices and hospital boards. He has been heavily involved in mergers of medical group practices, the formation of physician-hospital organizations and the analysis of corporate cultures.

- *Donald E. L. Johnson.* Don is the founder and president of The Business Word, Inc., a Denver-based publishing company that focuses on the health care industry. A former editor and publisher of *Modern Healthcare,* Don is editor of *Health Care Strategic Management.* His firm writes and edits the Marion Merrell Dow Inc. *Managed Care Digests* and Wyeth-Ayerst *Compendium of Hospital Economics.* In these capacities he has covered hospital and physician collaboration and integration. Don has been especially supportive of our previous publishing efforts and was a valued counselor during many phases of the preparation of this book.

- *Keith M. Korenchuk, JD.* An attorney with Parker Poe Adams & Bernstein in Charlotte, North Carolina, Keith specializes in working with physician group practices with emphasis on mergers and the formation of physician-hospital organizations (PHOs). His book, *Transforming the Delivery of Health Care: Mergers, Acquisitions and Physician-Hospital Organizations,* was valuable to us, especially in preparing Chapter 13, which deals with specific steps in moving ahead with the formation of a physician-hospital organization.

- *John F. Koster, MD.* John is a Vice President at Voluntary Hospitals of America and was recently Vice President of Network Development, Presbyterian Healthcare Services in Albuquerque. He is a frequent speaker at conferences on physician-hospital integration, and a leader in the field.

- *James R. Ludwig.* Jim is Sales and Marketing Director for Kaiser Permanente in Colorado, and formerly Executive Director of the Ochsner Health Plan in New Orleans, Louisiana. He was especially helpful in commenting on the relationship between health plan marketing and primary care development.

- *Lowell E. Palmquist.* Lowell is Senior Vice President, VHA Eastern Division in Washington, DC. A former hospital administrator and long-time friend of the authors, Lowell brought useful insights into the process of preparing this manuscript.

- *Janet Reich.* Janet is a registered nurse and health care consultant, and a leader in the Hospital Affiliated Practices Society (HAPS) of MGMA. She encouraged us to publish this research through the auspices of CRAHCA and was a continuing source of guidance throughout the process. We very much appreciate her interest and dedication to the concept of physicians and hospitals working together in new and different ways.

- *Ellen E. Stewart, JD.* Ellen, a long-time friend of the authors, is a health care attorney with the Denver firm of Gorsuch, Kirgis, Campbell, Walker & Grover. Ellen offered advice on the summary of legal issues facing organizations considering physician-hospital integration in Chapter 2.

- *Leigh Truitt, MD.* Leigh is an internist and head of an internal medicine group practice in the south Denver Area. In 1993 he was president of the Colorado Medical Society. He has had personal experience in organizing a variety of physician and hospital networks and joint ventures and has always been willing to share his thoughts on numerous health care issues.

- *Donald A. Wilson.* Don is President of the Kansas Hospital Association, and a supporter of the hospital industry. His organization, along with others, sponsored BBC's research into the factors driving health care costs.

MGMA and CRAHCA

We especially appreciated the support of Steven S. Lazarus, PhD. Steve, Associate Executive Director of MGMA and CRAHCA, worked closely with us in all phases of the research leading up to preparation of the manuscript and was especially helpful in encouraging organizations to participate in the case study process.

Anna Bergström, MSHA, Research Director of CRAHCA, supported Steve in this effort. We have always enjoyed working with Anna and are thankful for her contributions to this book. Lisa Pieper, Administrative Assistant in CRAHCA, reviewed the case studies and made many helpful suggestions.

Jeanine Barlow, MPH, CRAHCA Project Director, provided valuable insights and assistance in the publicity activities of the publication.

Within the MGMA Library, Barbara Hamilton, Library Resource Center Director; Donna Keslin, Assistant Library Resource Center Director; and Cynthia Kiyotake, Librarian, provided continuous support throughout the data collection stage. We found the MGMA Library to be an invaluable resource and we appreciate the research efforts of the staff.

Fred Graham, PhD, FACMPE, Senior Associate Executive Director and Dennis Barnhardt, Communications Director, two long-time friends on the staff of MGMA, participated in the initial discussions of this book and were supportive of this effort throughout the research and writing process. We very much value their friendship and support.

Mary Alice Krill, PhD, FACMPE, former Administrative Director and Director of Research of CRAHCA, provided invaluable editorial assistance. We very much appreciated her willingness to review the manuscript and offer numerous useful suggestions.

Kenneth Smith, FACMPE, Chair of the MGMA Research Committee reviewed the draft and provided valuable insights from the medical group practice field.

BBC and Others

Barbara J. Bendrick served as research associate for this project. Barbara's work was invaluable — collecting basic information on the growing number of physician-hospital organizations, reviewing the literature, listening to tapes of conferences on integrated delivery systems, checking references and obtaining permissions to publish case studies and other quotes, preparing the bibliography, and performing a myriad of other tasks involved in producing a book of this type. Barbara joined BBC in 1992, following completion of the MBA program at the University of Florida and has been involved in a number of health care assignments, including development of a physician-hospital organization and the merger of a medical group and hospital. She was truly the backbone of this undertaking.

David J. Keen, a BBC Managing Director, and a co-author of *The Crisis in Health Care: Costs, Choices and Strategies,* reviewed the entire manuscript and made numerous helpful suggestions. We appreciated his support throughout this endeavor. Joni Toenjes, a BBC senior associate who has participated in a number of projects involving the merger of medical group practices and the formation of physician-hospital organizations, was a valued resource person.

The administrative support staff provided a tremendous amount of help in preparing this book. Lynn Cook worked closely with the administrative assistants of many of the individuals in the case study organizations in arranging for field trips and follow-up approvals of the case studies. Rhonda Wyn and Kari Weiland, BBC's word processing staff, typed numerous drafts of the manuscript and case studies. Susan Pietri prepared the graphics.

Jim Hertel, President of HealthCare Computer Corporation of America, assisted us in addressing HMO issues in Chapter 6. Jim is a former president of an HMO, and a consultant to managed care organizations; we greatly appreciated his help. John Glassman, formerly with Stormont-Vail Medical Center in Topeka, Kansas, and a sub-contractor with BBC in 1992, reviewed various drafts and provided many useful comments and suggestions.

ABOUT THE AUTHORS

Dean C. Coddington is a founder of BBC Research & Consulting located in Denver, Colorado. He received his BS degree (1954) from South Dakota State University in civil engineering and his MBA degree (1959) from the Harvard Business School.

Coddington has written numerous articles, including four published in the *Harvard Business Review*. He is co-author of two previous books: *Market-Driven Strategies in Health Care* (1987) and *The Crisis in Health Care: Costs, Choices and Strategies* (1990). His research and consulting focuses on the factors driving health care costs, market research, economic feasibility studies and strategic planning for health care organizations.

From 1959 to 1970, Coddington worked as a research economist with the University of Denver's Research Institute. He is also past chairman of the board of trustees of Swedish Medical Center, Englewood, Colorado.

Keith D. Moore is a managing director of BBC, which he joined in 1982. He received his BA degree (1968) from the University of Texas in economics and his MA degree (1973) from Harvard University in city planning.

Moore's current consulting assignments include a number of projects involving the merger of medical practices, the merger of a medical group and a hospital and development of physician-hospital organizations. He has published several articles on health care subjects and is co-author of the two previous books mentioned above. He is a frequent facilitator at physician planning retreats and has worked with a large number of organizations in developing strategic plans.

Between 1969 and 1975, Moore was a senior consultant with a Denver-based consulting firm, a teaching assistant at Harvard University, and a US Marine platoon leader in Vietnam. From 1975 to 1981, he was head of the Industrial Economics and Management Division of the University of Denver's Research Institute, where he was responsible for research into technology transfer, R&D management, corporate planning, energy and resource economics and governmental management strategies. He is a past board member of Spalding Rehabilitation Hospital in Denver.

Elizabeth A. Fischer, also a BBC managing director, joined the firm in 1983. She has an AB degree (1981) in American studies and economics from Mount Holyoke College, and a masters degree (1983) in city and regional planning from Harvard University.

Fischer specializes in research and consulting in rural health care, long-term care, strategic planning and in physician-hospital relationships. Her experience includes the formation of health networks and the mergers of medical group practices. She has also conducted numerous market and financial feasibility assessments for health care clients regarding the development of new programs and services. Since joining BBC, she has completed over 50 assignments for health care organizations. She is a frequent presenter at professional meetings of various health care industry groups.

Prior to joining BBC, Fischer was an assistant planner for the City of Everett, Massachusetts where she coordinated a downtown revitalization program.

BBC Research & Consulting was established in 1970 to provide economic and policy analysis to clients in a variety of industries. BBC's health care practice focuses on strategic planning, financial feasibility assessments and market analyses for hospitals, medical groups and health plans throughout the country.

ABOUT THE CENTER FOR RESEARCH IN AMBULATORY HEALTH CARE ADMINISTRATION AND THE MEDICAL GROUP MANAGEMENT ASSOCIATION

The Center for Research in Ambulatory Health Care Administration (CRAHCA), established in 1973, is a section 501(c)(3) tax-exempt charitable organization as defined by the Internal Revenue Code. The purpose of CRAHCA is to improve ambulatory health care in general and group practice in particular through better administration. Its work focuses on new and innovative publications; education, research, and data services; and demonstration programs. The Center for Research in Ambulatory Health Care Administration is the research arm of the Medical Group Management Association (MGMA).

Founded in 1926, the Medical Group Management Association today comprises over 14,700 members and 5,900 medical groups involving about 111,000 physicians. It is the oldest and largest membership organization representing group practice administration. MGMA serves its individual and organizational members and their patients, and promotes the group practice of medicine as an effective form of health care delivery.

The relationships between medical groups, hospitals, and health plans are an important area of interest to CRAHCA. The more integrated the relationships among the three "legs of the stool", the greater the challenge is for CRAHCA to study ambulatory care in the new evolving organizational relationships in which physicians and group practices play an important role. These changes are posing significant challenges to CRAHCA and MGMA to change definitions as the environment is changing and to refocus its research agenda to meet the needs of these integrating organizations. In addition, CRAHCA has a mission to educate the ambulatory health care community on the changing environments.

To meet both of these objectives, CRAHCA is pleased to publish the book *Integrated Health Care: Reorganizing the Physician, Hospital, and Health Plan Relationship* as a very important and timely piece of work. Funding was provided from the CRAHCA Research and Development Fund. These funds were utilized to support the site visits and other data collection efforts of the authors, and in providing additional resources to them to analyze their findings, adding significantly to the value of this book.

We want to thank the organizations that shared their experience with the authors. They did this understanding the importance of sharing their learning experiences with the health care community, in general, and the MGMA membership in particular. It was important to focus the research on operating integrated health care systems as opposed to those that are in the nascent stages. The reader thus gets a perspective on the sets of circumstances and conditions important to an integrated organization.

We would like to thank the authors for taking the initiative to develop the idea for this text and for their interest and willingness in working with CRAHCA to publish it.

FOREWORD

For some of us, weaving together physicians, hospitals, ambulatory care, home health, nursing homes, management and the ability to insure enrolled populations is not new. We have spent decades building such systems and have demonstrated their impact on quality and costs. And we have seen first hand their unique power to stimulate innovation and learning.

In the past decade, under growing pressures from purchasers to control costs and document quality, many others in health care have begun to experiment with alternative approaches to integration. Now, a wide array of models can be found that link providers of care, economic incentives and enrolled populations. And, by shifting large populations of employees into integrated care environments, purchasers have sent strong signals that they value and will reward those who deliver care in such systems.

As a consequence, the historically fragmented American health care system is being transformed. In several parts of the country, integrated systems dominate health care delivery. Systems throughout the country are far from integrated; just over half the insured population of the country received their care in some form of managed care in 1992. However, the success of integrated systems in addressing quality and in managing costs, and their ability to create professional and patient care environments that stimulate innovation and learning, have sent a clear signal that more traditional forms of care have outlived their usefulness.

How do integrated systems achieve their impact? From the patient's perspective, the answer lies in seamlessness. In the ideal, the patient experiences an uninterrupted journey through the bewildering array of doctors, nurses, other health professionals, laboratories, imaging units, hospital care, nursing home care and home health care that characterizes today's complex medical care. Physicians have the information, support services, and financial incentives necessary to provide a strong, consistent focus on the problems of the individual seeking care. It is not the patient who must integrate the health care system, nor the primary care physician who must arrange it. Rather, when integration has been properly designed, the patient's experience is characterized by the right care being provided in the right place at the right time each time. The critically important relationship between doctor and patient is maintained and supported, but it develops within a context of specialists, diagnostic and treatment modalities, support functions, and financing all organized to provide care effectively (quality results) and efficiently (use of resources).

From an organizational point of view, the value of integration is even more readily apparent. The delivery of health care involves the blending of myriad systems necessary to support the unique act of patient care. The systems — financial, business, appointment making, laboratory, imaging, admissions, discharge, provision of prescriptions, and on and on — number in the thousands. Traditionally, they exist in isolation. One system may function well for what it is supposed to do, but may or may not integrate with or support other systems. A doctor in solo practice may have an excellent laboratory for routine tests, but the information obtained for a patient may not get to the hospital, or the referral specialist, or the emergency room, when needed. As systems are blended, coordinated and integrated, they become complementary. Simplification, ease of use for patients and providers alike, and reduction in waste and redundancy become possible. As those in other industries have demonstrated, these qualities are powerful tools for improving effectiveness and reducing costs.

In addition, integrated systems permit the exploration and gradual reduction of unnecessary differences in clinical practice among physicians and other professionals. As Wennberg and others have documented, variation in clinical practice contributes substantially to the spiraling costs of care and the uneven quality and outcomes that occur in American medicine. Clinicians, working together to examine episodes of illness, can determine what works best, where to provide the care, in what settings and with what professionals. Together, they plan their patients' care based on the best scientific information and the results of their own work that documents favorable clinical outcomes and cost effectiveness.

Tracking the impact of care, both on their patients and on the health status of the populations enrolled in their plans, provides the basis for the development of a science of population-based health care. This element has been a significant omission in most health care delivery for much of this century. Marrying such information with data on costs permits clinicians to make informed choices among alternative clinical approaches; such a decision is then based on an understanding of how to produce the best outcomes most efficiently.

In their definitive study of organizations that are working to integrate care, the authors of *Integrated Health Care: Reorganizing the*

Physician, Hospital and Health Plan Relationship, provide a rich description of the abundant experimentation under way in the United States. This is a much needed book. As significant health care reform occurs, the movement to integration will accelerate. Public policy makers and purchasers appear to have coalesced in support of integrated health care delivery. Developing a deeper understanding of how integrating organizations work, what elements have been incorporated into such systems and how they are managed and governed, is necessary background for anyone considering building or modifying such organizations, purchasing care or creating the legislative framework for health care reform itself.

The authors describe the complexity of integrated health care. Such systems are not simple to create. Nor are they easily managed. One cannot assume they will work well. Some certainly do not. Anyone involved in such systems knows there will always be ways to improve, to modify and to respond more effectively to patients and purchasers alike.

By analyzing the integration experiences of selected organizations, and bringing to that analysis the benefit of their considerable experience with the health care delivery system, the authors have made a significant contribution to the understanding of where such organizations fit into the health care system of the future. Those of us already involved in creating and managing integrated systems can learn from one another's efforts; those who wish to begin the journey now have a more solid, more carefully examined basis on which to build.

David M. Lawrence, MD
Chairman and Chief Executive Officer
Kaiser Permanente
Oakland, California

PREFACE

It is Thursday night. Two focus group interviews with patients are being held. The room is filled with internal medicine patients from a large group practice. A moderator leads a discussion of how patients were attracted to the group, what they liked and disliked about their care and what changes they would recommend. The patients are generally pleased with the services they received, and many express gratitude towards a particular physician or nurse. But there are some problems.

At lunch the following Monday, the videotape of the focus group is played for the office staff. There is time to enjoy the positive comments and words of gratitude expressed by several patients. Then, it is time to deal with the problems. Changes are discussed and the group agrees on a new way to handle "drop in" patients (patients not scheduled at least one day in advance). Changes are also made in how staff communicate with patients while they are in the waiting room.

Later that same day, the group practice administrator, a health plan manager and three hospital associate administrators discuss how to improve the patient flow for gastroenterology outpatients. There is also an inpatient nursing personnel problem that needs resolution.

On Wednesday morning, less than a week after the focus groups, the videotapes are played for a group of physicians. Several changes in scheduling are discussed and implemented. Whether involving physicians, hospitals, office staff or the health plan, most of the identified changes are implemented within two weeks.

One week later, the "Change Committee," a group of senior physicians, practice administrators and hospital and health plan managers, discuss how some of the lessons learned from the tape might be applied elsewhere within this integrated health care system.

A month later, it appears that approximately 30 changes have been implemented as a result of discussions that began with the focus groups. Three of the changes should improve future medical outcomes, 15 relate to better patient service, five look like they will lead to lower costs and the remainder made the workplace function more smoothly for employees.

Is this the year 2000? No, this happened in 1992. Is this an isolated incident? No, a series of events leading to changes in the way health care is delivered occur every month or so in this integrated health care system. A few of the changes are major; most are minor. What impresses the outside observer, however, is not the impact of any one change, but rather the relentless, cumulative pace of change and improvement in this integrated system.

The Power of Integrated Health Care

This book is about integrated health care — the process of physicians, hospitals and health plans coming together into new types of organizational relationships. Like the example above, the most successful health care systems are those in which two traditional adversaries — physicians and hospitals — are learning to function in ways that would have been unthinkable even in the early 1990s. Today's leaders in health care integration are going still farther and adding a third traditional adversary to the family — health plans.

There are several good reasons to form or participate in an integrated system today. One reason is that under many likely scenarios of health care payment reform, integrated health care systems would be required. The concept of "managed competition," for example, envisions competition among integrated systems organized around Accountable Health Plans (AHPs). In lieu of health care reform, many employers are pushing their local health care providers toward integrated systems. In discussion after discussion across the country, physicians and hospitals are making the argument, "How can we not get involved in an integrated system? This is going to happen. To be involved is to have a seat at the table in deciding our future. To not be involved is to let someone else decide our future for us."

There is, however, a far more powerful reason for pursuing integration in health care: it works. Integrated systems often times are more flexible and thus can adapt better to changes in the health care environment. They can identify the need to change and have the potential to respond to those needs far more rapidly than more traditional, fragmented health care delivery systems.

In our consulting practice, we have observed that physicians and hospitals working together almost always increase their market share, provide more coordinated care and better access to patients, have more favorable economies of scale, and are better positioned for the future. And, they are more likely to listen to their customers and promptly implement the changes needed to enhance their customer relations.

One of the key principles of integrated systems is the alignment of incentives to encourage cooperation rather than adversarial relationships among physicians, hospitals and health plans. Once this is done, the evidence is strong and getting stronger that integrated systems can be more cost effective than the traditional modes. Duplication in equipment and facilities can be drastically reduced or eliminated. The insurance "middle man" is no longer needed. New investment decisions can be viewed from a system-wide perspective.

To be sure, integration has its problems as well as opportunities. Large systems easily can become bureaucratic. Creating integrated systems requires enormous changes in organizational structures, financial arrangements, management information flows, interpersonal communications and personal outlooks. Nevertheless, integration can happen and, in most cases, is likely to happen; and the potential payoffs appear to justify the effort and risk that is required.

Realistically, today's integrated systems are only the beginning of a journey. Not a single one of the integrated systems discussed in this book is at its final destination. Therefore, this book is also about managing the process of continuous, often radical, change.

Overview of This Book

The purpose of this book is to further the process of integrated health care by offering insights into the experience of many of the organizations around the country that have embarked on this approach to the delivery and financing of health care. While none of the systems we researched are totally satisfied with their progress, physicians and hospital managers involved in developing integrated systems are of one mind that they are moving in the right direction.

In preparing this book we looked to the experience of organizations that had already achieved a measure of integration. There are examples of integration in various stages all around the country, and we have drawn from them at every opportunity. There is, however, a lack of systematically gathered, comparable information about these efforts. We have sought to meet part of this need by combining (a) information from over 60 organizations in various stages of integration, (b) the results of our experiences working with integrated systems and (c) systematically gathered data and insights from 10 in-depth case studies. The 10 case studies identified on Exhibit P-1 are of particular value in that they allow comparison of the experiences of several of the mature integrated systems. Of course, we also collected information on many additional organizations, interviewed a number of knowledgeable people in the field, attended conferences on the subject and performed a literature search using the resources of the comprehensive MGMA Library Resource Center.

Exhibit P-2 provides summary information about each case study organization. Factors considered in selecting the case study organizations are summarized in the introduction to Part B.

Part A of this book answers the question, "What is physician-hospital integration?" It explains how these types of organizations differ from more traditionally organized physician groups and hospitals. We discuss many of the challenges — legal, environmental, financial and personal — to achieving an integrated health care system.

Part B describes how integrated health care organizations function, drawing particularly on data from the case studies and many other organizations in various stages of the integration process. We outline the major issues identified in our literature search and case studies. For example, determining the most appropriate type of organizational structure is important, especially in the early stages of forming an integrated system.

Other issues discussed in Part B include developing a primary care network, achieving an appropriate balance between primary care physicians and specialists, management and governance of integrated systems (including the critically important role of physicians), financing the development of integrated systems, physician compensation, establishing a health plan, information systems and outcomes measurement. We have found that these are the issues that really make or break development of successful integrated systems.

EXHIBIT P-1
Location of Case Study Organizations

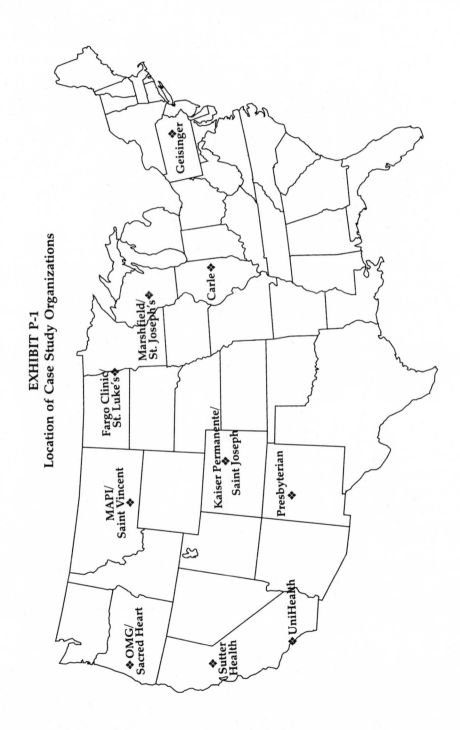

EXHIBIT P-2
Summary of Case Study Organizations, 1993

	Case Study Organizations	Total Number of Physicians	No. of Hospital Beds	No. of Lives Covered in "Owned" HMO	Comments
1.	Presbyterian Network, Albuquerque	450	628	55,000	Three hospitals in Albuquerque and 80 economically integrated physicians
2.	Fargo Clinic/St. Luke's Hospital	250	404	None	
3.	Marshfield Clinic/St. Joseph's Hospital	392	525	65,000	
4.	Carle Clinic/Carle Foundation Hospital, Urbana	240	288	68,000	
5.	Sutter Health, Sacramento	850	628	30,000	Data are for physicians in Sutter IPA and Sacremento facilities
6.	UniHealth America, Los Angeles	185* (affiliated groups)	3,003	180,000	Covered Lives is for Care America only
7.	Oregon Medical Group/Sacred Heart, Eugene	55	320	60,000	Number of physicians is for OMG only
8.	Geisinger System Danville, PA	500	803	143,000	Two hospitals - Danville and Wilkes Barre
9.	Kaiser Permanente/Saint Joseph Hospital, Denver	430	565	280,000	Number of physicians is for KP only
10.	MAPI/Saint Vincent Hospital, Billings, MT	110	285	None	Number of physicians is for MAPI only

* UniHealth America includes 4,258 physicians who use UniHealth hospitals.

Source: Data obtained by BBC, Inc. from the organizations listed as part of the case study process, March-July, 1993.

Part C is the "where do we go from here?" part of the book; it focuses on moving from fragmentation to an organized system of health care. Three chapters describe how to get started toward physician, hospital and health plan integration. In Chapter 15, we analyze the accomplishments of integrated health care systems, assess their cost effectiveness and discuss their potential for the future.

PART A.

OVERVIEW OF INTEGRATED HEALTH CARE SYSTEMS

The marketing manager of a hospital was befuddled:

At a recent chamber of commerce meeting I talked about physicians and hospitals coming together into integrated health care systems. A hospital chief financial officer and another health care administrator were present, and they didn't know what I was talking about. I was shocked!

It is not surprising that our friend was taken aback by the lack of knowledge and confusion about physician-hospital integration and integrated health care systems. The health care industry is at one of those points at which it is changing so fast that it can not keep its labels straight.

Part of the misunderstanding comes when we talk about "integrated delivery systems," "integrative management," "horizontal integration" and "vertical integration." These are all widely-used terms in the health care industry, especially among economists and strategic planners. For many physicians, hospital board members and administrators, however, eyes glaze over at the thought of trying to digest these obscure concepts. Within the category of vertical integration, hospital strategic planners often talk about "forward integration" (e.g., urgent care centers, health plans, primary care networks) and "backward integration" (including rehabilitation, long-term care and home health care).

The term "integrative management" refers to a managerial approach or style that seeks to include many perspectives. Integrated health care systems often are managed by persons who practice integrative management. But integrated systems use many tools other than a particular management style to reorganize the elements of health care delivery. For example, integrated systems are designed to insure that all providers of health care services — whether they are associated with physicians or hospitals or health plans — have common economic incentives. If one component does well financially, all do well.

Another frequently used term is "physician-hospital organization" (PHO). The term "PHO" often is used to describe a relationship, either formal or informal, between a physician organization (PO) and a hospital, often for the purposes of managed care contracting. A wide variety of organizational relationships, ranging from independent practice associations (IPAs) to clinics without walls to medical foundations, are sometimes referred to as PHOs.

There continues to be confusion between "collaboration" and "integration" in health care systems. The best example of collaboration may be Rochester, New York, where six of seven acute care hospitals participate in a consortium designed to reduce duplication of equipment and services, increase access and lower health care costs. The results have been impressive: health insurance premiums about one-third less than the national average, a significantly lower percentage of the population uninsured, 84 percent occupancy rates for hospitals, lower hospital admission rates per 1,000 residents and per capita hospital costs 41 percent below the state average (Pallarito, 1992, pp. 28-29).

But, integrated health care systems have not been formed for the purpose of hospital collaboration. Collaboration may be a natural by-product of building an integrated system, but it is not the objective. The reasons for the formation of integrated health care systems usually relate to positioning for the future, gaining competitive advantage, controlling costs, accessing capital and improving quality of care. Hence, "collaboration" is not the most appropriate term for describing the new combinations of physicians, hospitals and health plans that are being developed in many areas of the country.

Integrated health care systems, the subject of this book, combine the major elements of health care delivery — physicians, hospitals, related ancillary services such as outpatient diagnostic equipment, professionals such as physician extenders, and health plans — into one organization, or a family of organizations, that function as one. They seek to reorganize how health care is delivered and financed.

In Chapter 1, we discuss many of these definitional issues in more detail. It is our hypothesis that physician-hospital integration leading to the development of integrated health care systems is the central change needed to make the US health care system more cost effective. (Cost effective is not the same, however, as "inexpensive," "equitable," or even "sustainable." In a previous book, *The Crisis in Health Care: Costs, Choices and Strategies*, we agree that changes in the reimbursement system and in current patterns of cost shifting are necessary to produce a more sustainable health care system.) Integrated health care will also lead to improvements in the quality of care.

We show how physician practices often evolve into larger medical groups, both single and multispecialty. We discuss how these physician organizations come together with hospitals to form some type of physician-hospital organization (PHO). Finally, we describe how integrated organizations are positioning themselves to enter into "risk" contracting (i.e., the acceptance of financial risks for taking care of a group of patients, either on a discounted fee-for-service or capitated basis.)

Our second chapter describes the opportunities and challenges facing physicians and hospitals in their efforts to become integrated health care systems. We focus on the external environment — under what circumstances does developing an integrated health care system make sense? We discuss the major external factors — the presence of a "threat," growth in managed care, aggressive moves by competitors — that motivate physicians and hospitals to proceed with the development of these kinds of organizations. We also describe several of the more significant hurdles to integration including the legal issues of private inurement, fraud and abuse, and antitrust.

CHAPTER 1.

WHAT IS AN INTEGRATED HEALTH CARE SYSTEM?

Every decade or so a big new idea takes hold in health care and, like a fast-growing beech tree, begins to sink its roots deeply and spread its branches broadly. Such was the case with the notion of employer-based health insurance in the 1950s, health care planning in the 1960s, HMOs in the 1970s, and managed care in the 1980s. In the 1990s, the defining idea is organized or integrated networks of care.

— *Business & Health*, February 1993

The editor of a health care strategic planning newsletter asked us, "How many integrated health care systems are there?" Our answer: "It depends on how you define them." When an independent practice association (IPA) receives financial support from a hospital, does this constitute an integrated system? Most health care industry observers would say no. How about a 300-bed acute care hospital where 45 primary care physicians (out of a medical staff of 500) have formed a clinic without walls? This is a first step toward physician-hospital integration, but this organization does not possess most of the characteristics of an integrated health care system.

Most of the integrated health care systems studied in connection with the preparation of this book are at the opposite end of the spectrum from the independent community hospitals and solo practice and small group practices that are predominant in health care delivery in many parts of the country. Exhibit 1-1 shows one possible characterization of our present fragmented health care system.

Speaking at a national conference, a health care consultant noted that, "The fragmented health care system is being rejected everywhere you look. No one is satisfied with it. If you are looking for one statement that characterizes the present health care system it is 'fragmentation.' Physician-hospital integration has the potential to reverse the current situation. It (continuing the current fragmentation) is not an option" (Mason, 1992).

EXHIBIT 1-1
The Fragmented U.S. Health Care System

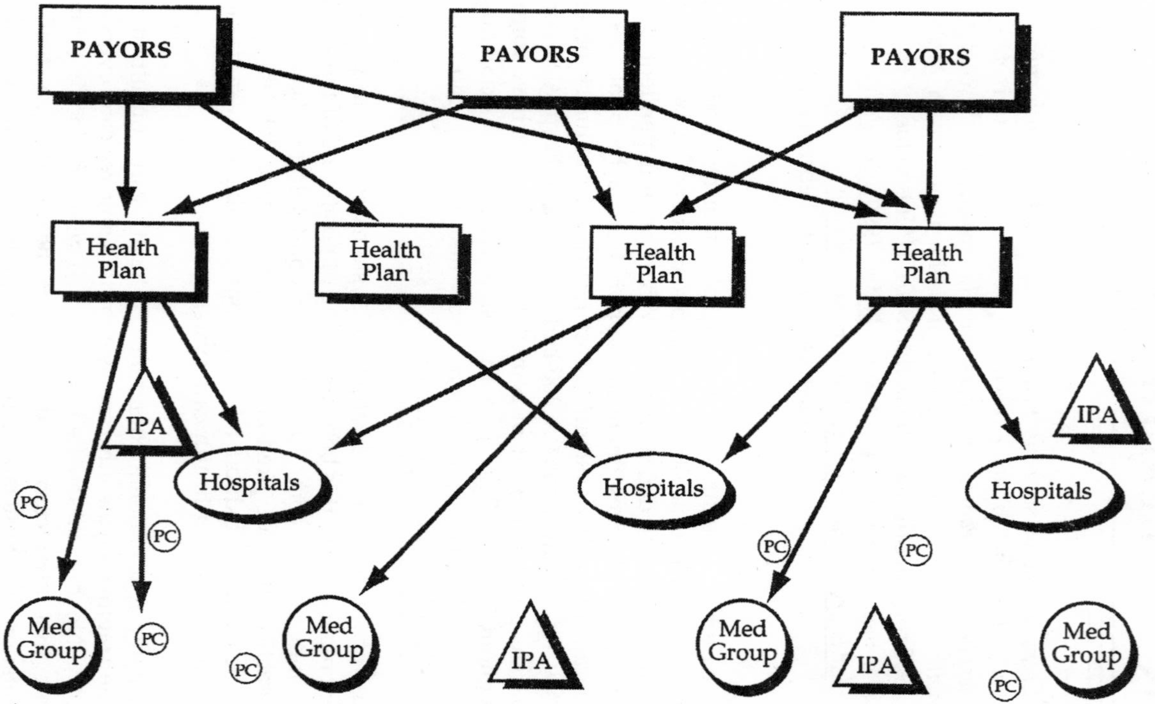

Source: Adapted from a chart by BBC Research & Consulting (reprinted with permission)

We agree; the present health care system is fragmented and uncoordinated. How, then, do integrated health care systems differ from the norm in many communities? What sets integrated systems apart?

Integrated Health Care Systems — Different Definitions

The Lovelace Clinic in Albuquerque defines integrated health care as a process in which the elements needed to provide all aspects of health care services to a population of people are brought together in a coordinated and accountable fashion (Pasternak, 1993). This sounds like the definition of a capitated health care system; Lovelace, with a 330-physician multispecialty group, its own hospital and a health plan that accounts for 75 percent of the revenues for physicians, is obviously well-positioned for a capitated environment.

Alta Bates Health Care System in Berkeley, California, spent two years developing its definition of integrated health care systems:

Integrated health care delivery systems are strategic alliances between physicians and hospitals, or health care delivery systems, which assume shared risk through common ownership, governance, shared revenue and/or capital, planning and/or management via a number of vehicles (management services organization, foundation, physician-hospital organization, joint venture, hospital division). Fueled by the presence or anticipation of managed care, integrated systems shift the focus of care delivery from hospital to health care system, from specialist to primary care physician, from acute intervention for the individual patient to accountability for the health status of defined populations (James, 1993).

Our definition. In reviewing the definitions used by Lovelace and Alta Bates, and those of several other organizations, we suggest that the essential ingredients of an integrated health care system would be defined as follows:

An integrated health care system combines physicians, hospitals and other medical services with a health plan (or the ability of the system to enter into risk contracts) to provide the complete spectrum of medical care for its customers. In a fully integrated system, the three key elements — physicians, hospital(s) and health plan membership — are in balance in terms of matching medical resources with the needs of purchasers and patients.

A few words of explanation. A fully integrated system positions itself to take full responsibility for the health status of its patients (or, as many say, a defined population); this includes typical medical and acute hospital services as well as other services, such as preventive care, mental health, pharmacy, rehabilitation and home health care. A few integrated systems even provide long-term care. However, it is not necessary for an integrated system to own all of the resources it uses; it can achieve its objectives by building networks or developing contractual relationships with other providers and health plans.

On the matter of balancing resources, it is important that an integrated system have an appropriate mix of physicians, especially a sufficient number of primary care doctors, in the right locations. Therefore, integrated systems will tend to provide good geographic coverage, making services available in convenient locations. It is also important that hospital capacity (including the number of beds, programs, equipment and personnel) be in balance — neither too much nor too little — with the needs of the population being served. Integrated systems work hard to eliminate unnecessary duplication of hospital beds, equipment and technology, and to add resources that are in short supply.

The higher the proportion of health plan subscribers using physicians and hospitals in the system, the more completely integrated the system will be. Many of the case study organizations analyzed in the preparation of this book were out of balance in terms of the number of subscribers to the health plans they own or control; their plans were small and represented a minor percentage of the patients using physicians and hospitals in the system. While it may not be necessary for an integrated health care system to limit medical services to the subscribers of its own health plan, the trend is in this direction.

Kaiser Permanente is a prime example of a fully integrated system; all of its patients are enrolled in its health plan, and the number of physicians and hospital beds are sized to meet the health needs of enrollees. For example, Kaiser Permanente adds an average of one new physician for each 765 enrollees. Other organizations, such as Lovelace, Inc. in Albuquerque and the Fallon Healthcare Organization in Worcester, Massachusetts, are close to the Kaiser Permanente model in terms of achieving a balance among physicians, hospitals and enrollees in their health plans.

A Matrix Approach to Describing Integrated Systems

Today there are many forms of organizations that consider themselves to be integrated health care systems or PHOs. Exhibit 1-2 illustrates how they relate to one another and to the concept of a fully integrated health care system. (We developed this matrix early in the process of preparing this book, and have subsequently seen several similar types of presentations. We apologize in advance for any appearance of plagiarism.)

The horizontal axis measures the degree of physician-to-physician integration. The most fully integrated physician organization (PO) is the multispecialty clinic in the lower right-hand corner. The vertical axis describes the depth of the physician organization's integration with a hospital. Physician-hospital organizations (PHOs) which participate in risk contracting are on the upper, or more integrated, end of this axis.

Many hospitals and physicians are positioned in the lower left hand corner of this matrix; they operate in the traditional manner (mostly solo practices or very small groups; minimal hospital financial support for medical practices) with little in the way of economic integration.

Over the past few years, physicians have moved across this matrix from left to right — solo practice physicians have merged with other physicians; IPAs have developed; small groups have become larger; single-specialty groups have merged into multispecialty group practices; multispecialty groups have grown. This trend has been well-documented.

There has also been a strong trend for hospitals to become more involved with physicians in the construction of medical office buildings, in joint ventures such as outpatient surgery facilities or diagnostic centers, in physician referral services, in computer linkages, and in joint marketing and managed care contracting. In the early 1990s, we witnessed an acceleration of these trends. At the same time, more and more primary care physicians have become employees of hospitals or hospital-controlled organizations. This might be called "hospital-physician integration," and is represented by the left hand vertical column on the matrix.

EXHIBIT 1-2.
Extent of Physician-Hospital Integration

	Economic integration with primary care groups; hospital-owned practices	Physician-hospital organizations engaged in risk contracting	Fully-integrated systems
	Medical Office Buildings (MOBs); subsidies; practice support;	Clinics w/o walls, MSO's; foundation models	Merged clinics and hospitals (usually positioned for risk contracting)
	Solo practices; small groups	Physician organizations; consolidation of groups	Significant group practices (multispecialty and single specialty)

Physician-Hospital Integration

Physician Integration

Source: BBC Research & Consulting

The various forms of physician-hospital organizations (PHOs) generally fall at the center of the diagram. They represent a variety of models for physicians and hospitals to achieve a closer working relationship. These include clinics without walls, management services organizations (MSOs), contractual networks and medical foundations. These types of organizations were represented among the case studies by the Sacramento Sierra Medical Group (Sac Sierra), Montana Associated Physicians, Inc. (MAPI), the Oregon Medical Group in Eugene, Presbyterian Network in Albuquerque, and several medical foundations associated with UniHealth America and Sutter Health.

At the same time, many large multispecialty clinics and multihospital systems are adding primary care offices to increase their size and market coverage, and positioning themselves to enter into risk contracting, either through their own health plans or single signature contracting with other HMOs, PPOs or with employers. Several of the case studies — Marshfield, Carle, Fargo and Geisinger health care systems — are representative of these types of organizations. Others include Fallon, Park Nicollet in the Twin Cities, Mullikin and Friendly Hills in Los Angeles and the Mayo Clinic in Rochester, Minnesota. Kaiser Permanente, more than any other organization, is viewed as a fully integrated health care system. Kaiser Permanente would be in the upper right hand corner of Exhibit 1-2.

Recently, the trend toward physician-hospital integration has accelerated. Physicians are joining with their colleagues to form physician organizations (POs) which have a united voice in dealing with hospitals and health plans. These physician organizations are entering into partnerships with hospitals to form physician-hospital organizations (PHOs) and ultimately contracting with a health plan, or starting their own, to become an integrated health care system. In short, physicians and hospitals are moving across and up the matrix, and diagonally toward the fully integrated model.

Characteristics of Integrated Health Care Systems

Producing high quality care in a cost-effective manner is the prime objective of most integrated health care systems. These two factors — quality and reasonable costs — are the measures of success. We have found that there are 10 major characteristics of integrated health care systems that help them reach for and attain success:

(1) Physicians play key roles in the overall leadership of the organization. This is listed first for a reason — it is the most important. We have yet to find an integrated system for which this is not true.

(2) The organizational structure provides common management and coordination of all elements of the integrated system. These elements include physicians, health plans managers and hospital administrators meeting regularly, joint strategic planning, and coordination of services through the corporate structure.

(3) Primary care physicians are economically tied to the system. In a fully integrated health care system, primary care physicians play prominent roles. Primary care physicians manage the deployment of most of the system's resources in the delivery of care. They are either economically integrated or are employees of the system.

(4) Primary care locations provide full geographic coverage of the system's service area. Integrated health care systems take medical services to the patients. All of the systems we studied have devoted years of effort and significant financial resources to developing their primary care networks.

(5) The system is appropriately sized. The number and mix of specialists and hospital capacity (primarily inpatient beds) are in balance with the needs of the market. Duplication of facilities and services is minimized.

(6) Physicians themselves are integrated. Physicians have been moving out of solo practice and into groups as the first step in the integration process. In today's more integrated systems, one or more large medical groups account for a high percentage of the patients served by the system. In the larger integrated systems, a single medical group often provides all of the medical services for customers.

(7) The system controls its own financing mechanism (usually an HMO), and/or has the ability to enter into "single signature contracts" with other health plans or large employers. This means that fully-integrated systems seek premium dollars rather than focusing on physician and hospital revenues.

(8) The financial incentives of physicians, hospitals and health plans are aligned. Most health care organizations operate in a

schizophrenic environment; they serve both fee-for-service and capitated patients, leading to confusion about what the organization is trying to accomplish. In fully integrated systems, all parties are working under the same financial incentives.

(9) Communications systems are in place to provide ready access to information. In most integrated systems, a common database is being developed to link all elements — hospital, physicians' offices, health plan and patients — to provide information needed to manage and coordinate care.

(10) The system has access to capital and the ability to allocate financial resources. This means that the system can invest in information systems, develop a primary care network and start a health plan. Without access to significant capital resources and the ability to use this capital without fear of regulatory or other intervention (e.g., threat of the loss of tax-exempt status for 501(c)(3) hospitals), there is little chance that physicians and a hospital can develop an integrated health care system.

What organizations are approaching full integration? Appendix A provides a self-administered questionnaire that can be used to rank a specific organization in terms of its current degree of integration. An organization's score on the questionnaire determines its "integration index." The higher the score, the farther a health care system has progressed toward becoming fully integrated. A perfect score is 100.

The authors completed this questionnaire for each of the 10 case study organizations detailed in this book and for several other physician and hospital groups. Which had the highest score? Kaiser Permanente of Colorado received 96 points out of a possible 100. Most of the other case study organizations were in the 55 to 88 point range. Exhibit 1-3 shows the ratings of each of the case study organizations in terms of how they meet the 10-part definition of an integrated health care system.

How did the other organizations we evaluated score? A 75-bed hospital and its 30 physicians in a community of 25,000 received a score of zero on the integration index. Many other hospitals and physician groups we have worked with rank in the 10 to 15 point range. The 300-bed hospital with a 45-physician clinic without walls mentioned earlier in this chapter received 23 points out of the possible 100.

EXHIBIT 1-3
Integration Index Scores, 10 Case Study Organizations

Characteristic	Presbyterian	Fargo Clinic/ St. Luke's	Marshfield/ St. Joseph's	Carle	Sutter Health	UniHealth	OMG/ Sacred Heart	Geisinger System	KP/Saint Joseph MAPI/ Saint Vincent
1. Physicians in key role	12	12	12	9	9	12	12	12	6
2. Organizational structure facilitates coordination	9	12	12	9	9	6	12	12	1
3. Primary care physicians economically tied to system	6	8	8	6	6	4	8	8	4
4. Geographic coverage through primary care locations	7	10	10	7	7	3	10	10	3
5. Supply of hospitals and specialists in balance with demand	0	8	8	4	4	4	8	6	0
6. Physicians are integrated	0	8	8	4	4	2	8	8	2
7. Owned financing mechanisms (HMO), and/or single signature contracting	6	4	6	6	6	6	6	10	2
8. Financial incentives same for all providers	6	3	3	9	9	6	6	12	0
9. Real-time communications systems and a common database	6	6	6	6	6	6	6	6	4
10. Access to capital and ability to allocate financial resources	6	9	9	9	9	6	12	12	6
Total	58	80	82	82	69	55	88	96	28

Source: BBC Research & Consulting

The weighting of questions in arriving at the index represents the authors' best judgement after completing the research presented in this book. Our thinking has changed as we have learned more from the experience of others. For example, as a result of this research, we have increased substantially the weight we place on the financing mechanism, often referred to as the third leg of the stool (along with physicians and hospitals). The financing mechanism is discussed further in Chapter 6.

Summary

Richard L. Clarke, President of the Healthcare Financial Management Association (HFMA), one of our co-authors on a previous book, succinctly described why integrated health care systems are important. "Health care reform leading to managed competition will require the development of networks of physicians, hospitals, clinics, other providers, and insurers (underlining added) to provide services to purchasing alliances" (Clarke, 1993, p. 12).

Integrated health care systems require physician-physician integration (POs) and "physician-hospital integration" leading to PHOs. Physician integration, including the formation of physician organizations (POs), represents a step toward the future in health care. Physician-hospital integration represents a second step. However, the systems that are working the best and have the greatest potential for the future include physicians, a hospital and a health plan.

CHAPTER 2.

THE CHALLENGES OF DEVELOPING AN INTEGRATED HEALTH CARE SYSTEM

We are now in our third attempt to form a single, integrated organization with the hospital. We know it's the right way to go. I just hope we can get it done this time.
—Physician and medical group president

If integrated health care systems are the wave of the future in health care, why isn't everyone jumping on the bandwagon? Part of the answer has to do with the environment — competition, presence of an external threat and the importance of managed care in the marketplace. In many health care markets, conditions are not yet right for encouraging the formation and growth of these more organized systems of care. Another part of the answer is that developing integrated systems is far from easy.

Integration is taking place in a legal and economic environment that was designed to promote fragmentation. Therefore, the legal and regulatory barriers associated with physician-hospital integration can be daunting. Such barriers include: possible loss of tax exempt status for not-for-profit systems if "private benefit" or "inurement" is found by the IRS, fraud and abuse laws, antitrust enforcement and esoteric employee benefit restrictions imposed by the tax laws relating to "qualified benefit and welfare plans."

What about the other challenges standing in the way of developing an integrated system? Is there a desire on the part of many physicians to retain their autonomy? Confusion over the possible impacts of health care reform? High initial investment? Are there emotional issues for physicians, medical group practice managers and hospital administrators, including fear of change and job security? We know from our own experience that these are all important challenges to moving forward with the development of an integrated health care system.

The External Environment

When it comes to forming an integrated health care system, the type of community served by a hospital and its medical staff can be the most important factor influencing the agenda for change. Factors making up the health care environment include:

- Presence of a serious external threat.
- Extent of managed care (mainly HMOs).
- Actions of competing hospitals and physician groups.
- Sophistication and proactive nature of local buyers of health care.

In our travels around the country and our work with physicians and hospitals in rural areas, in mid-size communities and in large metropolitan areas, we have observed huge differences in attitudes about integrated health care systems. For example, the presence of large managed care organizations and the high market penetration of capitated health plans in most large metropolitan areas in California, Minnesota, New Mexico, Oregon and Washington has driven the formation and growth of integrated systems. *community size*

At the other extreme, in many smaller communities in the Southeast, Midwest and Rocky Mountain regions, talk about forming integrated health care systems often meets with skepticism. If pushed aggressively by hospital administrators or others, the concept of integrated systems can generate a strong emotional negative response from some physicians. As one doctor told us, "I moved out here to be my own boss and to practice by myself. It is tough going at times, but it has its rewards and it's what I want. I do good quality work, patients get their money's worth, and they appreciate what I do. I'm not about to change. If I have to do what you are talking about, I'll hang it up." Based on our experience, this was a fairly typical attitude in many smaller communities in the early 1990s.

Presence of an external threat. One of the lessons learned by organizations that have invested substantial resources in developing an integrated health care system is that a recognizable external threat is a great help in motivating people to action. The main factor behind the formation of some of the largest integrated health care systems is competition from large group practices.

On the West Coast, Kaiser Permanente (often referred to by competitors as "the Big K") has done more to spur the development of integrated health care systems than any hospital CEO or health policy maker could ever dream of accomplishing. As one physician-administrator said, "You didn't have to be very bright to see what Kaiser was doing. We didn't have to do a lot of explaining to our physicians. They got the message every time patients requested a transfer of their medical records." Many physicians and hospital executives acknowledge that without the threat of Kaiser Permanente, it would have proven more difficult, if not impossible, to bring physicians and hospitals together into an integrated system.

In the Midwest an external threat can often come from a large clinic like Mayo in its purchase of Luther Hospital and a multispecialty group practice in Eau Claire, Wisconsin. The Fallon Clinic in Worcester, Massachusetts, the Carle Clinic in Champaign-Urbana (one of the case studies), or the Dakota Clinic in Fargo-Moorhead also serve as external threats to their competitors.

Managed care. The growth of managed care, particularly capitated payment, is a major stimulus to the growth of integrated systems. The next generation of managed care is likely to rely heavily on integrated delivery systems.

Managed care generally means health maintenance organizations (HMOs) and preferred provider organizations (PPOs). However, in some parts of the country, such as Southern California, managed care is synonymous with HMOs and capitation. One Los Angeles physician told us, "I don't consider PPOs to be managed care; they offer nothing more than discounted fee-for-service medicine." We agree with this physician.

With the expected shakeout in managed care (consolidation from several hundred health plans down to a dozen or fewer in most large metropolitan areas), surviving plans will have more market clout. These larger health plans will develop close working relationships with panels of physicians and a limited number of hospitals. Surviving managed care companies will not sign contracts with solo practitioners or small groups; they will favor larger group practices and integrated delivery systems. Furthermore, they will give preference to organizations that are positioned to commit the resources of a hospital and a large group of physicians to a single capitated contract. This was referred to in Chapter 1 as "single signature contracting."

Many physicians and hospital executives associated with integrated systems are questioning the value added of health plans, even HMOs. These leaders of provider organizations argue that as long as the health care system places physicians and hospitals at risk for the care of patients, providers may as well take over the insurance function. As one physician-administrator said, "When we are trying hard to be more cost effective, it doesn't make sense to lop off the top 10 or 15 percent and give it to someone else for performing administrative and marketing functions. We can do these things for less and become a more cost-effective organization in the process."

Aggressive moves by competing hospitals and physician groups. Watching competing physicians and hospitals form new organizations, such as an MSO or a medical foundation, is often a sobering experience, especially for physicians. The purchase of primary care practices by a competing hospital or an insurance company and the development of a primary care referral network are bound to set off strong emotions and strike fear into the hearts of non-participating physicians, especially specialists. (For example, in one of the case studies, three physicians were denied hospital admitting privileges in a small town where a large multispecialty clinic had an established branch. This triggered a strong response: the formation of a clinic without walls to compete with the larger clinic.)

Health care reform. At the time we prepared this book, the strong possibility of state and federal health care reform was motivating many physicians and hospitals to consider how they might work together, especially in the formation of integrated systems capable of serving large geographic areas. Health care reform is a compelling external "threat;" it grabs the attention of physicians, hospital board members and administrators and health plan managers.

The demands of health care reform, which favors the development of primary care networks, becomes increasingly difficult in light of the shortage of primary care physicians. Hospitals or health care systems must build and sustain a strong base of loyal physicians, especially primary care doctors. Most physicians just out of training, many of whom are female, are not interested in establishing their own practices or joining small groups; they want the income security and quality of life (e.g., relief from the burden of being on call every night, ability to take a vacation) associated with larger group practices. Autonomy is often less important to them than to older physicians.

Numerous environmental factors are converging to encourage physicians and hospitals to work together. At the same time, many hurdles to the development of integrated health care systems must be overcome.

Legal and Regulatory Hurdles

In discussing the legal and regulatory complexities of the merger with the Fargo Clinic, the CEO of St. Luke's Hospital in Fargo, said, "Despite the fact that we had the best attorneys available to help us through this merger, every time we opened a door we found two more that were locked. These issues were unbelievably complex."

The legal constraints and options for developing integrated health care systems are changing rapidly. Several issues have substantial financial implications. Organizations contemplating forming integrated health care systems are wise to secure competent legal and financial counsel early and to keep them involved throughout the process.

Anyone considering physician-hospital integration must also develop his or her own understanding of the key legal, tax and regulatory issues facing health care organizations as they consider moving forward in the process. In effect, these are some of the most important barriers to physician-hospital integration and have a major impact on the form a physician-hospital organization may take (e.g., MSO, foundation model). These barriers do not appear to be insurmountable; many of the organizations we analyzed are functioning under these constraints. However, they do add procedural difficulties to forming integrated systems, and they add otherwise unnecessary complexity to the organizational structure.

Legal and regulatory challenges often faced during the process of developing an integrated system include:

- Taking into account anti-referral and Stark legislation.
- Avoiding improper uses of tax-exempt status.
- Avoiding illegal and/or economically disadvantaged structures under Medicare.
- Avoiding antitrust concerns.
- Working within states' prohibitions against the corporate practice of medicine.
- Conducting legally defensible economic credentialing.
- Avoiding unworkable employee and owner benefits structures.

The challenge in designing an integrated system is to anticipate these hurdles and to develop creative ways to take them into account, <u>but not to let them deter the organization from achieving its fundamental goals or its potential.</u>

Taking into account anti-referral and Stark legislation. Anti-referral legislation seeks to remedy a recent problem in the delivery of health care. In a traditional model of health care delivery — small private practices, independent hospitals and insurers and perhaps independent diagnostic facilities — cross ownership among these services can represent an incentive to increase costs or even to create unethical referrals. A physician's ownership of a diagnostic service, for example, could be a source of revenue increases and improper gain if he or she referred patients to that facility without regard to the costs to patients or other benefits of competing alternatives, or of using no such facility at all.

In a traditional practice model, this possibility of unethical behavior is averted by Federal legislation that prohibits having an ownership interest in any of the following types of facilities and then referring patients to them (Section 13562, Physician Ownership and Referral, amending Section 1877 (42 U.S.C. 1395nn):

- Clinical laboratory services

- Physical therapy services

- Occupational therapy services

- Radiology or other diagnostic services

- Radiation therapy services

- Durable medical equipment

- Perenteral and enteral nutrients, equipment and supplies

- Prosthetics, orthotics, and prosthetic devices

- Home health services

- Outpatient prescription drugs

- Inpatient and outpatient hospital services

Unfortunately, laws that prevent inefficiency and possible unethical behavior in a traditional system present obstacles to cost effectiveness in an integrated system. In an integrated system, a key goal is to view all of these resources as part of one system and to efficiently manage them in concert with the provision of medical services. Therefore, it is necessary to design the integrated system so that either it fits under one of a limited number of exceptions that are provided for in the anti-referral legislation or physicians are excluded from profiting in any way from any of these revenues.

The heavy emphasis on joint ventures between physicians and hospitals and joint ownership of outpatient facilities (e.g., surgery centers, laboratories) plus leasing of space, equipment rental and management services has triggered a response under the general category of Medicare "fraud and abuse." This is one of the reasons the Fargo Clinic and St. Luke's Hospital decided to merge; they were engaged in a number of joint ventures and were concerned about the continuing hassles over the legality and propriety of what they were doing.

Avoiding improper use of tax-exempt status. Operating a hospital and providing indigent care fall within the definition of an acceptable public purpose for a tax-exempt organization. Thus, a majority of hospitals in the U.S. are tax exempt. However, operating a typical medical practice or health plan usually does not fall within the definition of public purpose for tax-exempt organizations. Medical and insurance services are usually provided by for-profit, taxable organizations. Thus combining physicians, hospitals and health plans usually requires considerable effort to separate out what is tax exempt and what is taxable.

If an integrated system is to be tax exempt, then it must have a primary purpose that falls within the definition of allowable public purposes — such as operating a hospital and providing indigent care, offering education and/or conducting research. As one attorney puts it, "Organizations that receive exemption from federal income taxes pursuant to the Internal Revenue Code (IRC) Section 501 (c) (3) are required to be organized and operated exclusively for charitable, religious, research, or educational purposes. Pursuant to this standard, an organization that has been determined to operate for private benefit will lose its exempt status unless such private benefit is found to be merely incidental to an overriding public benefit" (MacKelvie, 1990, p. 54).

In other words, activities such as providing physicians' services and providing health insurance must either be viewed by regulators and the courts as incidental to the provision of allowable public purposes or they must be organized in related but separate, for-profit entities. Related to this point, the Friendly Hills case is often cited as evidence that the Internal Revenue Service (IRS) has blessed, with tax-exempt status, the role of integrated health care systems. The IRS considered the Friendly Hills HealthCare Foundation's request for 20 months and issued its "determination letter" in January, 1993. We discuss this case further in Chapter 3 in the context of the medical foundation model as a vehicle for achieving physician-hospital integration.

Not only must tax-exempt organizations assure that their primary purpose is an acceptable pubic purpose, they must also insure that no benefits from their tax exemption inure to those in the for-profit sector. In developing an integrated system, using either an MSO or foundation model, the non-profit entity usually purchases all or a major portion of a physician's assets. To avoid violation of the Internal Revenue Code, tax-exempt systems can pay no more than fair market value for these assets. The Department of Health and Human Services has specific guidelines for determining fair market value in the purchase of physician practices. Avoiding violation of inurement includes determining the assets that are actually needed and how the evaluation was accomplished (*Report on Physician Trends*, 1993, p. 5).

The result of ignoring either the need to maintain an organization with an acceptable public purpose or the requirement to avoid inurement of tax-exempt benefits could be the loss of many millions of dollars; therefore, it is taken seriously.

Avoiding illegal or economically disadvantaged structures under Medicare. Medicare fraud and abuse statutes also have similar prohibitions against hospitals' or other facilities' providing undue remuneration to physicians in exchange for referral. The federal fraud and abuse statutes, which were strengthened by passage of the Medicare and Medicaid Patient and Program Protection Act of 1987, indicate, "that an individual or entity cannot knowingly and willfully offer, pay, solicit, or receive remuneration in order to induce business that is reimbursed under the Medicare or state health care programs" (MacKelvie, 1990, p. 50).

Medicare's reimbursement procedures pose an additional set of regulatory considerations in designing the integrated system. Certain physician services and allied professional services (e.g., physical therapy) are reimbursed at different rates by Medicare, depending on whether they are provided by a medical group or by a hospital. Generally, reimbursement is less favorable if these services are seen by Medicare as being provided at the hospital location and/or by a hospital corporation as opposed to a medical group.

When a patient visits a medical office and then is admitted to a hospital within the next three days, physician office services that previously were reimbursed by Medicare may not even be paid to the new integrated system. Instead, they may be viewed as covered under the hospital's DRG payment.

Avoiding antitrust concerns. The success of several integrated health care systems, in terms of their growth and gains in market penetration, can be a two-edge sword; it may make them vulnerable to charges of conspiring to monopolize a market and squeeze out solo practice physicians and small hospitals.

A number of management representatives of case study organizations expressed concern about dealing with accusations of antitrust violations. One financial officer said, "It's frustrating. We do a good job of serving patients and employers, and this attracts more business. But, when our share of the market climbs, as it has over the past five years, we get nervous because of possible attacks from our critics citing antitrust violations. We need more consistency from the various Federal agencies in their policies toward integrated systems — most like our approach, but they send us mixed signals — especially on antitrust issues."

With continued consolidation of the health care system likely to follow in the wake of state and national health care reform, antitrust accusations are likely to fly "fast and furious" and pose continuing problems for large integrated systems, as well as other provider groups. However, we believe that integrated systems should be large enough, and sufficiently in tune with the public interest to successfully cope with this threat.

Working within states' prohibition against the corporate practice of medicine. Approximately half of all states have laws making it illegal for a business corporation to employ physicians. In many states, these laws are not enforced. California, on the other hand, has one of the most stringent laws. Part of the rationale being that medical practice requires a license, and it is impossible for a business corporation to acquire a medical license (Sollins, 1988, p. 58).

At the same time, California is the state where most of the action is taking place with respect to the formation of medical foundations that contract with professional corporations for the provision of medical services (e.g., Sutter Health's five foundations involving the Sac Sierra Medical Group, Palo Alto Clinic and others). A California law requires that for a physician practice to become a foundation, the group must have a minimum of 40 physicians (27 full-time equivalents).

Economic credentialing. As new integrated systems are formed, the possibility increases that some physicians who are left outside the new entity may experience serious losses of patients and many will not be able to sustain economically viable medical practices. This means the potential for lawsuits charging unlawful enrichment leading to large damage claims. Designing and carrying out legally defensible credentialing processes becomes important. *any willing provider*

Avoiding unworkable employee and owner benefits structures. Combining organizations means consolidating benefits structures. The choice of the organization's legal structure, the relationships among organizations (in cases where there are more than one), and many other factors in negotiating the new system are often influenced by benefits issues. Ultimately, it is often prohibitively expensive if not legally impossible to maintain all parties' benefits at their current levels. When one group accepts a cut in benefits as a necessary condition for joining the new organization, it is often accompanied by a favorable concession in some other aspect of the negotiations.

Other Challenges

Based on our experience, other important hurdles to developing and growing integrated health care organizations include the relatively high front-end investment, lack of physician and hospital leadership, a medical staff dominated by specialists, and a fragmented medical community. These barriers to entry offer opportunities to those health care organizations that can overcome them.

Financial hurdles. It is expensive to pursue physician-hospital integration strategies. Start-up costs can be high in terms of payments to consultants, attorneys and appraisers. Physicians, especially those in leadership positions, can suffer a decline in income because of the time required to organize an integrated system. (We know of several cases when physicians devoted half of their time over several months to the formation of an MSO or similar type of arrangement.) Chapter 13 provides a sense of the complexities and time commitments required to develop a physician organization and PHO.)

If an MSO or foundation model is selected, the front-end investment required can be substantial — from hundreds of thousands to several million dollars to purchase assets and capitalize the new venture. Funds may be needed to form a primary care network, develop information systems and provide facilities that are convenient to patients. Chapter 5 discusses the costs of developing an integrated health care system in more detail.

Many hospitals, especially those in smaller communities and in the core cities of large metropolitan areas, lack the financial resources to invest in the development of an integrated system. Physicians, especially those in primary care, are unlikely to be a major source of capital.

In some communities, managed care companies, especially large HMOs, may provide front-end funding. Aetna's investment in primary care practices in several cities is an example. For-profit practice management companies, like PhyCor and Caremark International, also represent a potential source of capital. These kinds of firms have been acquiring medical group practices.

Leadership. In many communities, this may be the biggest challenge to achieving integrated health care. Are there physicians on the medical staff who are willing to risk their reputations and a possible drop in practice income in order to push for the formation of an integrated system? If these types of doctors are present, do they have the leadership ability and experience to do the job?

Are hospital administrators secure enough in their jobs to dive into the treacherous waters represented by the development of radically new relationships with physicians? Some hospital administrators and boards of trustees fear the power of strong medical groups. For many CEOs, the present fragmentation among physicians is just fine, thank you; please don't mess with it. However, we find that among the hospital CEOs of integrated systems, this is definitely not their attitude; these executives welcome the opportunity to work with strong and well-organized physician groups.

Managers of large medical groups also find it difficult to determine where to go next. This is a time of excitement and opportunity, but it can also be a time of personal insecurity. Can they be a force to promote integration?

Medical staff domination by specialists. Medical staffs dominated by specialists and sub-specialists may have a difficult time accepting the basic ingredients (e.g., increased role for primary care, emphasis on capitated contracts) of an integrated system. The encouraging note is that in the formation of several of the successful integrated systems, it was specialists who provided the initial leadership and who continue to provide mature management and governance.

As we discuss in Chapter 8, the bottom line is that strong physician leaders, whether they are in medical specialties or primary care, are absolutely essential for successfully forming and directing integrated health care systems. As the case studies show, physicians will step forward and provide this kind of leadership.

Physician autonomy. For many physicians, autonomy is an overwhelmingly important issue. Many of the initial efforts to form clinics without walls or MSOs were in response to physicians' desire for the benefits of group practice without the loss of independence. Therefore, clinics without walls and MSOs usually do not intrude upon practice locations, staffing and patient relations. To go farther than these initial steps would not have been accepted by most physicians, at least in the health care environment of the late 1980s and early 1990s. Other models, however, require physicians to give up some of their autonomy for income security and the benefits of being part of a large organization.

Summary

The problems associated with developing an integrated health care system are imposing, and the costs of turning a health care enterprise in a new direction are substantial. The legal challenges alone are enough to make the faint of heart turn back. And, what are the chances that a group of physicians can learn to work together, much less work hand-in-hand with a hospital and a health plan?

Nevertheless, systems are being formed and achieving success. The future for integrated health care systems appears to be extremely bright. As the case studies and the experiences of other organizations show, it is possible to make major progress in becoming a more fully integrated health care system. Part B focuses on the experiences of organizations that are meeting these challenges.

PART B.
COMMON CHARACTERISTICS OF INTEGRATED HEALTH CARE SYSTEMS

Sooner or later, every integrated system must deal with certain common challenges. To a great extent, how each system responds to these challenges essentially defines what the system is and its prospects for success. In developing case studies of existing integrated systems, we sought to determine how each organization had responded to these challenges:

- What is the best organizational form or model for structuring relationships between hospitals and physicians, now and in the future?

- What is the most effective way to work through the changing relationships between primary care physicians and specialists?

- What should we invest in and how?

- How closely do we affiliate with a health plan and what is the form of affiliation?

- How are physicians compensated?

- How is leadership and governance organized and carried out?

- How does the organization go about developing a strong corporate culture?

- How does the organization support itself with information and communications?

We also sought to identify patterns of what is working and what is not for the benefit of those who are or will be in earlier stages of developing their integrated health care systems. The first eight chapters of Part B are organized around the questions listed above. Chapter 11, the last chapter in Part B, summarizes what has been learned.

Although examples from other organizations are frequently cited, Part B relies heavily on the 10 detailed case studies of existing integrated organizations. Therefore we begin this part of the book with a further introduction of the case study organizations and their current situations. In selecting the case study organizations, we sought to include mostly systems that already have been in operation for several years. We also wished to include geographic diversity, a variety of approaches to integration (e.g., foundation model, MSOs, networking, merger), different settings (e.g., rural, urban, densely-populated metropolitan areas) and health care markets experiencing varying degrees of competition and growth in managed care.

Exhibit P-1 in the Preface contains background data on each integrated system studied. Exhibit B-1 (following page) presents information on the health care environments or marketplaces served by each of the case study organizations. Exhibit B-2 describes the major competitors for each of the case study systems.

Chapter 3 describes several organizational models for integrated systems — clinics without walls, MSOs, medical foundations — and the strengths and weaknesses of each. We found that many of the organizations have struggled, and continue to struggle, with their organizational structures. The threat of federal intervention (e.g., Internal Revenue Service, antitrust, and fraud and abuse) was constantly on their minds. In some cases, MSOs and clinics without walls were being converted to the foundation model, largely in response to regulatory concerns. Some mergers were being driven by a desire to be in more complete compliance with various federal and/or state laws.

Today's integrated systems are generally frank in assessing their strengths as well as their weaknesses. Some believe that in order to correct their weaknesses, they will have to undergo still more organizational change.

All 10 case study organizations were emphasizing development of their base of primary care physicians, and many have been developing or expanding their rural coverage for several years. Nearly all integrated delivery systems — case study systems and others — have taken giant steps in terms of shifting their mix of physicians to more sustainable levels for the long-term future under a new health care system. Chapter 4 is devoted to these important subjects.

Chapter 5 focuses on financial issues for integrated health care systems. The lack of capital for medical group practices, especially those in primary care, is an important factor driving medical groups to seek a closer relationship with a hospital or multihospital system. Of course, finding ways to finance the expansion of primary care is challenging to all of the organizations studied, primarily because of the high cost and special concerns over issues of private inurement (transferring funds from a tax-exempt organization to a taxable entity). In many instances, hospitals have purchased fixed assets and accounts receivable from medical groups brought into an integrated system. Chapter 5 reports on what financing mechanisms were used.

Eight of the 10 integrated systems had their own health plan; one that did not, Fargo Clinic, dropped its HMO in 1988 because of large financial losses. The other, MAPI/Saint Vincent Hospital in Billings, was studying the possibility of a community-based health plan. Having a financing mechanism is one of the most important aspects of an integrated health care system, and revenues and profits from these plans, as well as control over the flow of patients, were extremely important to most of the organizations. Chapter 6 discusses how health plans were formed and nurtured, and what they contribute to the overall success of integrated systems.

Physician compensation methods are important in terms of the flexibility afforded for the future when it is generally agreed that specialists will be paid proportionately less, and primary care physicians will earn more. And, commonly-used productivity-based compensation approaches do not relate well to a capitated payment system. As one Southern California group practice administrator said, "I tell our physicians that when they come in the morning and the parking lot is empty, they should be happy. This means that for the 14,500 lives we cover, we are making money. We need to worry when the parking lot is full; that is when we are using up valuable resources." Physician compensation is discussed in Chapter 7.

In preparing the case studies, it became obvious that the quality of leadership — both in medical groups and hospitals — was critically important in the success of these new types of organizations. Many of the leaders were physicians, and several of these individuals and their management styles are described in Chapter 8. We were interested in the changing role of physicians in hospital governance and management. Executives and physicians expressed concern about how an organization identifies and selects physician leaders and makes sure that it will have

Exhibit B-1.
Nature of Areas (Environment) Served by Case Study Organizations, 1993

	Case Study Organizations	Population of Service Area	Character of Service Area	Presence of Managed Care	Comments
1.	Presbyterian Network, Albuquerque	500,000	Metro area	High (>50%)	
2.	Fargo Clinic/St. Luke's Hospital	300,000	Urban core; rural	Minimal (<10%)	
3.	Marshfield Clinic/St. Joseph's Hospital	300,000	Rural	Moderate to Minimal (<20%)	
4.	Carle Clinic/Carle Foundation Hospital, Urbana	1,000,000	Urban to rural	Moderate (25-50%)	
5.	Sutter Health, Sacramento	> 10,000,000 (1,500,000 in Sacramento)	Large metro to urban	High (>50%)	
6.	UniHealth America, Los Angeles	15,000,000	Large metro area	High (>50%)	
7.	Oregon Medical Group/Sacred Heart, Eugene	250,000	Urban	Moderate (25-50%)	
8.	Geisinger System Danville, PA	2,200,000	Urban to rural	Moderate to Minimal (<20%)	
9.	Kaiser Permanente/Saint Joseph Hospital, Denver	1,800,000	Large metro area	High (>50%)	
10.	MAPI/Saint Vincent Hospital, Billings, MT	350,000	Urban to rural	Minimal (<10%)	

Source: Data obtained by BBC, Inc. from the organizations listed as part of the case study process, March–July, 1993.

EXHIBIT B-2
Major Competitors of Case Study Organizations, 1993

Case Study Organizations	Competitor Medical Groups	Competitor Hospitals	Competitor Health Plans	Competitive Integrated Systems
1. Presbyterian Network, Albuquerque	Lovelace Medical Clinic (350 physicians)	St. Joseph-3 hospitals; Lovelace	Lovelace; FHP	Lovelace
2. Fargo Clinic/St. Luke's Hospital	Dakota Clinic (140 physicians)	Dakota Medical Center	BC/BS	Dakota Clinic & Medical Center
3. Marshfield Clinic/St. Joseph's Hospital	Mayo Clinic in Eau Claire (60 physicians)	Wausau Hospital Center	Several indemnity plans	Mayo Clinic
4. Carle Clinic/Carle Foundation Hospital, Urbana	Christie Clinic (90 physicians)	Covenant Hospital	Personal Care (HMO)	None
5. Sutter Health, Sacramento	Permanente Group; Mercy	Mercy; Kaiser; U.C. Davis Medical Center	KP; Foundation Health	KP; Mercy
6. UniHealth America, Los Angeles	Permanente; Mullikin; Friendly Hills	>200 Hospitals in L.A.	KP; many others	KP; Friendly Hills, Mullikin
7. Oregon Medical Group/Sacred Heart, Eugene	Eugene Clinic (60 physicians)	McKinzey-Williamette Hospital	Capital Health Care	None
8. Geisinger System Danville, PA	None	Hospitals in Wilkes-Barre, Hershey, Harrisburg, and in service area	Blue Cross (2 plans)	None
9. Kaiser Permanente/Saint Joseph Hospital, Denver	None	Rose; Swedish/PSL; St. Anthony; others	TakeCare; numerous HMOs and PPOs	None
10. MAPI/Saint Vincent Hospital, Billings, MT	Billings Clinic	Deaconess Medical Center	Blue Cross/Blue Shield of Montana	Billings Clinic/Deaconess Medical Center

Source: Data obtained by BBC, Inc. from the organizations listed as part of the case study process, March-June, 1993.

strong leaders in the future. And, we were impressed with the transition in thinking made by several hospital chief executive officers (CEOs) and medical group practice managers.

From the start, we were interested in the unique aspects of the corporate cultures of integrated systems. The corporate culture includes the way physicians and managers in these systems communicate, their basic attitudes toward change and the role of physician-administrators who wish to continue their medical practices. Chapter 9 summarizes many of the unique aspects of the corporate cultures of the organizations studied.

We also found that all of the case study organizations were investing huge sums of money in developing information systems, generally viewed as one of the most important aspects of integrated health care. Some of this investment relates to being able to measure medical outcomes. A major reason for revamping and expanding the information system is to be able to control patient utilization under a managed competition payment system. This emphasis on database development and information systems, combined with high levels of interest in the potential for improving quality, led us to devote Chapter 10 to three related subjects — information systems, continuous quality improvement and outcomes measurement.

Chapter 11 summarizes our insights or lessons learned. Several of these insights were sprinkled throughout the previous eight chapters. This chapter represents a more focused approach to our analysis of the experiences of many integrated health care organizations, and we have been more liberal in offering our personal opinions about what we have observed.

CHAPTER 3.
DESIGNING INTEGRATED HEALTH CARE SYSTEMS

The only way to truly effectively compete with organized systems of care like Kaiser is to build organizations of your own.

— *Reece Report,* October 1991

The research for this book demonstrated that there are many more organizational models being used than the commonly-referred to "PHO," "clinic without walls," "MSO" and "foundation model." We counted more than 50 different organizational structures, and there are probably more.

Here are four examples from among the case study organizations:

- The for-profit Oregon Medical Group in Eugene and a not-for-profit hospital system (Sacred Heart) are linked through a not-for-profit management services organization (Oregon MSO). The health plan, SelectCare, is a for-profit HMO owned by Sacred Heart.

- In Albuquerque, the Presbyterian Network is part of Presbyterian Healthcare Services, a not-for-profit multihospital system. Those physicians who are the most closely integrated economically operate from several for-profit professional corporations; they receive administrative support from Presbyterian. The health plan, Health Plus, is a for-profit entity owned by Presbyterian.

- In Urbana, the Carle Clinic Association (a for-profit multispecialty group practice) leases facilities from the Carle Foundation, a not-for-profit organization that owns and operates the hospital. CarleCare, a for-profit HMO, is owned by the Clinic.

- In Long Beach, the Harriman Jones Medical Group (for-profit) provides medical services for the UniHealth Long Beach Foundation, a not-for-profit entity. UniHealth America, the unifying multihospital system, is also a not-for-profit. Its major health plan, CareAmerica, is a for-profit HMO under UniHealth Ventures, UniHealth America's for-profit subsidiary.

Complicated? Confusing? You bet. However, a certain degree of complexity is necessary in developing an integrated system in the legal and regulatory environment of the mid 1990s. Crafting the right organizational structure to meet a specific set of circumstances can be a challenging and somewhat artful process. The choice of organizational structure needs to reflect the actions and strategies the integrated system intends to pursue. It also has to reflect the level of commitment that physicians, hospitals and other participants are willing to make at the time the integrated system is formed and the level of financial risk that each party is willing and capable of assuming.

Because of today's legal and financial incentives in health care, the organizational design process usually entails a balancing of several competing considerations. For example, what would work best from a strategic perspective? What would be easiest to operate? What would maximize physician benefits and yet limit tax exposure? What would minimize legal exposure? What would maximize reimbursements and minimize costs? What is politically acceptable? In addition, as in the examples above, most systems have to think through the relationships between their not-for-profit and for-profit lines of business.

In this chapter, we consider six common approaches to building an integrated health care system. These include the clinics without walls, MSOs and foundations noted above, as well as models of integration based on networking, physician employment and medical group-hospital mergers leading to the creation of an integrated system. Exhibit 3-1 shows how the medical groups in each of the 10 case study organizations are linked to the hospital(s) and health plan(s) typically comprising the integrated health care systems. We draw heavily on these case study examples to illustrate the basic principles of each model and discuss the advantages and disadvantages of each.

We have not included Kaiser Permanente among the six models discussed even though it is perhaps the most completely integrated health care system in the country. In several of its 12 regions, Kaiser (a not-for-profit foundation) owns and operates clinics, hospitals, and a health plan. The Permanente medical groups in each region are for-profit professional corporations under exclusive contract to provide medical services to Kaiser Permanente members. In effect, Kaiser Permanente is a closed system, and one that has achieved a balance between the needs

EXHIBIT 3-1
Organizational Form, Case Study Organizations, 1993

Case Study Organizations	Hospital Ownership	Medical Group Assets	Medical Group Income	Health Plan Ownership	Control of Integrated Delivery System
1. Presbyterian Network, Albuquerque	NFP	PC	PC	NFP	NFP System Board (community based)
2. Fargo Clinic/St. Luke's Hospital	NFP	For Profit	For Profit	None	NFP Association (community based)
3. Marshfield Clinic/St. Joseph's Hospital	NFP (Ministry Corp.)	NFP	NFP	NFP	NFP System (physician governed)
4. Carle Clinic/Carle Foundation Hospital, Urbana	NFP Foundation	NFP	For Profit Clinic	For Profit Clinic	NFP Foundation (community based) and clinic
5. Sutter Health, Sacramento	NFP	Foundations (5)	PC	For Profit	NFP System (community based)
6. UniHealth America, Los Angeles	NFP	Foundations (3)	PC	For Profit	NFP System (community based)
7. Oregon Medical Group/Sacred Heart, Eugene	NFP (Health & Hospital Services)	NFP; MSO	PC	For Profit	NFP System/MSO
8. Geisinger System Danville, PA	NFP	NFP	NFP	501(c)4	NFP System (community based)
9. Kaiser Permanente/Saint Joseph Hospital, Denver	NFP	PC	PC	NFP	One of 12 regions of KP; Sisters of Charity of Leavenworth
10. MAPI/Saint Vincent Hospital, Billings, MT	NFP	PC	PC	N/A	Physicians and Sisters of Charity of Leavenworth

Source: Data obtained by BBC, Inc. from the organizations listed as part of the case study process, March-July, 1993.

of its health plan members, employer groups, and its physician and hospital provider organizations.

We have also not included several more traditional methods of linking hospitals and physicians, such as independent practice associations (IPAs) and preferred provider organizations (PPOs). Although there are exceptions, IPAs tend to be physician-owned and managed entities. (In Chapter 4 we discuss the importance of a hospital or multihospital system offering a variety of services to medical groups and physician organizations, including IPAs.) PPOs are restricted networks of physicians and hospitals, and can be owned by physician groups, insurance companies, employers or hospitals. The models discussed in this book go beyond these types of organizations and focus on those in which there are stronger ties between physicians and a hospital.

Clinic Without Walls

For several years, perhaps the best known clinic without walls in the country was the for-profit Sacramento Sierra Medical Group (also referred to as "Sac Sierra") formed in 1984 by 25 primary care physicians and two cardiologists. The Montana Associated Physicians, Inc. (MAPI) could also be considered a clinic without walls although the organization prefers not to use that terminology. MAPI is owned by 38 medical practices and was established in 1986.

Sac Sierra and MAPI were formed with the encouragement and support of hospital-based health systems (Sutter Health in Sacramento and Saint Vincent Hospital in Billings). However, in both cases the clinics without walls were owned by physicians, and intended to be financially self sufficient. It was not originally anticipated that either of these organizations would require on-going financial support from a hospital or health care system.

Exhibit 3-2 depicts how a typical clinic without walls functions. The assets, patient records and managed care contracts remain under the ownership of the various professional corporations. In most clinics without walls, non-physician employees continue to work for one of the professional corporations. The professional corporations pay an administrative fee to cover the expenses of centralized services, such as payroll, collections and purchasing.

EXHIBIT 3-2

Schematic of Typical Clinic without Walls

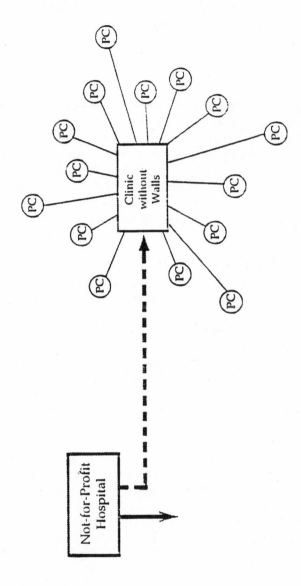

Note: Clinic without walls provides billing services, collections, payroll, marketing, and administrative support. It does not own contracts, accounts receivable, patient records, or other assets. Support staff may or may not be employees of clinic without walls.

Sac Sierra. Since Sac Sierra was the prototype clinic without walls, we followed in the footsteps of hundreds of other physicians, hospital administrators and consultants on a pilgrimage to Sacramento to find out why it was formed and how it worked. We were surprised by what we heard.

"The clinic without walls, at least the way it was implemented in Sacramento, is a failed concept." These are the words of Gary Susnara, the Sutter Health executive responsible for the new Sutter Medical Foundation, the entity created in early 1992 to support Sac Sierra and other for-profit medical groups. The clinic without walls was unable to live up to its original purpose as described by one of its founders, "the common vision was to organize an effective single business entity to maximize economic clout and yet preserve some traditional values of autonomy" (Forster, 1988, p. 12). The reasons:

- Sac Sierra had too many practice sites (at one point, there were 70 locations). Many of these were clustered around the medical center so they did not provide broad geographic coverage.

- Because of these multiple locations, Sac Sierra was unable to realize significant revenues from centralizing ancillary services, such as laboratory and radiology. There were no economies of scale. In fact, because of the central administrative offices, overhead was higher than it would have been without the association.

- Primary care physicians' net incomes were falling. The organization lacked a funding source to prop up these incomes to be competitive with what other physicians were earning in the Sacramento marketplace.

- Sac Sierra failed to develop a corporate culture among participating physicians. Physicians continued to practice in their own office settings and had little reason to share their experiences with others in the group.

- Including specialists in the organization did not yield the additional hoped-for source of revenue to support primary care physicians. Specialists eventually left the group with the blessing of the primary care physicians and Sutter Health.

In a sense, Sac Sierra was a loose association of physicians. One Sutter Health executive described Sac Sierra as, "a chamber of commerce for small businesses. The physicians united in response to a common vision but really did not come together from a cultural and operational point of view."

Montana Associated Physicians, Inc. (MAPI). This 110-member association of physicians was generally successful. Originally formed in 1986 in response to competition from the Billings Clinic (a 95-doctor group which merged with Deaconess Medical Center in 1993), MAPI has doubled in size and has achieved broad geographic coverage through the development of 38 practice sites.

MAPI has focused a substantial amount of attention on building strong relationships with independent primary care physicians in 40 smaller communities around Billings. Through television commercials, MAPI has encouraged residents of these small towns to use their hometown doctors.

MAPI has also devoted resources to an "assault on overhead of individual practices." Another major financial benefit: group purchasing of medical malpractice insurance leading to a large reduction in rates for most medical specialties.

On balance — clinics without walls. In terms of the advantages and disadvantages, this organizational model represents a first step toward physician integration in situations where physicians place a high value on their autonomy and have not previously collaborated. There also may be modest benefits in terms of economies of scale (e.g., group purchasing of malpractice insurance). In comparison with solo practice, a clinic without walls offers advantages in managed care contracting, and to varying degrees, guaranteed patient flow.

On the other hand, the clinic without walls does not provide access to capital, and it fails to provide a vehicle for supporting primary care physicians in situations when they need financial assistance. As the MAPI example illustrates, a clinic without walls can work in markets where primary care physician incomes are strong. However, this model is ineffective in competing with more highly integrated systems that can pay a premium for primary care physicians.

Management Services Organization (MSO)

The management services organization, or MSO, can be organized in a variety of ways — as a hospital-based organization, a joint venture between physicians and a hospital, a free-standing corporation, or under the auspices of an insurer, HMO or investor.

Exhibit 3-3 describes the initial flows of capital and asset ownership, and shows how revenues and expenses flow among an MSO, medical practices and a hospital. The MSO owns the real estate and other tangible assets. An MSO may or may not purchase intangible assets, such as patient medical records, managed care contracts and covenants not to compete (Grant, 1993, p. 13).

The MSO employs most or all non-physician personnel and provides administrative services and facilities. Stronger versions of the MSO model provide all services and facilities to all medical practices. As with the clinic without walls, the MSO may offer a menu of services and practices may choose which services they wish to receive and pay for. For example, a practice may choose to participate in the joint purchasing of malpractice insurance and joint contracting with managed care while refusing to have the MSO employ its nurses.

Physicians usually form a single professional corporation to function as the physician partner in an MSO structure. The professional corporation employs the individual physicians, holds the provider number and owns the managed care contracts. Insurers contract separately with the professional corporation and hospital for services. However, managed care contracting efforts are usually coordinated in an MSO model.

In many instances the MSO is jointly owned and governed by participating physicians and the partner hospital. This "joint venture" MSO more readily encourages a partnership approach between physicians and a hospital. Some organizations have established MSOs which are wholly owned and operated by a hospital or health care system.

Another approach to management services is a free-standing for-profit corporation, such as PhyCor, Pacific Physician Services or Caremark International. These proprietary companies purchase the assets of the physician practices, assume all management responsibility and contract with the professional corporation for medical services.

Finally, another variant is the for-profit MSO which is affiliated or owned by an HMO. While few examples of this model presently exist, we anticipate that more will emerge as insurers bid for control of the health care delivery system. Insurance companies, such as MetLife and Aetna, are investing in primary care delivery networks through an MSO or other arrangements (Fine, 1993).

Clearly the MSO concept has an almost infinite number of variations. However, since we were most interested in MSOs which involved a partnership of physicians and a hospital, the Oregon Medical Group and Sacred Heart Hospital case study provided the model we have analyzed in greater detail.

Oregon MSO. The Oregon MSO came about as a result of the desire of physicians and Sacred Heart Hospital to put a structure in place that would allow them to effectively compete for managed care contracts and to help build the base of primary care physicians in Eugene.

The founders of the Oregon Medical Group, which included physicians in eight different primary care practices, evaluated a number of different organizational approaches, including the formation of a medical foundation. They chose the MSO model, primarily because it let them retain their existing practice locations, gave them a significant voice in the governance of the new organization (four representatives out of eight on the MSO board) and allowed them the flexibility of terminating their relationship if things didn't work out. In other words, the formation of the Oregon Medical Group (OMG) and the Oregon MSO was not viewed as an irreversible decision. Under this model, the physician organizations largely retain their autonomy and independence as well as the value of their respective medical practices.

How does this MSO work? The not-for-profit Oregon MSO purchased most of the tangible assets and accounts receivable of the participating medical groups; some of the groups elected to retain ownership of their buildings. The initial investment approximated $2 million for the eight practices. Physicians did not receive payment for goodwill, nor did they receive income guarantees.

Once established and operating, the billings for work performed by OMG physicians are channeled through the professional corporations (PCs); the Oregon MSO bills the PCs for services provided. The former non-physician employees of the medical groups became employees of the MSO. Physicians in each medical practice participating in the Oregon Medical Group have the responsibility for dividing up the compensation pool (the residual after paying expenses).

EXHIBIT 3-3
Initial Flow of Capital and Assets,
Management Services Organization (MSO)

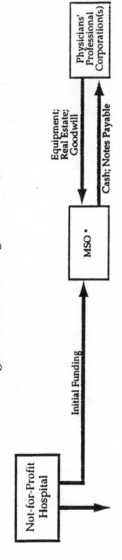

EXHIBIT 3-3(b)

Flow of Funds from Operations, MSO

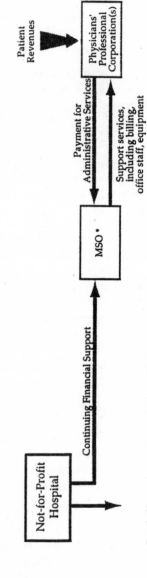

* Board of hospital representatives and physicians.

On balance — MSOs. Like clinics without walls, MSOs allow physicians to practice as they have in the past and retain much of their autonomy. In fact, one of the OMG physicians interviewed said that when he is asked with which medical group he is associated, he responds, "Westmoreland Family Medicine Group" (his former and on-going group) rather than the Oregon Medical Group. Physicians hold on to the value of their practice as represented by managed care contracts, accounts receivable, patient records and other on-going business interests.

As noted earlier, physicians retain a strong voice in the governance of the Oregon MSO. For example, they have equal representation (with Sacred Heart) on the board. The administrator of the MSO is generally regarded as the OMG group practice administrator. Even though his salary is paid by the MSO, his primary loyalties are to the physicians he serves.

An MSO structure with hospital participation can provide access to capital, which helps meet the expenses of consolidating practices, recruiting new physicians and supplementing physician incomes.

The disadvantages of an MSO are similar to those of a clinic without walls. In the case of OMG and the Oregon MSO, there were limitations on the medical group's ability to receive ancillary income from laboratory and radiology since these two potential income sources were subject to prior joint venture agreements between Sacred Heart and its pathologists and radiologists. Changes in Stark anti-referral legislation make it more difficult for groups to own ancillary services under the MSO model.

The MSO arrangement is usually weak with regard to promoting a common corporate culture. The day-to-day contact among many physicians in the group, which is typical of the larger multispecialty clinics, is often lacking.

From a legal perspective, the MSO model appears to be especially vulnerable to accusations of inurement (shifting funds from a tax-exempt entity for the benefit of private physicians or a for-profit organization). As attempts are made to adequately fund primary care practices from not-for-profit funding sources, this problem continues to surface.

The Contractual Network

Some organizations have found it effective to offer a pluralistic approach to physician-hospital integration and have combined several of the approaches noted above with other forms of assistance to physicians.

The Presbyterian Network. Among the case studies, Presbyterian Healthcare Services (PHS) provided the best example of linking physicians, hospitals and health plans through a series of contracts or networking relationships. The Presbyterian Network example is especially interesting in that most physicians in Albuquerque were in solo practices or small groups; there were few large clinics other than the Lovelace Medical Foundation, Presbyterian's major competitor.

By becoming a Network physician, (410 out of 650 physicians applied for membership) doctors agree to attend Network meetings, participate in continuous quality improvement projects, and allow the Network to pick and choose among its members in assembling provider panels for specific managed care contracts. Physicians selected for the Network sign a network affiliation agreement, a binding contract for as long as the physician meets the terms of Network membership.

There are several levels of involvement with the Presbyterian Network, varying from collaborative services (e.g., medical records, purchasing, information systems), to managed care contracting, to practice management services, to full economic integration. (This type of "pluralistic" approach was used by several of the integrated health care systems studied and is discussed in more detail in Chapter 4.)

At the most integrated end of the spectrum, Presbyterian Network had over 70 primary care physicians participating in practice development agreements. This arrangement has some of the characteristics of an MSO — non-physician employees and practice managers are employed by PHS, and the physician compensation pool is a function of residual funds after covering practice overhead. However, in the Presbyterian case, physicians own the assets and lease them to the not-for-profit parent organization (PHS); therefore, physician owners generate lease income from their fixed assets which supplements their practice income. (In most cases examined, the not-for-profit hospital or health care systems purchased physician assets and leased them to the MSO; lease payments were an MSO expense and deducted from net revenues.)

Presbyterian Network physicians who are economically integrated may lose their ability to choose a practice location; the Network has the authority to assign them where they are needed within the Albuquerque area. In general, physicians are more closely managed than in typical MSO arrangements. However, physicians remain "at risk" for a large portion of their earnings; they are not on salary and are not employees of PHS.

On balance — the network model. The primary advantage of the network model is its ability to be flexible in meeting the needs and preferences of a physician population that is skeptical of too much integration too fast. Network models can theoretically operate simultaneously with one group of physicians that is interested only in managed care contracting, another group interested in management services, and another group that is interested in closer economic integration with a hospital.

The network model in Albuquerque links the success of primary care physicians with the success of the Presbyterian Healthcare System. A primary care physician who was economically integrated cited several advantages of the network approach. He found that the Presbyterian Network:

- Creates a partnership approach.

- Articulates the expectation of a long-term relationship.

- Creates a sense of security for both parties (physicians and hospital).

- Improves physician productivity and lessens worries about office operations and income.

- Facilitates contracting with managed care companies.

- Improves benefits (e.g., pension plan funding) for physicians.

This physician said that his decision to enter into a practice development agreement with PHS was driven by a number of factors including the erosion of his financial base. He also cited the growing "hassle factor," inability to recruit new physicians, lack of funds for the group's pension plan and a feeling that they were losing control of their practice. He added, "We needed a bigger, tougher older brother, and we saw this in PHS."

The weaknesses of a network arrangement include the perception among some physicians that those doctors who are economically integrated have "sold out" to PHS. Other problems are created between the "innies and outies." And PHS has found it difficult to accommodate the income expectations of all physicians.

Most of all, operating a network model can be exceedingly cumbersome. For all of the above reasons, the network model is often seen as a transition stage that a group of providers may go through in reaching another, more fully integrated model.

Medical Foundation Model

The foundation model, usually a not-for-profit 501(c)(3), is a stronger organizational arrangement than the MSO or clinic without walls in terms of binding physicians and hospitals together in an integrated health care system. The foundation model may also be less vulnerable to Internal Revenue Service (IRS) challenges provided it can demonstrate a community purpose. Foundations often include teaching and research functions which contribute to a showing of how the foundation benefits the community.

Exhibit 3-4 shows the structure of the typical foundation model, including the flow of funds at the time of formation and once it is operating. Under this model the foundation owns all the tangible and intangible assets, receives all the revenues and employs all the non-physician staff. The physician group, often organized as a professional corporation, contracts with the foundation to provide medical services. The professional corporation has no assets other than the clinical skills of its members.

The foundation is the contracting entity for managed care and maintains the provider number for Medicare purposes. It is governed by a board of community representatives with limited physician representation. In California, the law requires that 80 percent of the board members of a foundation be community representatives and that no more than 20 percent can be physicians.

Medical foundations are receiving increasing attention across the country, especially in California where they have sprung up in response to an aggressive managed care environment and California's unique legal framework. Russell Coile, a health care futurist, says the foundation

EXHIBIT 3-4
Initial Flow of Capital and Assets, Medical Foundation

EXHIBIT 3-4(b)
Flow of Funds from Operations, Medical Foundation

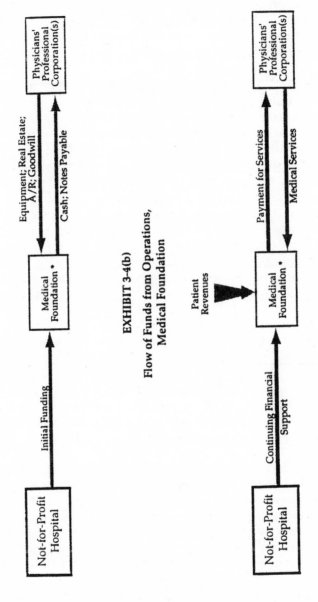

* Board dominated by community representatives.

concept has applications throughout the country. "Physicians are open to a new approach to hospital-MD relations that will protect their clinical freedom and ability to control their own practices. The nonprofit medical clinic foundation may be a new umbrella concept under which hospitals and doctors can unite" (Coile, 1992, p. 66).

Tax-exempt status for the entity that engages in the practice of medicine is the key distinguishing feature of the foundation model. Obtaining tax-exempt status is difficult; today's requirements are more strict than in the 1930s and 1940s, when many well-known multispecialty groups, such as the Mayo and Cleveland Clinics, received tax-exempt status. The IRS approval of the Friendly Hills HealthCare Foundation was believed by many to be an important step forward in the acceptance of this type of organization. The IRS considered this application for tax-exempt status for 20 months before issuing an approval in January, 1993.

The key question addressed by the IRS in the Friendly Hills case was whether the foundation would benefit the community. Factors considered were the operation of an emergency room available to all, open medical staff, governance and control (no more than 49 percent of directors could be interested parties), lack of non-compete clauses in physician contracts, participation in Medicare and Medicaid, appropriate valuation of assets and medical education and research (Grant, Hanlon and Margulis, 1993, pp. 4-7).

To illustrate the workings of a medical foundation, we describe Facey Medical Group which provides medical services in partnership with Northridge Hospital, part of UniHealth America in Southern California.

Facey Medical Foundation. The Facey Medical Group, established in 1923 in the San Fernando Valley, is a 60-physician group with an emphasis on internal medicine and pediatrics. Its shareholders examined their future in light of their payor mix (80 percent managed care) and decided they needed access to capital in order to succeed. As the president of the medical foundation, a gastroenterologist, relates, "We needed a partner ... We could see that we needed $5 to $7 million over the next five years for a new main building, computer systems and imaging equipment." The group decided to associate with UniHealth America, a not-for-profit, multihospital health system serving many parts of the Los Angeles area.

How does this type of foundation work? The foundation, governed by a board of community representatives, purchased all of the assets of Facey Medical Group. It had a 20-year contract with Facey, the professional corporation, to provide medical services. Facey received a three-year guarantee that physician compensation would not fall below a fixed percent of net revenues. In comparison with an MSO, the contractual ties are stronger and extend over a longer time period. As one UniHealth executive summed up, "We are in it together for the long haul."

On balance — medical foundations. The foundation model has two potential strategic advantages over an MSO model. First, the physicians are more integrated with one another; they usually function in a manner similar to a multispecialty group. Second, the foundation model is a way to provide physician services and related activities in a tax-exempt setting.

From a physician perspective, the major advantage of the foundation model is that it opens up one or more sources of capital for expansion and other needs of the medical group practice. As with the MSO model, the foundation model provides participating medical groups with the ability to be a part of a larger system, achieve economies of scale and have improved access to managed care contracts, especially those involving risk sharing.

Physicians are at less financial risk in a foundation model (they are often on salary) and enjoy a more predictable income. Another advantage is that it is easier for new physicians to be attracted to a group practice setting since buy-in requirements to become part of the group are less; all of the assets are owned by the foundation.

Doctors in a foundation structure find that the trade-off for security and access to capital may be less autonomy and independence. Physicians no longer directly control the hiring and firing of administrators, where they practice, hours of practice, call schedules or other factors. (However, they usually retain control of clinical decision-making and patient care.) The foundation model also removes physicians as a major voice in the formal governance structure of the organization.

The foundation model is particularly popular in California, where there is an enforced prohibition against the corporate practice of medicine. Legislation enabling the establishment of medical foundations was enacted as a means of facilitating practicing in a manner similar to a corporation yet practicing in a tax-exempt setting. In California, foundations require that medical groups have at least 40 physicians (or 27 full-time equivalent doctors).

Physicians Employed by a Hospital

None of the case studies involved significant numbers of physicians being directly employed by a hospital or multihospital system. (Geisinger started out this way, but its 1981 reorganization created a separate clinic which had equal status with the Geisinger Medical Center.) However, employing physicians, especially primary care doctors, is becoming commonplace. For example, the Premier Hospitals Alliance, Inc., headquartered in Chicago reports that, "It is becoming more convenient for physicians to come in with an employment arrangement, and it's easy for the hospital to do, particularly when we are placing physicians in primary care settings affiliated with the hospital" (Premier Hospitals, 1993, p. 5).

In the case of Sisters of Providence, a multihospital system with hospitals in Alaska, Washington, Oregon, California and Montana, several of the hospitals have moved more aggressively to put primary care physicians on the payroll. The CEO of one hospital said, "The arrangement is incredibly simple — we employ the doctors." As of mid 1992 there were 70 primary care physicians in 11 clinic locations, all part of the hospital.

The CEO of a large hospital that is moving aggressively toward employing primary care physicians said that there were several major stumbling blocks. There is the expectation of physicians about the goodwill value of their practice; this can make such a move financially unfeasible for the hospital. Another problem is development of a compensation model that stimulates productivity, works well under capitation, and provides the kind of base salary attractive to physicians who are considering alternatives, such as being employed by the larger clinics or in a staff or group-model HMO. Finally, specialty physicians feel threatened by the hospital organizing its primary care base; however, this threat is off-set by the mutual need of the hospital and the specialists for a strong primary care base.

Dr. James Todd, President of the American Medical Association said that, "One of the big concerns is the numbers of hospitals literally buying up practices and making physicians hospital employees. We do not think that physicians should be employees of hospitals. They should be partners with hospitals" (Clarke, 1993, p. 23).

On balance — direct employment of physicians. In our view, the direct employment of physicians by a hospital has several drawbacks. Direct hospital employment of physicians can reduce incentives for productivity and typically does not encourage the same degree of risk-sharing as other models; thus it leads to a less effective alignment of financial incentives. It often skews the balance of power to the hospital rather than toward physicians, and in the long run this can lead to less innovation.

On the other hand, we respect the track record of several large integrated systems, as well as many hospitals in rural areas, that use this approach. The direct employment of physicians appears to create few, if any, regulatory or legal problems in states that do not enforce corporate practice of medicine prohibitions. Even though we are more impressed with other arrangements, we expect direct employment of doctors to increase.

Becoming an Integrated System Through Merger

In an effort to achieve higher levels of integration, some hospitals and physician organizations have merged. The product of the merger is a unified system, with common goals, in which neither hospital nor physicians are thought of as having the upper hand. The Fargo Clinic/St. Luke's Hospital case study is an example of a merger between a for-profit clinic and a not-for-profit hospital, with the surviving organization being the not-for-profit St. Luke's Association.

There are different pathways to unifying a physician group and hospital. In Fargo, in nearby Bismarck (Q&R Clinic and Medcenter One), and in Billings (Billings Clinic and Deaconess Medical Center), the pathway was the merger of a large multispecialty group and a hospital. The Geisinger System was formed by a hospital's first employing physicians, then later forming a medical group to work as an equal partner, then, in late 1992, reorganizing the day-to-day management of the system to facilitate all organizations acting as one. In Worcester, Massachusetts, the Fallon Clinic took over Saint Vincent Hospital. Some medical groups have started their own hospitals.

St. Luke's Association. Why would a medical group like Fargo Clinic consider merging with a hospital? In the case of the Fargo Clinic, the major reasons were:

- A preference to join hands with its neighbor and supporter, St. Luke's Hospital to focus resources in the marketplace. The two organizations have been co-located for 70 years, and the clinic accounts for more than 99 percent of the hospital's admissions.

- A hope of achieving economies of scale through less duplication. A consultant retained at the beginning of the merger discussions told the two entities that these economies would not be sufficient to justify the pain and expense of the merger. However, at the time the case study was prepared, the clinic and hospital had identified 20 areas for consolidation, including human resources, security, plant maintenance and information systems.

- An ability to position the organization for capitation, including the ability to sign "single signature contracts" covering both physician and hospital services.

- The need for the clinic to gain access to capital through the not-for-profit hospital. As is true with most medical groups, the Fargo Clinic had not retained capital nor strengthened its financial position.

- A desire to do what is best for the people of the service area. Several physicians, hospital administrators and board members said that they believed that patients would be better served by coordinated care of the type offered by the new organization.

Geisinger. Within Geisinger, 11 separate organizations are operated as one. The missions of the organizations — including a medical group, a hospital and a health plan — are integrated. The officers of each organization are common. According to Geisinger's chief financial officer, "We examined the possibility of combining these organizations into one. We found that we could have reduced the number from 11 to perhaps four. We couldn't get by with fewer than four without running into tax and reimbursement problems. So we decided the best approach was to keep the 11 separate organizations but to operate the entire system as a single entity."

On balance — the merger model. While a merged organization offers a compelling example of an integrated system, this approach is also one of the most difficult to achieve. It is easiest to implement in instances like Fargo or Fallon when the medical staff is organized into a single professional corporation that represents the vast majority of admissions to a hospital.

Even then it is complex and difficult. It requires combining missions, cultures and people, usually including strong egos on both sides. Knowing that the merger in Fargo might be the end of a for-profit medical group managed by doctors, one of the physician directors of the Fargo Clinic said, "When I first heard the idea of the merger I was vehemently opposed to it. I thought we were giving up too much. However, the more I thought about relinquishing control to a community-based board of directors, the less it bothered me. I thought that these people are going to try to do what is best for the community, and that we could work together to achieve the same ends."

On the other hand, the unified model resulting from a merger offers mutual benefits to physicians and the hospital. It enhances the ability of the two organizations to focus their energies on the needs of the marketplace without concern over internal competition. The merger assures the hospital and its physicians of being a major player in the health care system of the future. And, the merger better positions both groups to bid on capitated contracts. The hospital is able to lock in its medical group and assure its flow of patients.

Today's merger of a medical group and a hospital almost always leads to a single corporate entity that manages a hospital, a medical group and other related services. Like Geisinger, the designers of the new system are likely to conclude that there are too many legal and financial incentives to maintaining separate entities for engaging in hospital and physician activities. Designing the best merger structure for a particular set of circumstances involves tradeoffs. Which structure:

- Is the most cost-effective way to comply with Stark anti-referral legislation? Generally speaking, the options are (a) to separate physicians from receiving any of the net revenues from ancillary services, (b) to fit under an exception according to the Stark legislation that allows physicians to own an interest in a hospital, or (c) to fit under an exception that allows physicians to participate in these revenues if the services are wholly owned and directly supervised by the physicians.

- Minimizes the tax liabilities of the participants?

- Minimizes the risk of inurement challenges?

- Enables physicians to maximize retirement benefits without imposing prohibitive benefits costs on the organization?

- Maximizes reimbursements under Medicare? Certain services are reimbursed more favorably if submitted by a medical group as opposed to a hospital. Also, for those systems that do not have separate entities for physician and hospital services, Medicare will not reimburse for medical office services when patients see a physician and are then admitted within three days.

Selecting a Model

There are so many models to choose from — which one to choose? As the prior discussion illustrated, the "best" model for an organization often depends on a number of underlying factors:

Composition of medical community. In situations where physicians are mainly in solo or small group practices, it may not be feasible to move directly toward development of a foundation model or the unified, merged system. The founders of Sac Sierra reflect that they would never have become a medical foundation if they had not first gained experience as a clinic without walls. Patrick Hays, the CEO of Sutter Health, says, "In 1984, when the clinic without walls was initiated by a bunch of solo practice physicians and small groups, that was as far as they wanted to go in terms of losing their autonomy. But, if the group hadn't gone through that first step in what has been an evolutionary process, we wouldn't have the Sutter Medical Foundation and the ability to consolidate these physicians into the three locations where we need them."

On the other hand, in markets where physician integration is advanced, organizations such as the Fargo Clinic and the Q&R Clinic in Bismarck have looked to models which expand the depth of integration by uniting with a hospital or health plan. These organizations have found that more complete integration of a medical group and hospital can expand market share and simplify managed care contracting.

The autonomy/security trade-off. This will vary by market; also, every medical group is different. In the upper Midwest, where many practitioners come out of the Mayo tradition, physicians tend to place a higher value on group practice. However, the same is not true in other parts of the country. Independent-minded physicians are more apt to embrace the concept of a clinic without walls or MSO, both of which preserve physician autonomy and control. Other physicians, especially recent graduates, are likely to give greater weight to economic security and stability — characteristics associated with a foundation, a single professional corporation or direct employment.

The trade-off has its roots in the governance structure. Management services organizations like the Oregon MSO offer physicians a strong voice in governance. On the other hand, in an MSO, physicians' incomes are more at risk. A foundation model offers considerable economic security, but the degree of formal physician representation on the governing board is less.

The need for capital. The ability to finance the development of an integrated delivery system is an obvious consideration. At one end of the spectrum, the clinic without walls offers little prospect for access to capital. In the 1980s, Sac Sierra failed to appreciate its need for capital for practice expansion or physician recruitment. On the other hand, Facey Medical Group recognized that it needed funds and this need pushed the group toward UniHealth America and the foundation model.

The managed care marketplace. Since capitation is rapidly gaining ground, models offering the greatest prospects for building a primary care base, increasing geographic coverage and controlling costs may be the best answer. These are likely to be the more integrated models, such as medical foundations and mergers of physician groups and hospitals.

Legal barriers. Depending on the legal climate, not all of the options may be available. Many of the issues involved in developing a foundation model relate to obtaining IRS approval of tax-exempt status. The Friendly Hills HealthCare Foundation approval is an important step forward in the acceptance of the concept of a foundation model.

Taking the next step. In this chapter we have touched on six of the numerous organizational models that are being employed to achieve greater physician-hospital integration. Adjustments and refinements are possible within any of these models. In addition, most of those in "established" integrated systems readily admit that they may well need to undergo further structural adjustments in the future.

Once a general determination of the best direction is made, there is a need to balance the legal and financial considerations to arrive at the most appropriate structure for a given situation. The legal system was not put in place with integrated health care systems in mind; therefore, substantial balancing is sometimes necessary. Still, despite the problems in selecting a model that fits the needs of physicians and the marketplace and is legal, many integrated systems are pushing on and getting the job done.

CHAPTER 4.

POWER SHIFTS: PRIMARY CARE PHYSICIANS AND SPECIALISTS IN INTEGRATED SYSTEMS

If we can't control our sources of referral and control utilization of our health plan, we are in big trouble. Primary care locations are the answer to this problem.
—Physician CEO of a large multispecialty clinic

Based on our review of actions taken by the 10 case study organizations, none were more important than the decision to build or expand their primary care base. As will be discussed in Chapter 5, this can be an expensive strategy; in fact, for most of the organizations studied, expansion of primary care was, and continues to be, very costly. However, nearly all of the organizations agreed that the efforts they have made to add primary care doctors and to expand their referral network geographically were among the most significant accomplishments of the last decade.

This chapter discusses four closely related issues:

- Why have many of the large integrated systems increased their emphasis on primary care, especially family practice?

- How have these organizations gone about developing primary care networks that provide adequate geographic coverage? Locating their own physicians? Acquiring existing practices?

- How can an organization emphasize the development of its primary care base and, at the same time, avoid antagonizing its specialists?

- Looking ahead, how do the large integrated systems intend to achieve an appropriate balance between primary care and medical specialists?

Exhibit 4-1 shows the proportion of primary care physicians — defined as family practice, internal medicine, pediatrics and OB/Gyn — in each of the case study organizations and the number of primary care

EXHIBIT 4-1
Primary Care Initiatives, Case Study Organizations, 1993

Case Study Organizations	Proportion of Primary Care	Number of "Controlled" PC Locations*	Year Began PC Initiatives	Major Funding Sources for PC Initiatives
1. Presbyterian Network, Albuquerque	25%	8	1988	Hospitals
2. Fargo Clinic/St. Luke's Hospital	30%	30	1983	Specialists; ancilliaries
3. Marshfield Clinic/St. Joseph's Hospital	30%	23	1980	Specialists; ancilliaries; health plan
4. Carle Clinic/Carle Foundation Hospital, Urbana	33%	10	1974	Specialists; hospital; ancilliaries; health plan
5. Sutter Health, Sacramento (Sac Sierra Medical Group only)	60%	70	1984	PC Physicians; health system
6. UniHealth America, Los Angeles	30%	8	1990	Hospitals; health plans; ancilliaries
7. Oregon Medical Group/Sacred Heart, Eugene (OMG only)	100%	7	1988	PC Physicians; health system
8. Geisinger System Danville, PA	30%	43	1982	Specialists; health plan; hospital; ancilliaries
9. Kaiser Permanente/Saint Joseph Hospital, Denver	50% **	13 **	1969 **	Health plan; specialists
10. MAPI/Saint Vincent Hospital, Billings, MT	35%	2	1986	Hospital; MAPI

* Some of the locations also include specialists.

** KP only.

Source: Data obtained from the organizations listed as part of the case study process, March-July, 1993.

branches away from the main campus. (Incidentally, the variation in terminology used to describe these outlying facilities is interesting — satellites, branches, care centers, network sites, medical offices, family practice offices, primary care pods, regional clinics, rural clinics.) The exhibit also shows the approximate time frame when each of the 10 organizations initiated its primary care strategies.

Emphasis on Primary Care

Prior to performing the research for this book, we had the preconceived notion that the Marshfield, Fargo, Geisinger and Carle Clinics, four members of the prestigious "Clinic Club" (an informal organization of 11 clinics including Duluth, Scott & White, Sharp Rees-Stealy, Park Nicollet, Palo Alto, Wichita and Virginia Mason), were staffed by medical specialists who concentrated on taking care of the most complex cases referred to them by independent physicians practicing in the hinterlands.

The extent to which the case study clinics and other major integrated systems have already emphasized the development of primary care, particularly family practice (FP), surprised us. In our research and consulting, we frequently hear specialists criticize family practice doctors by saying things like: "Patients would be better off if they came to me first." "I've seen too many cases where FPs treated a patient too long without specialist input and really messed things up." At the same time, not a primary care meeting goes by without expressions of fear of being associated with "specialist-dominated organizations." Why, then, have prestigious multispecialty clinics emphasized family practice and primary care? What do the large integrated health care systems know that others have failed to recognize?

First, these organizations realize that primary care physicians are essential for the organization to compete in a managed care environment with or without health care reform. Since many of these systems are also continuing to expand their own health plans, usually HMOs, they need a distribution network they can control. Thus, primary care physicians must be economically integrated into the large organization and located where needed to serve health plan subscribers. Second, they fear that competitors might buy the loyalty of primary care physicians in solo or small group practice since these practice settings probably are not economically viable in the long term. The result is that some of the large health care systems risk losing important referral sources. Third, and most important, they know that many primary care doctors practice high quality medicine and are an asset to any medical organization. Finally, integrated systems are well aware that primary care physicians are a scarce resource. The number of new primary care physicians in the pipeline has been shrinking and organizations must compete aggressively to build a strong provider network.

All four of the large clinics that were part of the case study research have devoted substantial resources — money, management time and energy, and physician leadership — to reaching out to primary care doctors in general and family practice physicians specifically. And, these efforts have been evolving for at least a decade. Furthermore, when physician leaders and clinic administrators were asked about their key strategic moves of the past 10 or 15 years, development of a geographically diverse primary care network was among the top two or three initiatives cited.

Building the primary care base. The development of a primary care base began incrementally for most organizations but has accelerated in recent years given the increasing need to control a broad geographic area. In some cases, the primary care network evolved in response to requests from other physicians or communities. For example, local community leaders in the sparsely populated area of north central Wisconsin asked the Marshfield Clinic to sponsor primary care in their towns.

In the case of the Fargo Clinic during the 1983 through 1985 period, several primary care groups in outlying communities decided they would like to become a part of a larger clinic. This movement was spurred by the efforts of the competing Dakota Clinic to establish a referral network in small communities in Minnesota and North Dakota. One of the executives of the Fargo Clinic said, "If we hadn't been willing to work with these primary care groups, we probably would have been left at the starting gate. Now they form an important part of the clinic, and they give us excellent geographic coverage of the region."

Dr. Jack Pollard, a cardiologist and long-time CEO of the Carle Clinic, said that in 1975 it was hard for patients to get in to visit any one of the Carle physicians. "At the same time we could see that people were flocking to family practice docs; patients were voting with their feet. Some of us concluded that if we had some of these types of physicians it would help us with our work load."

One of the physicians at Carle Clinic noted that it was "gutsy" for Dr. Pollard to introduce the idea of family practice to the Carle Clinic in the late 1970s. "This was not a popular decision with many of the physicians at that time." The first family practice physician at Carle was brought into the main campus in Urbana. As Dr. Pollard recalled, "It was important for our staff to get to know the first family practice doctor and what he could do. This helped change minds about family practice."

Times have changed at Carle; one third, or slightly more, of the physicians at the Carle Clinic were in primary care in 1993. Also, three of the six members of the Carle Clinic board of governors were primary care doctors, including one in family practice.

How well have family practice physicians fit in? The answer: very well. For example, the president of the Marshfield Clinic, Dr. Richard Leer, is a family practice physician. Three out of eight members of the Fargo Clinic board of directors are primary care physicians.

At Geisinger, family medicine was introduced in the late 1960s, but the initial efforts failed. In the early 1970s, a family practice physician was recruited to try again to establish a family medicine clinical area; this physician accepted the offer on the condition that family practice would be part of the residency program. This gave the program more credibility, and it succeeded. In 1993, Geisinger was considering adding family medicine as the eighth clinical division in the organization.

The Primary Care Feeder System

Based on our analysis of the case study organizations, a common theme is the concentration of resources in the development of a primary care feeder system for specialists and hospitals. Even more important, the primary care network enables the integrated systems to deliver care and control utilization in system-owned HMOs (see Chapter 6).

Depending on whether the integrated system serves a rural, urban or heavily populated metropolitan area, there are differences in how this strategy is implemented. In general, integrated systems serving rural areas have more branches, or primary care sites, and the facilities are smaller (two or three physicians is common). The integrated systems in more heavily populated areas tend to follow the Kaiser Permanente (KP) example of a limited number of fairly large clinics or offices, usually with some specialty coverage, but predominantly primary care. For example, in the Denver Area KP's medical offices average 12 to 20 physicians each, with only one large specialists' facility located adjacent to Saint Joseph Hospital.

Rural networks. As shown in Exhibit 4-1, some of the more rural integrated systems have very well developed referral networks. For example, the Fargo Clinic has 30 locations, most staffed exclusively with primary care, and a few with specialists, over a 90-mile radius including portions of Minnesota and North Dakota.

Exhibit 4-2 shows the distribution of the Marshfield and Gundersen Clinic's medical practice sites in Wisconsin. Gundersen Clinic also has a number of primary sites in Iowa. This exhibit is intended to demonstrate the extent of geographic coverage achieved by these two integrated systems.

In the case of the Marshfield Clinic, the initial primary care offices were in nearby communities that had lost their doctors through death or retirement. "The local people pleaded with us to come in because they weren't having any success in recruiting a doctor" according to Fritz Wenzel, former Executive Director of the Marshfield Clinic. "While this was our initial motivation, we quickly realized that this was a good long-term strategy, and we began pursuing it more aggressively." In 1993 Marshfield had 23 practice locations in north central Wisconsin.

Montana Associated Physicians, Inc. (MAPI) has used a different approach in that it has cultivated its relationship with primary care physicians in 40 small towns through promotion of the concept that residents of rural areas should use their home-town doctors. MAPI also has been insistent that its members communicate with these physicians when a referral is made to a MAPI physician and that patients are promptly returned to their primary care provider.

Combination urban and rural areas. Case study examples that fall in this category include the Carle Clinic and Geisinger. These systems serve areas that have many small and medium-sized communities but that normally would not be considered rural.

The Carle Clinic primary care network is referred to as a "hub and spoke" system. Carle has 10 practice sites plus its home base in Urbana. The clinic has branches as far as 60 miles from Urbana. Some of these branches have been informally designated as hubs and will have clusters of small primary care offices surrounding them. This system benefits the Carle-owned HMO, CarleCare, in that it constitutes an important component of the needed provider delivery system and represents a significant source of referrals to specialists located at the main campus.

EXHIBIT 4-2
Distribution of Marshfield Clinic and
Gundersen Clinic Primary Care Sites in Wisconsin, 1993

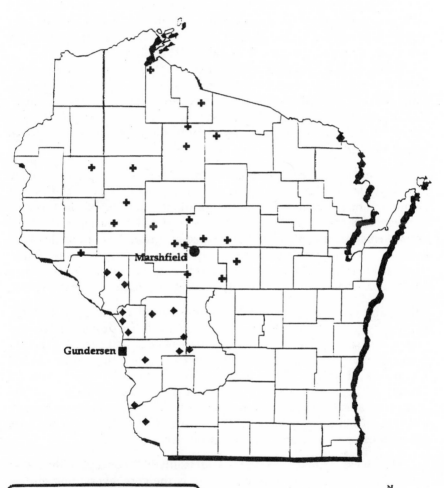

+ Marshfield Clinic Primary Care Sites
♦ Gundersen Clinic Primary Care Sites

The head of CarleCare remarked that, "Managed care and branching strategies are synergistic. The HMO, branches and our emphasis on family practice are all part of a tripod that has been the key to our success and an important building block for the future."

Geisinger has 43 outpatient locations in central Pennsylvania. In 1978, when Geisinger Medical Center was designated as one of four tertiary care centers for the state, it was on the condition that Geisinger reach out to serve the people of northeast and central Pennsylvania. According to the Senior Vice President of Operations for Geisinger's Central Region, this was the initial impetus needed to start the primary care network. Geisinger calls its primary care locations "network sites." Continued expansion of the primary care network from 1985 to 1993 was largely stimulated by a desire to provide more convenient access to members of the Geisinger Health Plan.

Densely populated metropolitan areas. The experience of one of the case study organizations — Sutter Health in Sacramento — shows that having too many small primary care locations can backfire. In 1990, the Sacramento Sierra Medical Group (Sac Sierra) had physicians in 70 locations. "This was not efficient and the medical group lost out on ancillary income," according to a Sutter representative. Under the new Sutter Medical Foundation, most of the primary care physicians in Sac Sierra will be concentrated in three suburban locations in the Sacramento area.

UniHealth America is implementing a similar strategy within the densely populated Los Angeles area. UniHealth has designated several Organized Delivery Systems (ODS) in places like Long Beach and the San Fernando Valley. Each ODS is anchored by an existing large medical group (e.g., Harriman Jones Medical Group and the Facey Medical Group). These groups will, in turn, expand their coverage of the immediate area through additional practice sites; Harriman Jones already has two sites and Facey has one. These sites will include primary care, but will also offer a more comprehensive array of services.

The role of primary care in the UniHealth ODS concept is illustrated in Exhibit 4-3. As shown, primary care is the core; everything else — specialty care, acute care, sub-acute care — emanates from this core.

According to Dennis Strum, Senior Vice President for Planning and Development, the ODS approach allows UniHealth America to concentrate its resources in building depth and market share in more limited areas rather than "deploying assets" (military terminology used by several UniHealth staff members) over the broad front of the entire Los Angeles area and its 15 million residents.

EXHIBIT 4-3
UniHealth America's Organized Delivery System

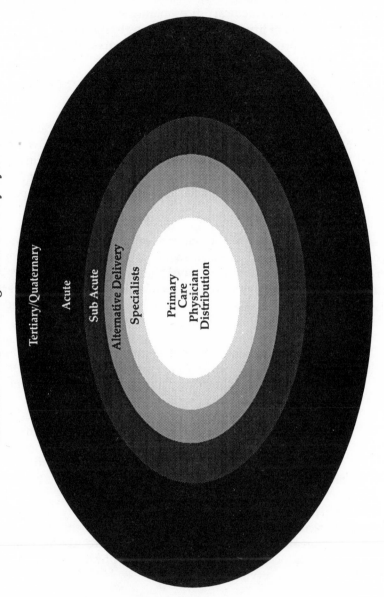

Tertiary/Quaternary

Acute

Sub Acute

Alternative Delivery

Specialists

Primary
Care
Physician
Distribution

Source: UniHealth America, 1992

In the case of Kaiser Permanente in the Denver Area, the organization includes 13 medical offices mainly staffed with primary care physicians. The mix of primary care physicians to specialists throughout the system is approximately 50/50; this is representative of Kaiser Permanente 's 12 regions.

A Pluralistic Approach in Serving Physicians

With all of the investment in, and emphasis on, primary care practice development and distribution, what about specialists? How does a hospital or integrated health care system avoid showing favoritism to a limited number of primary care physicians? How can a hospital keep its specialists from feeling abandoned and from taking their patients elsewhere?

A physician member of the Sutter Health board of directors, Dr. Harold Ray, an OB/Gyn specialist, said that in the early days the Sac Sierra Medical Group upset many physicians, primary care doctors and specialists alike. Physicians feared that the group would retain referrals and build up its own core of specialists. Similar types of concerns surfaced in Eugene when the Oregon Medical Group was formed.

Many of the case study organizations have faced this issue and have developed what several referred to as a "pluralistic approach." Here is what several of the organizations provide in the way of support for others on the medical staff:

- *Sutter Health.* Sutter encourages and has provided support to a number of IPAs through an IPA management company. In addition, Sutter has a group that provides practice support for any physicians desiring this service.

- *UniHealth America.* UniHealth provides a variety of services to physicians practicing at its hospitals, including practice management support and managed care contracting. It supports local IPAs and includes many physicians in the health plan panels serving its two HMOs.

- *Presbyterian Healthcare Services.* The Presbyterian Network (390 physicians) offers six different levels of integration ranging from managed care contracting to full economic integration of primary care doctors.

- *Sacred Heart.* In addition to its investment in the Oregon MSO, Sacred Heart supports the Lane IPA; most of the physicians on the medical staff of the hospital participate in the IPA.

- *Saint Joseph Hospital.* Sister Marianna Bauder, CEO of 565-bed St. Joseph Hospital in Denver, said, "It would not be smart to alienate a portion of our loyal physicians, especially since many of them are our best customers. In addition to our contract with Kaiser Permanente (which accounts for 55 percent of admissions to Saint Joseph), we have a group of physicians who are interested in at-risk contracting, a PPO which is supported by 200 of our specialists, and an investment in a 45-person multispecialty group practice."

Sharp Healthcare in San Diego includes the Sharp Rees-Stealy Medical Group (220 physicians and nine clinic sites), plus relationships with 12 other multispecialty clinics and 135 primary care sites in San Diego County. The CEO said, "On the North coast, we have an association with the Mission Park group. They have 77 primary care physicians and a total of 20 sites." In eastern San Diego County, Sharp has an IPA with 90 primary care physicians and 280 specialists. In central and southern San Diego, Sharp has primary care medical groups with 36 sites. In addition, Sharp has another 140 physicians under contract for various services ("Sharp Healthcare...", 1992, p. 8).

Achieving the Proper Balance Between Primary Care and Specialists

One of the MGMA staff members who worked with us on this book said, "The most frequently asked question I hear relates to when specialists should be brought into a primary care group." Several of the case study organizations have faced this issue.

A related question, and a delicate one at that, is: "How does an organization downsize its base of specialists?" An article in *Medical Economics* quotes a hospital administrator who said, "There are two to three times too many specialists for managed care. They're (specialists) right to be worried" (Slomski, 1993, p. 138).

Adding specialists. One medical group practice manager in southern California, a market dominated by capitation, said, "Deciding when to add specialists is really a 'make or buy' decision. We know how much we pay out-of-pocket for specialists' services. When this reaches the point at which we can support a specialist in-house, we might consider adding one. However, if it is less costly to contract out for specialist services, this is the route we take."

To physicians and hospital managers operating in more traditional markets, dominated by indemnity insurance or PPOs, this may sound weird. At least up until 1993, the smart strategy for most hospitals was to encourage specialists to cluster around the facility in order to generate more inpatient admissions and patient days.

Along a similar vein, for a primary care group practice in a fee-for-service environment, or when Medicare is disproportionately important, it is tempting to add specialists to help generate more revenue to cover practice overhead and add to the compensation pool. It is generally recognized that specialists require less administrative support, generate higher fees for the time they spend with patients and contribute a larger percentage of a medical group's net income.

A physician friend of the authors, an internist, told us, "This is a terrible time to consider adding specialists to a group. If you do it you are often locking in a new physician at a high salary. This flies in the face of every trend out there regarding the forthcoming drop in specialist compensation. This is like signing a long-term $3 million per year contract with a pitcher who has a history of shoulder problems."

Jeff Goldsmith, a health care consultant, speaker and writer, comes to the same conclusion. "It would be foolish for the hospital or other healthcare organization to grandfather specialist incomes that could fall by 30 to 50 percent during the Nineties" (Goldsmith, 1993, p. 40).

Downsizing the number of specialists. Several of the physician leaders interviewed as part of the case study research had given thought to this possibility and some had interesting contingency plans.

The president of the Marshfield Clinic said that the clinic had a policy of not laying off physicians.

> But, there are a number of things we can do. We can reduce specialists' compensation so it is more in line with primary care. Our salary deliberations include consideration of the market, and we have a mechanism for making salary adjustments. Also, many of our specialists are capable of

providing some primary care. We could have our staff, who arrange appointments, fill up some of the gaps in specialists' schedules with primary care visits.

The CEO of the Carle Clinic had a similar observation. "In some parts of the country specialists' incomes are way out of line. However, our salary spread is not as wide, and we will be able to adjust compensation according to market demands without any great convulsion in the organization. We can also use some of the specialists to help out in primary care if we get into a crunch."

The Senior Vice President for Clinical Operations at Geisinger said that shifting the mix of primary care physicians and specialists is one of the major issues facing the organization. He said, "Figuring out how to manage the specialty areas is complex. In some cases, they may be more cost effective than primary care. For example, our studies indicate that when a pulmonologist manages an inpatient case, costs are likely to be lower." Geisinger is intensely involved in studying its future need for specialist services; much of the analysis relates to the likely growth of its health plan and whether or not Medicare will shift to risk contracting.

Sutter has reduced the number of specialists in the Sac Sierra Medical Group which became part of the Sutter Medical Foundation in 1992. One physician on the board of Sac Sierra said, "It really never worked well having primary care physicians and specialists intermingled in this kind of organization. The specialists were not willing to financially support primary care, and their presence muddied the water for Sutter as it attempted to develop its primary care network in Sacramento."

Uwe Reinhardt, Princeton professor and noted health care speaker, says, "One of the sleepers embedded in managed competition, and one surely well known to organized medicine, is the impact that the spread of tightly managed, fully integrated health care plans could have on the market for medical professionals . . . a substantial enrollment of Americans in such systems could trigger a sizable physician surplus in the fee-for-service sector." Reinhardt goes on to note that under a group-model HMO scenario, the country may have twice as many physicians as needed, with specialists constituting most of surplus (Reinhardt, 1993, p. 190).

Summary

One of the lessons learned is that hospitals and specialists are taking a significant risk if they continue to rely on a traditional system where primary care physicians, usually operating independently in solo practices or small groups, refer patients to specialists who are major users of the hospital. The factors that have historically driven referral patterns (e.g., reputation for quality of care, friendship, school ties, physical proximity, members of the same medical staff) are losing their impact. Managed care, with its increasing use of limited panels of providers, has already driven a wedge into the old referral patterns.

The trend toward integrated health care systems means that the number of primary care doctors practicing on their own will shrink. The continued deterioration of the financial condition of many primary care practices is also driving this trend. The end result is that primary care physicians will soon lose the last vestiges of their freedom to refer patients to the specialist of their choice. This is a sobering thought for those hospitals and medical groups that have yet to take the first steps in terms of securing their primary care base.

Related to this point, even IPA-model HMOs, dependent on contracts with primary care physicians to staff their delivery network, may have problems keeping their networks together. This will drive managed care companies into seeking relationships with primary care physicians (this is already happening), or with hospitals and physicians that are pursuing integration strategies.

Based on our research, we believe that many of the organizations in integrated health care systems, especially the large multispecialty clinics, will be able to cope with the expected drop in demand for specialty medical services and adjust their compensation schedules and mix of physicians accordingly. The ratio of primary care physicians to specialists in these organizations tends to be more in line with the demands of a capitated system. And, the compensation formulas used by these large clinics allow for adjustments based on changes in national and regional payment trends for physicians.

The next chapter discusses the financing of an integrated health care system, with emphasis on how to pay for the development of primary care networks.

CHAPTER 5.
FINANCING THE INTEGRATED HEALTH CARE SYSTEM

Physicians are increasingly pressuring healthcare managers (after hours and out of earshot of their colleagues) to bail them out — by increasing their subsidies, providing them paid administrative roles, or simply buying them out.
— Jeff Goldsmith in *Healthcare Forum Journal*
March/April 1993

Goldsmith is right; primary care physicians all over the country are asking their hospital administrators to bail them out. This can mean substantial front-end investments to acquire the assets of a practice and a long-term commitment to supplement the earnings of many physicians.

But, the financial problems of primary care are but one of the issues relating to the financing of integrated health care systems. This chapter focuses on four broad topics:

(1) The front-end investment in professional fees; purchase of physicians' buildings, land and equipment; buying accounts receivable; building new primary care branches; providing working capital; and the most controversial of all, paying for "goodwill."

(2) Other investments in starting a health plan and underwriting operating losses for the first few years (this can easily cost $10 million or more), developing a comprehensive information system and establishing a malpractice insurance subsidiary.

(3) Covering operating expenses, including the overhead associated with running primary care practices, guaranteeing the compensation pool, agreeing to systematically contribute to profit sharing and pension plans, and other operating expenses.

(4) Sources of funds for both the initial capital investment and for year-to-year operating deficits, especially for primary care.

Front-End Investment Required for Physician-Hospital Integration

The front-end investment required to develop an integrated health care system can be substantial. This part of Chapter 5 begins with an overview of the magnitude of dollars involved and then discusses the various types of financial requirements to get started down the road to integration.

Professional fees. The professional fees for attorneys, consultants, property appraisers and others required to put together even the most basic physician-hospital organization can run several hundred thousand dollars. As one physician told us, "This is a very expensive and time-consuming activity to get involved with. Don't jump into it lightly."

Based on our experience, and from what we have learned from the organizations studied, this initial funding is usually provided by a hospital or health care system interested in achieving a new relationship with its physicians. In some cases physicians are willing to contribute to these costs in order to preserve their independence, but this option is the exception rather than the rule.

Goodwill. Of all of the issues we have dealt with in financing the development of integrated health care systems, goodwill is the most explosive. Most physicians are well aware of the payment of goodwill (really a payment for a portion of the capitalized value of future earnings) when a practice is sold to another physician. Articles discussing the amount of goodwill and how to calculate it are prominent in magazines such as *Medical Economics, Healthcare Financial Management,* and the *MGM Update.*

There are a variety of viewpoints on goodwill, when such a payment is justified, and when it is not. Incidentally, when it comes to the subject of physician-hospital integration, it is difficult to find examples of situations where parties will admit that payment for goodwill occurred. In one case we were told that "another hospital" in the community paid primary care physicians $250,000 each to join their system.

A physician-administrator of a hospital system that is purchasing the assets of primary care groups and making them employees of the hospital said, "Yes, goodwill is being paid, but it is not large. It is usually twice the value of accounts receivable and varies from $5,000 to $40,000 per physician." He went on to say that all of the equipment that has been used to generate ancillary income for physicians would be owned by the hospital, and the hospital would retain all income. "We told the physicians, 'we realize that you have been scrambling for income, and this is one of the ways you have survived. However, we aren't going to be doing things like this in the future; you won't need ancillary income.'"

In another example, primary care physicians entering into a relationship with a hospital were able to negotiate a premium based on the present value of a projection of future earnings. As one of the physicians said, "I don't care what anyone says, this practice is worth something more than just the value of its hard assets. This group has existed for 50 years and has a large base of loyal patients. The name of the group has real prestige and value in the community. We aren't going to walk away from all of this without some financial consideration."

It is our observation that payments for goodwill to physicians joining an integrated health care system are becoming smaller and less common. A decision to become a part of an integrated system is not the same as selling a practice to a younger physician, and retiring. Physicians who join an integrated system do so to gain the benefits of economic integration, and these advantages are significant and likely to be long lasting. It is becoming more difficult to justify the on-going value of a small medical practice, especially when that practice is not part of a larger system and poorly positioned for the future.

Front-end negotiations between physicians and not-for-profit hospitals seldom go far without the question arising as to whether goodwill payments would be illegal — i.e., that they would represent the inurement of benefits from a tax-exempt entity to a for-profit organization or private individual. This is a rapidly changing area of legal interpretation; therefore, an updated legal opinion should be sought. As of this writing, the most common legal opinion appears to be that some form payment for non-tangible assets can be made as long as it does not exceed market value.

The market value of a medical practice, as with any other business, can be estimated through a combination of three approaches:

- Future earnings potential — projecting the future revenues and expenses of the organization and then discounting them back to the present (determining a net present value).

- Replacement cost — estimating what it would cost to build a practice like the one being acquired if the new organization had to start from scratch.

- Comparable sales — researching what others have paid under similar circumstances.

Care must be taken in applying these approaches. For example, not-for-profit hospitals may be well advised to use comparables of medical group practice purchases by groups such as PhyCor, Pacific Physician Services or Caremark International where there is no hospital ownership. This helps avoid accusations that the comparable sales are in any way influenced by the physicians' potential to refer patients to the hospital.

Buildings and equipment. There are major differences among the organizations studied in how payment or leasing of physicians' buildings and equipment has been handled.

- In Albuquerque, Presbyterian Healthcare Services leased buildings and equipment from its economically integrated primary care physicians, and paid rent to the doctors for use of these assets. This helped stabilize the income of primary care physicians by giving them an adequate return on their investment in fixed assets.

- In most other cases, the new organizations — whether an MSO or a medical foundation — purchased physicians' assets. The price paid was based on an appraisal of the current market value of these assets.

- In the case of the Fargo Clinic, clinic assets were acquired by the new St. Luke's Foundation at book value. This was less than market value as determined by appraisals. Part of the physicians' motivation for accepting these kinds of terms is a desire to avoid even a hint of physicians' profiting from the sale of assets to a not-for-profit organization.

One hospital administrator involved in organizing an MSO that purchased physicians' assets commented that the system did not carefully evaluate what it was buying. "Some of the telephone systems were so outmoded that you couldn't hook up a computer modem. Other office equipment was on its last leg. What it amounted to was that in order to achieve any kind of progress toward integration and standardization, we basically junked a lot of what we bought. We weren't hoodwinked or anything like that; it was just a matter of the old equipment not meeting the needs of the new organization."

Real estate. Real estate holdings are a necessary aspect of most physician-hospital integration efforts. In many communities, physicians own more real estate than they use for their practices. They often view the formation of an integrated system as the ideal opportunity to cash in; to get themselves into a liquid position after many years of being tied down with mortgage payments, or to pull out the appreciated value of a property they have owned for years. In many instances the integrated system may not be interested in these properties, and this can become a point of contention.

We are familiar with a group of physicians who borrowed $5 million to build a new office building. They were not able to sell their old building, which was worth around $2 million, and it was being leased to tenants for uses such as a dance studio, cooking school and a pizza restaurant. None of the tenants could justify the kinds of rentals that the building could have commanded if used as a medical office building. Since several of the long-time members of the medical group had the largest financial stake in the old building, they were adamant that any sale of assets and formation of a physician-hospital organization include the sale of the old building. They prevailed and received the $2 million from the hospital.

Although the hospital board balked at having to include this transaction as part of the deal with the physicians, an appraisal indicated that the market value of the old building was $2 million, and they believed that they could sell it for that amount within a reasonable period of time.

From another perspective, reducing the physician group's investment in real estate often helps in the recruitment of new doctors. Individuals coming out of medical school and training usually lack the capital needed to purchase their share of these kinds of assets.

Accounts receivable. For many medical practices, accounts receivable are the largest asset. We have seen a variety of arrangements for handling this asset including outright purchase, purchase with payment spread over a fixed period of time, say 12 months, or allowing physicians to collect and keep the receipts of these payments. On the latter point, this requires a working capital advance to the new organization since accounts receivable will soon build back up to their former levels.

When accounts receivable are purchased, there is usually a discount involved, based on the age of the outstanding receivables and the types of payers from whom they are due. Since the value of accounts receivable can usually be realized by the purchaser, typically a hospital, within a few months, this part of the financial transaction is relatively straightforward.

Other Investment Requirements

Merging the medical group or groups with the hospital is the beginning of the early investments, not the culmination. Several other forms of investment are needed at or near the beginning of the development of the new integrated system.

New primary care offices. In most cases it is necessary for integrated systems to invest in new and larger primary care facilities. Existing primary care offices are often small and not in the most appropriate locations. This was evident in several of the case studies.

In Sacramento, for example, Sutter Health was investing millions of dollars in three ambulatory centers situated in parts of the metropolitan area where primary care physician coverage was inadequate. Many of the primary care physicians who had been operating in their own facilities in older parts of the city moved to the newer and larger office buildings in the suburbs. One of the advantages of the new offices: sufficient volume to justify installation of diagnostic equipment and thus increased income from ancillary services, such as laboratory and radiology. However, substantial capital investment is required to obtain these types of facilities and geographic coverage.

Robert Nelson, Executive Vice President of the Harriman Jones Medical Group in Long Beach, said, "From our perspective, we were seeing the market change, and it was going to take capital to continue to compete. For example, it costs us about a half a million dollars to establish a satellite office, and we needed more of them. We saw UniHealth America as a strong system; a survivor. That's why we started talking with them."

In Denver, Kaiser Permanente invested over $60 million in five medical offices during the 1985 to 1987 period. These funds were available as a result of KP's decision to cancel construction of its own hospital. KP Senior Vice President and Regional Manager, Chris Binkley, said that the decision to invest these funds in primary care offices was a key factor in the growth of the health plan in the late 1980s and early 1990s. As noted earlier, KP staffs each of these medical offices with 12 to 20 primary care physicians.

In Albuquerque, primary care physicians participating in the Presbyterian Network agreed to be assigned to practice locations deemed most appropriate by the Network. The Network, in turn, spent large sums of money in building or refurbishing medical office space. The same was true in other systems studied. For example, Fargo Clinic, Marshfield Clinic and Carle Clinic were all investing substantial amounts in improving the quality of their primary care locations.

As a rule of thumb, we believe that each primary care practice established in quality facilities in a metropolitan area requires a $200,000 investment per physician spread over the first two or three years. This covers facilities, equipment and initial shortfalls in revenues. In California, it is estimated that this amount approaches $300,000. In rural areas, it may be less.

Recruiting primary care physicians. All of the organizations studied have active recruiting programs for bringing in new primary care physicians. In fact, the inability to recruit new primary care doctors was an important motivating factor driving the formation of some of these systems, such as the Oregon Medical Group and MAPI.

What does it cost to recruit new physicians? Who pays the recruiting and moving expenses? How about covering the short-term loss of income experienced by existing physicians when a new associate is added? How much does all of this cost? One internist who expanded his practice from seven to 11 doctors in one year said, "We each took a hit by being so aggressive. You can't bring in that many new doctors and expect them to be busy with patients immediately. Therefore, our patient base is spread over more physicians while we wait for them to build their own practices."

As a general rule, hospitals and health care organizations seeking to expand their primary care base can expect to pay $50,000 to $75,000 for the first year a new doctor is in practice. This covers recruiting, moving and compensating existing partners in the practice for the loss of income from dilution in the patient base.

Working capital. One of the nearly universal truths about medical group practices is that, other than accounts receivable, funds are not set aside for working capital. Integrated systems, on the other hand, cannot operate this way. These types of systems have to have access to substantial amounts of working capital in order to operate effectively.

How much working capital is needed? As a general rule we found in our research that medical groups need to have enough working capital to cover 90 days of operation. In other words, working capital should equal the value of bills sent out over a 90-day period. On an individual physician basis, this would mean $60,000 to $75,000 (primary care).

Investing in information systems. The amounts being invested in information systems are truly astounding. Among the case study organizations, the range was from $3 million to $8 million per year over the next few years. There is little in the way of "off the shelf" software available; all of the organizations were developing their own systems. As one individual said, "Our information system is the glue that holds this organization together. But, what we have isn't good enough for the future, especially when we are at risk. We simply have to invest now to prepare for the future or we won't be competitive in the marketplace." (Information systems are discussed in more detail in Chapter 10.)

Self-insurance for malpractice. Carle Clinic has its own malpractice insurance company and Marshfield Clinic has a self-insured trust. While the capital requirements are modest (less than $2 million), the amount in reserves has built up to the point where it now exceeds $10 million in each clinic.

The reasons for committing this capital are obvious: significant annual savings in malpractice premiums. In both clinics, malpractice expenses are several hundred thousand dollars per year less than if premiums were paid to an independent company.

Starting a health plan. All but one of the case study organizations had experience at establishing a health plan, and all invested several millions of dollars before these plans began to return a profit. Our experience in analyzing the financial performance of HMOs and calculating the initial capital requirements is that a minimum of $5 million is likely to be needed before achieving break even. As noted in the next chapter, Fargo Clinic invested nearly $10 million and did not come close to achieving profitable operations.

Other bailouts. We noted in the case studies that hospitals and health systems, usually the biggest source of capital, have had to bail out IPAs and other physician organizations. This is all part of giving fair treatment to all types of physicians on the medical staff — the pluralistic approach discussed in the previous chapter.

In at least one of the case studies, the health system had to step forward and provide funding for an 800-physician IPA. The IPA had lost money during the previous two years, and the health care system invested several million dollars in the organization to get it back on a sound financial footing. IPAs, like most physician organizations, tend to be undercapitalized and susceptible to poor utilization management requiring infusions of capital, especially when they assume the risks associated with capitated contracting.

Covering Operating Costs

We have noted differences of opinions among physicians and hospital CEOs about the necessity of providing continuing financial supplements to primary care practices. However, we also note that among the 10 case study organizations, all were paying more to primary care physicians and for the expenses associated with operating their practices than they were directly receiving back in revenues.

Is this a subsidy? It depends on whom you talk to. In one organization, a physician leader vehemently objected to using that term. He said, "We take a systems approach and, to have a successful system, we have to have a good primary care feeder network. We don't consider this a subsidy." We tend to agree with this observation. Nevertheless, for organizations contemplating physician-hospital integration, but aren't there yet, some form of long-term financial assistance will be necessary for primary care.

Annual financial short-falls in primary care. Primary care doctors in the case study organizations were generally well paid, at least in comparison with primary care physicians in other practice settings (see Chapter 7). Primary care doctors were making at least $100,000 to $120,000 a year from day one of joining an integrated system. Two of the case studies — Sac Sierra and Oregon Medical Group — demonstrate the point that primary care physicians' net incomes must be stabilized at something close to these amounts or there is risk of losing a significant number of physicians to other integrated organizations like Kaiser Permanente.

As a general rule, based on both the case studies and our experience elsewhere, we estimate that the shortfall in primary care net incomes ranges from $10,000 to as much as $40,000 per year. An average might be around $20,000 annually. These are not the extra dollars that we think primary care physicians are entitled to be paid; these are the amounts that an integrated system has to cover to keep its primary care network intact.

Higher administrative expenses. Another finding from the research conducted as part of this book is that there are few, if any, economies of scale in assembling a network of primary care physicians. In fact, when primary care physicians become part of a hospital system, or integrated delivery system, overhead is more likely to go up than down.

However, we are talking about "apples and oranges" when we compare administrative expenses before and after physician-hospital integration. The level and quality of support services received by primary care physicians in an integrated network is likely to be substantially higher than when they were in solo practice. This was definitely true with Sac Sierra, the Oregon Medical Group, MAPI in Billings and with the economically integrated physicians in the Presbyterian Network.

A third factor: When an integrated system's mix of physicians becomes more heavily weighted toward primary care, its overhead is likely to increase. Overhead expenses in a typical primary care practice are 65 percent of net revenues; for specialists, the ratio is more like 50 percent. (The higher overhead for primary care practices has to do with the cost of serving a large volume of patients, relatively high staffing levels and low payment for each patient encounter.)

Funding pension and profit sharing plans. In most of the integrated systems, contributions to pensions plans have been stabilized and improved. For example, in the case of the Fargo Clinic/St. Luke's Hospital merger, funding of the pension plan was a major issue. In this case, the clinic's plan was funded more generously than the hospital's plan; clinic physicians insisted that the hospital bring its funding up to that of the clinic. The added cost: $3 million per year.

In other cases, one of the factors that motivates primary care physicians to consider joining an integrated system is to be able to make regular financial contributions to their pension plans. In the past, money for funding these plans has often not been available. As in the case of physician compensation, this additional expense is part of the price that integrated systems pay for building and retaining their primary care referral networks.

Funding Sources

In the first half of this chapter we have spelled out the many up-front and continuing financial requirements of an integrated system. The next question: Where does the money come from?

Hospitals or health systems. In the case study organizations, tax-exempt hospitals and health care systems were the major source of funding for the integrated system. Most clinics and medical group practices do not retain earnings; nor do they have strong balance sheets. They basically operate on a cash flow basis; whatever money comes in is paid out.

The hospital serving as a source of capital has a strong need to establish a mutually accepted "playing field" for financial negotiations. For example, will the transaction be "another form of physician bail-out," or will it be a "true risk and gain-sharing partnership?" One clinic manager referred to the hospital as the "bank." Another person described the not-for-profit hospital as a "giant 401 K." Of course, this is also a sensitive issue given concerns about private inurement.

A physician-manager of a large hospital-owned primary care group practice on the West Coast said, "Our hospital administrative staff and the board recognize that rather than buying new equipment or adding to facilities, the future need for capital will be for primary care practice development."

We agree with this assessment. Given health care reimbursement patterns of the 1990s and the predominance of not-for-profit hospitals, it is likely that hospitals and hospital systems will be the primary source of capital for primary care practice development. Hospitals and multihospital systems are usually the organizations with the strongest balance sheets, and many have access to the tax-exempt bond markets. (For-profit hospital systems and management companies have access to capital, but it may be more costly.) Without a source of capital, attempting to achieve physician-hospital integration and the benefits of an organized, coordinated delivery system is probably not feasible. The lack of capital may slam the door on many aspiring integrated systems.

Specialists. We found several cases in which specialists were willing to support primary care physicians even though it meant lower income for themselves. We conclude that one of the secrets of success of several of the large organizations studied is that they have corporate cultures that encourage this kind of sharing.

Marshfield Clinic is a prime example of an organization in which specialists, by agreeing to a rather narrow salary range, are helping fund the primary care network. In the case of Marshfield, specialists also are subsidizing a large medical research and education foundation. The reason for this may be found in the early culture of the organization; up until 1980 all physicians were paid the same salary. And, in 1977, physicians became convinced of the importance of retaining earnings. This led to the development of a strong balance sheet for Marshfield Clinic and its ability to fund the entire system. As of September 1992, Marshfield Clinic had $177.5 million in assets and a net worth of $73.8 million.

Health plan profits. In several of the case studies, profits from health plans were contributing to the cost of expanding the primary care network and to maintaining the incomes of primary care physicians. This was most noteworthy in the cases of Marshfield, Geisinger and Carle Clinics where HMO profits were relatively large. Kaiser Permanente uses the cash flow generated by its health plan to help cover the costs of maintaining its system of primary care offices throughout most of the metropolitan areas it serves.

Ancillaries. Net income from the operation of ancillaries often is used to support other activities in an integrated system. Ownership of ancillaries was an interesting issue in nearly all of the case studies. In the Marshfield and Carle Clinic cases, the hospitals generate very little ancillary income; nearly all of it goes to the clinics who own or control radiology, laboratory and pharmacy. This added income contributes to the ability of these clinics to support their primary care networks.

In another case, the loss of ancillary revenues by the Oregon Medical Group contributed to the organization's inability to maintain physician compensation at competitive levels. Although it was the original intent of the hospital to involve OMG physicians in ancillary income, prior agreements with radiologists and pathologists prevented such a shift. And, as noted earlier, failure to capture significant amounts of ancillary income contributed to the financial problems of the Sac Sierra Medical Group.

As indicated in Chapter 2, integrated systems must carefully analyze their compliance with Stark anti-referral legislation in determining their approach to ancillaries.

Other sources of funding. It is possible that other funding sources for the development of integrated delivery systems might develop. These could include large health insurance companies, such as Aetna, that take a leadership role in assembling such delivery systems. In mid 1993, it was announced that Aetna was acquiring primary care practices in four metro areas.

Another possibility might be a for-profit practice management company, such as PhyCor, Pacific Physician Services and Caremark International, that have access to the public capital markets. While PhyCor has been active in acquiring the practices of specialists, can it earn an attractive return on investment on primary care practices? Perhaps not in the present environment, but with a capitated payment system and the potential to dramatically improve primary care compensation, the for-profit management companies are likely to become more important players.

Summary

One of the major points of this chapter is that it requires a substantial amount of capital to develop and operate an integrated health care system. Not only are the funding requirements large, they are different. Huge sums will be needed for "soft" investments like information systems and primary care. Starting a health plan involves a venture capital mentality. Many hospital board members are likely to be uncomfortable with allocating funds for these kinds of high risk, intangible endeavors.

Health care systems, including hospitals and medical groups, that do not have access to capital, run the risk of being locked out of the health care system of the future. But, we shouldn't be surprised by these findings. All businesses, whether they are large or small, require access to capital if they are to grow and be successful. The integrated health care system is no different. But, some key elements of the "system" — namely primary physician practices — have been starved for funds for many years, and the requirements of the future make it imperative that these types of medical practices be bolstered, not relegated to the poor house of medicine.

that's why hospitals are still central.

CHAPTER 6.

THE THIRD LEG OF THE STOOL — HEALTH PLANS

In our system we no longer think about hospital revenues; we think in terms of perimum dollars.
— Multihospital system CEO

If it isn't clear to everyone yet, it will be soon. The process of physicians and hospitals coming together is but one element of developing an integrated health care system. Ownership of a health plan, or what is often referred to as controlling the "financing mechanism," is viewed by nearly every integrated system as critically important. We cannot envision a successful integrated system in the future that does not include a strong, close relationship with a health plan.

Stephen Shortell, professor and health care researcher, and several of his co-authors define an organized delivery system as owning or having close ties with a health plan:

An organized delivery system is a network of organizations that provides or arranges to provide a coordinated continuum of services to a defined population and is willing to be held fiscally and clinically accountable for the health status of that population. It owns or has a close relationship with an insurance product (underlining added) (Shortell [and others], 1993, p. 20).

Paul Starr, author of *The Social Transformation of American Medicine,* says that the framework of managed competition "is designed to encourage the integration of health insurance and health care provision into the same organizations (the health plans). The more integrated the plans, the better able they will be to control cost and quality" (Starr and Welman, 1993, p. 11). Most of the case study organizations would agree with this assessment.

One person we interviewed said that physicians and a hospital are but two legs of a stool, and that the third leg is the health plan. A speaker at a national conference on integrated health care recently used the same analogy. (He quickly added that he thinks one of the legs of the stool is getting shorter — acute care hospitals!)

This chapter discusses five issues related to the role of a health plan in the integrated delivery system:

(1) The reasons integrated systems decided to own a health plan, both at the time their health insurance product was initiated and in the environment of the 1980s and 1990s. Why was ownership of a plan viewed as important?

(2) The financial performance of health plans owned by integrated systems.

(3) Analysis of the contributions of health plans to the overall success of integrated health care systems.

(4) The lessons learned in terms of developing a profitable insurance product that represents a significant number of patients for the integrated system.

(5) Options available for organizations that aspire to become integrated systems but started too late in developing their own financing mechanisms.

Exhibit 6-1 summarizes the number of subscribers, and the percent of system revenues represented by each health plan among the 10 detailed case study organizations.

Why Establish a Health Plan?

Were the reasons for establishing a health plan based on a vision of the future? Or, were these plans established as a result of some of the "me too" thinking of the 1970s and 1980s? Remember the hospitals that re-organized themselves into health care systems made up of numerous corporate entities, only to find that this made life more complicated from a governance and management perspective? Federal legislation and funding in the late 1970s encouraged the formation of HMOs, and many hospitals and physician groups jumped on the band wagon.

In our 1987 book, *Market-Driven Strategies in Health Care*, we cautioned strongly against hospitals investing in HMOs. We saw how difficult it was to hold down physician rate increases and utilization when the hospital found itself negotiating with its best customers, the members of the IPA, who also happen to be the key members of the

EXHIBIT 6-1
Summary of Health Plans, 10 Case Study Organizations

	Case Study Organizations (Name of Health Plan)	Year Established	No. of Subscribers Spring 1993	Percent of System Revenues Represented by Owned Health Plan	Comments
1.	Presbyterian Network, Albuquerque (Health Plus)	1986	88,000	25%	Profitable
2.	Fargo Clinic/St. Luke's Hospital (MedCenters HMO)	1985	None	None	Fargo Clinic lost $10 million before ceasing operations in 1988
3.	Marshfield Clinic/St. Joseph's Hospital (Security Health Plan)	1971	65,000	25%	Profitable
4.	Carle Clinic/Carle Foundation Hospital, Urbana (Carle Care)	1980	68,000	33%	Profitable
5.	Sutter Health, Sacramento (Sutter Preferred Health Plan)	1985	30,000 in Sacramento	Small	Omni Health Plan, an HMO, jointly owned with St. Joseph in Stockton
6.	UniHealth America, Los Angeles (CareAmerica & PacifiCare)	1985 Late 1970s	180,000 in CareAmerica 912,000 in PacifiCare	Small	Own 54% of Class A voting stock of PacifiCare, a publicly traded company
7.	Oregon Medical Group/Sacred Heart, Eugene (SelectCare)	1978	65,000	25%	Sacred Heart purchased in 1983; profitable
8.	Geisinger System Danville, PA (Geisinger Health Plan)	1973	145,000	20%	Geisinger began pushing HMO in 1985; profitable
9.	Kaiser Permanente/Saint Joseph Hospital, Denver	1969	280,000	100% for KP	Profitable
10.	MAPI/Saint Vincent Hospital, Billings, MT (Yellowstone Community Health Plan)	1993	None	None	

Source: Data obtained by BBC, Inc. from the organizations listed as part of the case study process, March-June, 1993.

medical staff. Frankly, we did not see the typical hospital of the 1980s as having the ability and the political leverage to organize or sustain health plans that would be sufficiently aggressive to succeed in the market.

Several hospitals that did invest heavily in health plans at that time were generally unsuccessful, and the red ink flowed. Perhaps the two prime examples were found in two national proprietary systems, AMI and Humana. However, this experience was certainly not limited to the for-profits. For example, one otherwise strong and well managed not-for-profit hospital with which we are particularly familiar invested in an HMO in the early 1980s. Substantial losses were incurred. Physician-hospital relations suffered many setbacks, and the HMO eventually failed. Few tears were shed when the HMO closed its doors in 1988.

Was our thinking correct in the 1980s? We still believe it was not appropriate for the typical hospital in that time frame to own an HMO. Why, then, do so many of the large integrated systems believe it is absolutely essential that they own their own health plans? The answer goes to the core of the difference between the hospital acting alone and the integrated health care system — with a hospital, physicians and health plan acting together within a structure that is moving toward one patient care philosophy, one management and one set of financial incentives.

Patrick Hays, the CEO of Sutter Health, said that his board was happy when Sutter purchased an equity interest in Foundation Health Plan in 1985 and then sold it three years later for a $70 million profit. But, rather than patting himself on the back, Hays said, "This was probably the best financial decision we ever made, but it was our worst strategic decision. It delayed us in getting started with the development of our own financing products." By the early 1990s, Sutter had begun marketing its Sutter Preferred Health Plan and had also purchased a 50 percent interest in Omni Health Plan, an HMO developed in Stockton, California in the mid-1980s. There were approximately 30,000 Sacramento residents in this plan as of year-end 1992. However, the size of Sutter's health plans were small relative to the size of the system, and this was a matter of concern in terms of positioning Sutter for the future.

Carle Clinic participated in the formation of a not-for-profit HMO in 1980. At the time, the local health care marketplace was dominated by indemnity insurance. Carle's motivation was to comply with the spirit of federal legislation, and to be able to offer employers an alternative. Also, a competing clinic had established an HMO, and this spurred Carle to react.

SelectCare, a community-based IPA-model HMO in Eugene, Oregon, was originally established in 1978 at the urging of a group of university staff members. However, Sacred Heart Hospital bailed out the financially troubled organization in 1983, largely at the urging of physicians on the medical staff. The hospital CEO saw the HMO as an opportunity to attract patients and to position Sacred Heart and its physicians for the future.

In Albuquerque, Presbyterian Healthcare Services established Mastercare in 1972, but discontinued it in 1981. The primary reason: flack from specialists on Presbyterian's medical staff and problems of controlling utilization. One physician said, "We weren't used to taking discounts and couldn't see the need for it. Oh, for the good old days! The shocker was that when the HMO closed, two-thirds of the 25,000 members immediately switched to Lovelace. We thought we had the loyalty of our patients. However, we found out that many of them liked the concept of an HMO better than they liked us."

Presbyterian then established Health Plus, an HMO, in 1986. Health Plus has since grown to cover 88,000 lives, and its gross revenues were $56 million in 1993. The plan is profitable and is a key part of Presbyterian's strategy of controlling premium dollars.

Geisinger Health Plan was established in 1973 as a joint venture with a Blue Cross system. To avoid threatening independent physicians who referred patients to Geisinger specialists and the Geisinger Medical Center, the health plan was limited to a single county. In 1985, after 13 years, the plan had only 12,000 members, two-thirds of whom were Geisinger employees and their families.

In 1985, Blue Cross dropped out and Geisinger decided to get serious with marketing and managing its HMO. This also meant a commitment to expanding its "distribution system," the network of primary care sites in the counties surrounding Danville. Enrollment grew rapidly, and soon the Geisinger Health Plan was the largest HMO in rural America with 145,000 subscribers in mid-1993.

When Kaiser Permanente (KP) came into the Denver Area in 1969, the California-based HMO positioned itself as an alternative to Blue Cross and Blue Shield of Colorado, the dominant indemnity insurer at the time. KP used a low-key approach in that it did not advertise; its marketing director had the title of "Director of Enrollment." KP suggested to employers that they could offer their employees a choice without additional cost. A former hospital CEO who was in Denver in the 1970s said that he and his colleagues did not take KP seriously. "We never dreamed they would become the competitive force they are today."

These examples reflect a variety of reasons for either establishing an HMO, sticking with it during difficult times or deciding to expand its coverage and base of subscribers. These motivations don't necessarily reflect a vision of where the health care system would be headed in the mid- to late-1990s. One might say that many of the decisions to establish and own a health plan were fortuitous or the result of external competitive pressures.

On the other hand, there is a common theme in the above examples as to who was successful and when. Health plans owned or controlled by integrated systems begin to be successful when (a) the key physician decision makers are fully behind the plan, (b) physicians become convinced that having a successful HMO is a key to their future financial success, (c) the number of physicians committed to the plan reaches a critical mass, and (d) physicians and hospitals commit significant dollars to market the plan aggressively and cease worrying that it will draw from their indemnity business. Without these critical success factors in place, a managed care plan can fail today just as it would have in the 1980s. However, the integrated health care system can deliver these success factors.

Profitability of System-Owned Health Plans

The profitability of the health plans, all HMOs, owned by the integrated systems studied, was generally impressive. For example:

- CarleCare, with 68,000 subscribers in 1992, posted over $7 million in profits from revenues of $86 million.

- Security Health Plan with 65,000 members is owned by the Marshfield Clinic. In 1992, profits were in the $7 to $8 million range on revenues of $90 million.

- Geisinger Health Plan, with revenues of $152 million in 1992, contributed $2.3 million to the bottom line of the system.

- Health Plus, the 88,000 member health plan owned by Presbyterian Healthcare Services, earned $700,000 in 1992 and provided an additional $2 million to participating physicians in the form of withholds; revenues were $56 million.

- Kaiser Permanente's Colorado Region earned $19.5 million on revenues of $430 million in 1992. (As an overall system, Kaiser Permanente earned $796 million on revenues of $11.0 billion in 1992. This represented a 7.2 percent return on total revenues.)

The capital investment in these plans (other than KP) typically ranged from $2 to $10 million; this includes the start-up capital and operating losses during the initial years. As noted earlier, the Fargo Clinic absorbed a $10 million loss on its HMO over a three-year period.

The physician-administrator of the Geisinger Health Plan said that he would not want to try to establish an HMO without the availability of $4 to $5 million in capital. "But," he said, "there are so many variables that influence what it takes to achieve a break-even level of operations that it is hard to generalize."

How Integrated Systems Benefit From Owning a Health Plan

In addition to profits, what else has health plan ownership contributed to the success of integrated health care systems? What are the major elements of value added from ownership of an HMO?

The double benefits of owning a health plan. In addition to profits from a health plan and control of a segment of the market, integrated systems owning health plans benefit in terms of the dollars that flow to their physicians and hospitals. In the case of many HMOs, this was the primary motivation of hospitals and medical groups for establishing this type of health plan. An HMO provides physicians and hospitals with another pathway to patients.

For example, in the case of CarleCare, of the $86 million in HMO revenues in 1992, 40 percent came back to the Carle Clinic in the form of payment for physician services. This represented one fifth of the $164 million in revenues of the clinic in that year. Clinic physicians received a substantial share of their patients and revenues from health plan patients and also earned a significant profit on the HMO.

The same is true for the Marshfield Clinic. Of the clinic's $230 million in revenues in 1992, one third came from payments for patient services provided to subscribers of its HMO. The clinic, then, received a substantial portion of its revenues from HMO patients, and profits from the health plan (after replenishing reserves) also flowed to the clinic.

Experience in capitation. From our perspective, one of the most important contributions that comes from owning and managing a health plan has been the experience gained in dealing with capitation. Most of the integrated systems welcome capitation. They believe they can perform well in a capitated environment. Part of this confidence comes from their experience in running an HMO. Most of these organizations admit that they have already made their share of mistakes and have undertaken the subsequent adjustments needed to achieve profitability.

One southern California internist who owns and manages a 1,500-physician IPA that is responsible for the health status of 100,000 lives told us:

> We have several million member-months of experience in our computer. We can pretty well predict what it will cost to take care of the health care needs of this group. By the end of the year we will have all of our sub-specialists paid on a capitated basis. When they see our database they are more confident they can do the job for a fixed amount of money.

This is an example of having the know-how to be effective in a capitated environment.

The CEO of Saint Vincent Hospital in Billings, James Paquette, agreed. "One of the main reasons we are exploring a community health plan is to allow us to work with our physicians, especially those in MAPI, in getting ready to compete in a capitated environment. We know it won't be easy, but it's something we have to do and I'm confident it will be a valuable experience." A physician-administrator agreed: "This is tremendously important."

Controlling the flow of premium revenues. The control over a substantial number of patients and their payment source is also important. In several of the case studies, the proportion of hospital and physician revenues derived from system-owned health plans was substantial. It was 25 percent in the case of Marshfield, and 33 percent for Carle (see Exhibit 6-1 presented earlier).

Geisinger derives 20 percent of its revenues from its health plan, management's priority is to double this percentage. One executive said, "This will help us control our payment sources and speed us along toward the goal of being successful in a capitated environment. Right now we have our feet in both the fee-for-service and capitated environments, and it doesn't work well. It keeps us from sending the right messages to our physicians and others in the system."

Becoming more cost effective. One physician who serves as director of medical affairs for a hospital-based system told us that during a recent strategic planning effort, hospital and physician leaders focused on what could be done to make the system more cost effective. One of the major sources of savings identified was consolidating the role of the insurance segment by having providers — physicians and the hospital — assume risks and thus take over the role of insurance companies and health plans.

> By taking over this function, we could see the possibility of taking as much as 20 percent out of our costs of delivering health care services. We can't get that kind of savings from the hospital alone, or from physicians. The only way we can hope to attain this improved efficiency is by controlling the entire system, including the health plan.

The experience of Park Nicollet Medical Center, a large integrated system in the Minneapolis-St. Paul market, was similar. A manufacturing executive told the CEO of the clinic that he was tired of buying health care through a middle man and would like to buy direct from Park Nicollet. However, before jumping in, clinic management wanted to make sure that it could provide quality care at rates below those of HMOs in the community. Dr. James Reinertsen, the former CEO, said:

> We wanted to make sure that our fees, at 100 cents on the dollar, times the volume of our services, plus the cost of the hospitalizations we order, plus 3 or 4 percent for a third-party administrator to process claims, would actually wind up being a good deal for the purchasers.

The actuarial firm hired to advise Park Nicollet said that its calculations showed that the clinic was five to 10 percent lower in total costs than the lowest-priced HMO premium in town. "Since then, even without any marketing effort, companies have been lining up at Park Nicollet's door" (Holoweiko, 1992, p. 112).

In Chapter 15 we devote several pages to the cost effectiveness of integrated systems. These two examples and others (Kaiser Permanente, Fallon) indicate that integrated health care systems can function well when it comes to managing the health care of a defined population.

Other benefits of owning an HMO. Ownership of an HMO is also viewed by some of the organizations as a plus factor in recruiting new primary care physicians. One physician told us, "It sets our organization apart and adds to the impression of overall financial stability. We are in control of our own destiny. We can't be whipsawed by the health insurance industry. Physicians considering joining our group recognize this."

Aurora

Many of the plans also have name recognition in their market areas and have broad consumer acceptance. This bodes well for continued acceptance of both the plan and the delivery system behind the plan under a future of managed competition.

Another benefit of health plan ownership is access to data on patient utilization of the full continuum of health care providers. One physician said that this type of information is especially valuable for credentialling, new product development, capital planning and physician education.

Lessons Learned from Owning a Health Plan

The lessons learned from establishing and successfully turning around a health plan are numerous. The experiences of three of the case study organizations and Fallon are summarized here:

CarleCare. The director of CarleCare said, "There are two issues involved in running a profitable HMO — underwriting and management, especially the control of utilization. When we started the HMO, the underwriting criteria were too loose; we ended up with a pool of high-risk patients and lost money. It doesn't matter how good a job of managing you do; if you have a poor risk pool, you won't make money with an HMO."

He went on to describe several ways in which the Carle Clinic and Carle Foundation Hospital contribute to the profitability of the health plan:

(1) Continuum of care: "This means you can match the patients' needs with the most appropriate level of care."

(2) Emphasis on outpatient care: "This is the most cost-effective way to do things."

(3) Hub and spoke branching system: "This is an efficient way to provide primary care services and assure the appropriate use of specialists. Also, only 10 percent of the expenses were paid to physicians who are not part of the Carle system."

(4) Lower overhead: "The health plan can share the costs of certain services, such as personnel, accounting and purchasing."

(5) Greater use of physician extenders (e.g., physician assistants and nurse practitioners).

(6) Centralized leadership and governance: "This reduces competition and gives everyone the same sense of direction."

Marshfield Clinic's Security Health Plan. This plan was originally owned by Marshfield Clinic, St. Joseph's Hospital, and Blue Cross and Blue Shield United of Wisconsin. However, the plan experienced financial difficulties in the years leading up to 1986, and Marshfield Clinic bought out its two partners.

According to the medical director of this HMO, "The plan was community rated until 1986, and this led to serious problems of adverse selection. Once we switched to experience rating, profitability improved." *adverse selection?*

There are 800 providers on the panel, meaning that roughly half are not part of the Marshfield Clinic. These providers are paid on a discounted fee-for-service basis. However, payments to outside providers represent only two to three percent of expenses, and control of utilization has not been a problem.

Geisinger. The secret of success in managing the health plan is controlling physician utilization; this is the opinion of the physician-administrator of the Geisinger Health Plan (GHP). He said that 90 to 95 percent of subscriber encounters were with Geisinger physicians (there were 350 non-Geisinger doctors on the panel), and that the Geisinger doctors were learning how to practice effectively in a capitated environment. "We don't have to police them or look over their shoulders. This helps keep our administrative costs down." (On this point, he noted that the HMO's administrative staff was about half the size of that of most HMOs with equivalent membership.)

The GHP executive also noted that one of the key factors in expanding health plan membership in the past has been the number of primary care locations. He added, "The Geisinger name has also been a powerful marketing force." Looking ahead, he said that in order to expand the size of the HMO, Geisinger would need to add several more primary care practice sites and that the health plan had already identified where some of these sites should be located (a good example of the interaction of a health plan and clinic within the framework of an integrated health care system).

Fallon. Allan Stoll, FACMPE, Executive Vice President of the Fallon Foundation in Worcester, Massachusetts, said that Fallon established its health plan in 1977; enrollment had reached 163,000 members by mid-1993. Stoll said that Fallon established the first HMO in the area and it took several years before it was accepted. He noted, however, that "we built a better mouse trap and we were swamped with persons wanting to subscribe." He said that physicians at Fallon have had a strong commitment to primary care going back as far as the 1960s and that this set the stage for the success of the HMO. A decision to build a distribution network (Fallon has 27 branches) added to the accessibility for subscribers. And, most important, physicians and managers quickly came to see that it was possible to practice cost-effective, high-quality medicine; the two are not in conflict.

Building a Financing System in Other Ways

All this about owning and growing a health plan is fine for those organizations that had an early start or operate in markets where it is still possible to launch a successful HMO. But what about physician groups and hospitals in situations when establishing a health plan is not practical? What are they to do?

For example, Mullikin Medical Centers, a 400-physician medical group headquartered in Artesia, California, owns 99-bed Pioneer Hospital but does not own a health plan. John McDonald, Mullikin's administrator, said, "It would mean competing with the insurers we do business with. We wouldn't want insurers to start practicing medicine." In the fall, 1992, Mullikin provided care to 165,000 enrollees in 22 HMOs

(Burda, 1992, p. 42). Many other organizations share McDonald's viewpoint.

Several integrated systems have positioned themselves to be successful in providing physician, hospital and other needed services to capitated health plans. This is one of the strategies of both UniHealth and Sutter Health and of their respective medical foundations. In the highly competitive California marketplace, neither of these systems was self-sufficient in terms of a large proportion of their patients coming from their health plans. To succeed as providers of services to health plans means that physician-hospital systems need an appropriate panel of physicians (i.e., reasonable balance between primary care and specialists), good geographic distribution, especially for primary care, and the ability to provide cost-effective services.

Another approach is single signature contracting. This simply means that the provider network is organized and that one individual has the authority to commit the various participants in the network to a provider contract for a fixed amount of money. The Presbyterian Network, in particular, is an example of an integrated health care system using this approach to augment its HMO and related health plans. One physician-administrator said, "This is what the employers in this community want, and we have to give it to them or they will go elsewhere."

What about the old traditional IPAs? Can they compete effectively in an environment dominated by an emphasis on cost-effective care and capitation? We are aware of IPAs that capitate both primary care physicians and specialists, and do it successfully. Although these organizations tend to have large panels of physicians, the management of these IPAs usually have the authority to deal with sub-groups of physicians who demonstrate that they can meet certain performance criteria.

The successful IPA-model HMOs are reinventing themselves. The physician-owner of a Southern California IPA told us, "I may have 1,500 physicians on my panel, and some of them are not practicing cost-effective medicine. These doctors simply won't see any of our patients." The physician-owner managers of a highly successful North Carolina IPA-model HMO told us that, "We were successful because of aggressive, credible physician leadership in getting the organization through its lean years." Now that same aggressive physician leadership is beginning to introduce the incentives necessary to weed out physicians whose economic performance is causing problems for the group.

Other hospitals and physicians groups are joining together to own IPA-model HMOs or PPOs and to provide third-party claims services administration. Although these strategies have been around for several years, the more successful organizations are getting better at controlling utilization. The marketing director of a large staff-model HMO told us, "These kinds of organizations can't be written off as being ineffective. They are learning from their mistakes, and becoming much more of a competitive force. We certainly don't take them lightly." We believe that some successful IPA-model HMOs will soon be in a position to participate in more fully integrated systems.

The bottom line is that even if it is not feasible to own an HMO or directly control a large group of patients, there are other alternatives. The question boils down to good management and strong physician leadership in order to position an organization to be successful as a provider of health care services to health plans and other entities that control the financing mechanisms. It is usually better to take the first step toward forming the ultimate integrated system with all three legs of the stool, even if it is an incremental advance.

Summary

Two of the case study organizations that do not have a health plan or who moved into health plan ownership too late — Fargo Clinic/St. Luke's and Sutter Health — admit that they may have made a mistake by not giving ownership of an HMO a higher priority. It is all part of an increasing recognition that integrated health care systems are positioning themselves to compete for premium dollars. To accomplish this, these organizations need to have health insurance products, marketing expertise and experience in the management of capitated health plans.

The competitive advantages enjoyed by Kaiser Permanente, which not only owns its health plan but channels all of its revenues toward providing care for the individuals covered by the plan, have not escaped the attention of other integrated systems or those groups considering the formation of such systems. They view the Kaiser Permanente approach — combining health insurance, a medical group practice and hospitals all in one organization — as the most cost-effective and highly competitive model for the future. But, for most health care systems desiring further integration, the Kaiser Permanente model may be an impossible dream. Other integrated systems will have to settle for different approaches (e.g., forming an IPA, developing an IPA-model HMO or networking with other provider groups as part of a delivery system to contract with well-established HMOs).

Aside from the profitability which accompanies the ownership of a mature and well-managed health plan, the integrated systems stand to benefit from the patient base under contract, by the name recognition and reputation of their health plans, the data base developed on patient care and financing, and by the experience gained in operating in a capitated environment. Many of the integrated systems believe that by owning a health plan, the next steps required to perform well under health care reform will be manageable. They welcome the challenge.

CHAPTER 7.

PHYSICIAN COMPENSATION IN INTEGRATED HEALTH CARE SYSTEM

Physicians care about medical outcomes, quality improvement and other efforts aimed at improving quality. But, when it comes right down to it, they really want to know how any proposed change will affect their income.
— Medical group administrator of integrated system

Physicians considering involvement in an MSO, medical foundation, multispecialty clinic or other organized system are interested in how such a move will affect their compensation, both in the immediate and in the long-term future. Several issues relate to physician compensation in integrated health care systems:

- How do the large clinics and other integrated systems determine physician compensation?

- How do the earnings of primary care physicians in integrated systems compare with those who are in solo practice or small groups?

- What is the range of earnings between primary care doctors and sub-specialists in integrated systems? How does this compare with more traditional practice settings? How is this range of earnings likely to change in the future?

- What sorts of compensation guarantees are given to a physician who shifts from solo practice or a small group into a larger integrated system?

- Under a new type of health care system, emphasizing capitation rather than fee-for-service medicine, how will the incentives for physician compensation and productivity change?

Let's look at how integrated health care systems have wrestled with these issues.

Physician Compensation in Integrated Systems

In most solo practice settings, physicians take home what is left over after covering expenses; as a result, their incomes may vary substantially on a month-to-month basis. Even in most medical group practices, physicians do not retain earnings or large cash balances, so there is little cash to cushion monthly variations. Several physicians, especially those in primary care, tell us that in some months there is nothing left to take home after paying expenses.

As expected, most of the integrated organizations have formalized systems for determining base salaries (or draw) and other financial payouts. Physician compensation does not usually fluctuate, and there are likely to be bonuses or other cash distributions at the end of the year. Here are some examples:

Carle Clinic. Physicians at Carle receive a monthly salary which is based on their earnings of the previous year. The clinic's compensation formula weighs productivity at 70 percent and length of service with the clinic at 25 percent. A portion of the remaining five percent is allocated to department heads for distribution to physicians in their department; there are no predetermined criteria for allocating these departmental funds.

Kaiser Permanente - Denver. Dr. Toby Cole, Medical Director of the Colorado Permanente Medical Group, described KP's physician compensation policy as being straightforward. "We hire physicians, using comparable rates in the community. This may place us above the average for new primary care doctors, but overall we are not that much different. Salaries increase automatically for six years." Dr. Cole said that in a good year there is a four to five percent bonus paid to physicians. "In an exceptional year, it might run a percent or two above that, but this does not represent a whole lot of money for our physicians."

Fargo Clinic. Fargo Clinic subscribes to what it calls a "market-driven approach." Its compensation committee annually reviews a variety of data sources, including the Medical Group Management Association compensation surveys and data from other members of the Clinic Club (an informal association of 11 large clinics), in arriving at physician payment. There is little differentiation within specialties (i.e., most orthopedic surgeons earn the same amount).

Marshfield Clinic. Marshfield Clinic was founded on the philosophy of an equal distribution of earnings to all physicians. While this approach had the advantage of developing a strong corporate culture, the system had to be changed in order to recruit radiologists. From this modest beginning of a four percent premium, the size of the differential has widened, and income variations between specialists and primary care doctors have continued to grow. While most physicians earned $150,000 to $250,000 per year, the salary range was from $110,000 to $425,000 in 1992.

Geisinger. Geisinger has two different compensation methods — one for physicians at the main campus and a different one for doctors in its 43 network sites. Physicians in locations away from Danville are paid based on productivity. For those physicians in Danville, the compensation arrangement is more complex in that many of the doctors perform research, teach and spend time on administration or other activities other than direct patient care. Therefore, the Geisinger compensation program is more individually oriented for physicians in the network, and more departmentally oriented for those in Danville.

Physicians in these and other integrated systems can sleep easier at night knowing that their incomes are more predictable and secure. Gone are the monthly uncertainties and fluctuations which physicians in solo practice or small group practices experience. As one physician commented, "I can take a vacation without taking a hit in my paycheck."

How Physician Compensation in Integrated Systems Stacks Up

Not only do physicians in integrated systems have a more stable source of income, if they are primary care doctors, they also have more money to take home. Based on the case studies, we found primary care physicians in integrated systems were almost always earning more than most of their counterparts in private practice. In fact, compared with solo practitioners, and especially solo practitioners in markets dominated by managed care, incomes were considerably higher. These higher levels of income run counter to the national experience of primary care physicians. As discussed in several previous chapters, the incomes of primary care physicians have been losing ground to specialists for quite some time.

Many factors have contributed to this decline in primary care incomes including a high proportion of Medicare patients (they take more time and in the mandated fee schedule, compensation for primary care is relatively low), increasing managed care, and higher overhead, to name a few. In fact, over the last decade the inflation adjusted income of the average family practice doctor was up less than one percent per year compared to an average across all specialties of 2.2 percent. Family practice doctors and other primary care physicians are on the bottom rung of the income ladder, earning only half as much as surgical specialists who are at the top.

Interestingly, despite the wide geographic variation among case study organizations, most of the systems studied had a similar going rate for primary care physicians. Family practice doctors typically earned annual incomes in the $100,000 to $120,000 range. This exceeded the incomes of over half the primary care physicians in the country. Needless to say, these salaries look pretty attractive to the graduate just coming out of residency.

In addition to a larger and more secure earning base in an integrated system, physicians also receive significant benefits for joining and staying with the organization. Some groups offer a signing bonus of several thousand dollars to recent residents as well as to practicing physicians who join a medical group. Others offer an enriched package of benefits, including substantial time off for continuing medical education and personal leave. Pension plans and other benefits are nearly always superior to that of physicians in traditional solo practices.

Range of Earnings: Primary Care Physicians and Specialists

One of the characteristics of several of the integrated systems studied was that they have limited the range of specialists' earnings over that of primary care physicians. (In the typical fragmented medical staff situation, dominated by solo practitioners and small groups, the range of earnings between specialists and primary care physicians can reach five to one or more.) The experience of the case study organizations is shown below.

- *Fargo Clinic.* Fargo Clinic has sought to balance its market-driven approach with the desire to avoid large disparities in income. In fact, the range of physician compensation at the clinic is not as wide as in most multispecialty clinics. Until two years ago, the compensation of specialists did not exceed that of primary care physicians by more than 50 percent. However, in the past two years market pressures have been given more weight in compensation discussions, and the clinic has relaxed its guidelines in order to attract and retain certain specialists. Even so, the range from the more highly paid specialists to the lower paid primary care physicians is less than three to one.

- *Geisinger.* This organization has a relatively narrow compensation range according to Dr. Stuart Heydt, Geisinger's president. Specialists earn somewhat less than they might in private practice, and primary care physicians earn more. Primary care physicians earned $90,000 to $120,000, and a limited number of specialists earned as much as $375,000.

- *Carle Clinic.* The Carle system, with its emphasis on productivity, results in an income spread of seven to one (the highest-paid specialist earns seven times the amount earned by the lowest-paid primary care doctor), although most of the salaries at Carle fall within a three to one range. The clinic's leaders would like to narrow this range but the present marketplace mitigates against it. But, as the physician-CEO of the clinic noted, "Our salaries reflect the external environment. When the market for physicians changes, our salaries will also shift."

Compensation systems like those used at the Fargo Clinic, which are based on a market survey of physician incomes to establish compensation levels, have considerable flexibility so that can respond to changes expected in the future. As market forces brought about by health care reform drive primary care incomes up and specialist incomes down, compensation levels can be adjusted accordingly. One of the physician members of the compensation committee at the Fargo Clinic noted, "With our compensation system, we should be able to make these kinds of adjustments. We are not locked into a system that pays specialists more; the market place will be the driver."

Specialists among many of the case study organizations profiled earn less than what they would in other settings. A Fargo Clinic physician said, "People who come here know they are not going to make as much as they might in another situation." When Carle Clinic physicians compare their compensation to that of their specialist colleagues at a competing multispecialty clinic, they find they make about one-third less. This stems, in part, from the financial support specialists provide to their primary care colleagues. A physician-administrator notes that specialists know that, "The subsidy is a two-way street. Primary care physicians keep the specialists busy."

Specialists who join integrated systems usually take a long-term view of the situation. They recognize that their ability to serve patients has become increasingly dependent on primary care referrals, and that they can assure their own success, now and in the future, by joining forces with primary care physicians in an integrated system.

There are other advantages to working within an integrated system which offset lower incomes. These include security, a more stable income, and a steady supply of patients. This fact prompted one specialist to remark, "I may not make as much money at this clinic as I would elsewhere, but I make enough."

Some organizations, such as Marshfield Clinic, have built in flexibility which will soften the blow when specialist incomes begin to decline relative to primary care. Marshfield has a policy of not laying off physicians. As one physician-administrator said, "If times get tough, everyone will take pay cuts, but there will be no lay-offs. Furthermore, many of our specialists can help out in primary care if the need arises." Physicians are not penalized for handling more primary care patients, making the conversion to a primary care-dominated system more feasible — a major advantage over a system in which physician practice patterns are more narrowly prescribed.

Guaranteeing the Compensation Pool

When physicians join a physician-hospital organization or an integrated health care system, they are often successful in bargaining for some sort of income guarantee, at least for two or three years. This usually is expressed as a percentage of net revenues that will be available in the compensation pool. Physicians are often worried about the increase in administrative expenses when a hospital gets into the medical practice business; therefore, they seek guarantees limiting the amount of overhead coming out of the compensation pool.

Integrated systems have responded to these concerns in a variety of ways. Some systems have guaranteed the size of the compensation pool (or physician salary levels) to provide physicians with a measure of income stability, particularly in the early stages of physician-hospital integration. For example, economically integrated physicians in

Presbyterian Healthcare Services in Albuquerque receive a salary based on past years' compensation and current year incentives. Physicians know the minimum amount of income they can expect and it is up to them to exceed this amount. Primary care physicians participating in this arrangement report that they earn more than when they were in solo practice or small groups.

Other systems have guaranteed a portion of the physician compensation pool. For example, part of the Fargo Clinic/St. Luke's Hospital merger agreement stipulated that the physician compensation pool would not fall below 40 percent of net revenues for the first three years of the merger. Under such an arrangement, physicians are protected from the down-side risk of increased administrative expenses, but retain a strong incentive to increase revenues.

A guaranteed compensation pool offers another measure of security for physicians. The value of the guarantee can be significant to physicians who have been in solo or in small group practice settings and have watched their overhead ratios climb year after year. One case study organization offers a compensation pool guarantee at a rate that is specific to each deal; the ratio has ranged from 46.5 percent of net revenues for one group to 51 percent for another group. Another organization has built in shared financial incentives for the hospital and physicians. The guaranteed percentage to the compensation pool established base earnings, while profits from the system were equally divided among the two partners (the hospital and the physician group).

For a hospital to be able to provide this guarantee, there must be an economic justification for assuming the risk. This is one of several considerations in developing a new organization's business plan and structuring the financial flows.

Physician Compensation in the Future

With the shift to a capitated payment system, and away from fee-for-service with its corresponding emphasis on productivity, how will physician compensation be determined in the future? As one physician-administrator reflected on the clinic's productivity-based compensation formula and the advent of capitated care, "This is a key issue for the future of the organization. Will we be willing to change the compensation system so physicians personally feel the pressures of capitation?"

As one administrator noted, regarding the present state of affairs, "We have our feet in both worlds — the fee-for-service world where we are rewarded for having patients in the hospital and the capitated world where we are rewarded for keeping them out." Not only is it frustrating, it is costly for the hospital and for the physicians.

The standard approaches to physician compensation existing in the market may not suffice in a market dominated by managed competition and capitated care. Many compensation philosophies which reward productivity were developed in the era of fee-for-service medicine when the guiding principle was, "The more patients you see, the more revenue you generate, and the more money you make." In a capitated environment the attitude behind this approach is a recipe for disaster.

John McDonald, the administrator of the Mullikin Medical Center in southern California, described the issue of changing incentives in this way: " . . . groups must modify physician compensation and scrap production-based systems. Compensation must be tied to quality, not to any type of system where the individual can control the supply side of the equation, as in the fee-for-service system." Mullikin Medical Center compensates its physicians from three sources:

- From practice: Physicians are compensated for the amount of time they spend seeing patients and providing quality care in a cost-effective manner.

- From management: Physicians in administration are compensated for management responsibilities.

- From capital: Physicians have the right to a return on investment for capital invested in the business, equipment, and facilities" (Grant, 1991, p. 32).

The physicians who participate in Alta Bates Medical Resources in Berkeley, a physician-hospital sponsored MSO, have devised a point system for determining compensation. Points are awarded based on stated criteria related to physician work effort, capitated enrollment, time allocation, hospital and specialist utilization and other factors. Depending on how well they score on these criteria, family practice physicians may see a difference of $20,000 to $30,000 in their annual incomes.

The physician-administrator of a hospital in a health care market dominated by capitation said that the compensation formulas for employed physicians are simple. "The base salary is the average of the past three years, and includes what they earned from ancillaries before they joined us. At the end of each year salaries are adjusted. The only factor considered in terms of base salary is the number and type of patient encounters, not revenues." In addition there will be financial incentives based on the number of "members per month" served by the group, and the number of capitated lives cared for by each physician.

Some integrated systems have begun to put the pieces in place to make the transition to a capitated environment. For example, at Presbyterian Healthcare Services, there is a risk-sharing agreement between physicians and the network. If practice net income after payments to physicians — the true bottom line for a medical practice — exceeds the budget forecasts for the year, one quarter of the surplus goes to Presbyterian and three quarters is divided among the physicians. Several systems are considering changing to this approach for arriving at the overall physician compensation pool and then shifting to an approach similar to Medicare's Resource-Based Relative Value Scale (RBRVS) for allocating the pool among physicians.

This type of approach puts the incentives in place for rewarding cost-effective medicine. With capitated care expected to become the dominant source of revenues, the budgeting process and risk sharing plan can adapt accordingly to further encourage high quality, cost-effective patient care.

Other administrators fear that the change to a capitated system could lead to lower productivity. Most physicians work very hard, which enables clinics to see more patients and be more profitable. If the payment system is changed, physicians may cut back on the hours they are willing to work. This could require hiring more physicians to accommodate the same number of patients.

The Bottom Line on Physician Compensation

Primary care physicians in more fully integrated systems are clear cut winners in terms of achieving a secure and rewarding income, exceeding what they could expect on their own in a managed care marketplace. With incomes near the median level for their specialty, they generally earn more than their counterparts, and often considerably more, usually $10,000 to $20,000 per year, than new residents starting out in solo practice. Month-to-month variations usually are reduced or eliminated. Of course, a big part of the increase in earnings for primary care physicians participating in integrated systems is due to the availability of external funding sources to stabilize the finances of these medical practices.

Specialists working with integrated systems may not be optimizing their incomes in the short term. However, most specialists recognize this possibility, and are taking a longer-term view. Also, specialists in the integrated systems we examined tend to be aware of the value of their primary care referral network and are willing to forego income so that this referral system can continue to develop. Furthermore, we believe that most integrated systems will find ways to keep valued specialists and already have the mechanisms in place to adjust compensation levels to reflect the marketplace of the future.

When physicians decide to become part of a physician-hospital organization or an integrated system, it is common for them to expect some guarantees, at least for two or three years, to protect the compensation pool from the incursions of higher overhead. Most of the systems we studied recognized that higher overhead costs were a distinct possibility, and were willing to make some accommodations to their physicians on this matter. However, in the future physicians may be expected to share more of the financial responsibility for the success or failure of the integrated health care systems they join.

Physicians participating in integrated systems also are likely to be ahead of their counterparts in solo or small group practice in terms of being part of a compensation model that is adjusting to capitation. Although different organizations are trying a variety of approaches, no one seems to have the answer in terms of maintaining productivity and, at the same time, practicing cost-effective care. Nevertheless, we believe integrated health care systems are well positioned to adjust to this new paradigm (making more money by keeping people healthy) in the health care industry.

CHAPTER 8.

LEADERSHIP AND GOVERNANCE

If physicians do not take the leadership in forming and managing our efforts to form an integrated system, nothing will happen.
— Hospital administrator of integrated health care system

This chapter describes the people and organizational structures that make integrated health care systems work. In reviewing the 10 case studies and the experiences of many other organizations, one characteristic that distinguishes integrated systems from the more traditional hospital-based systems is that physicians are at the core of the organization, expanding their bounds of responsibility beyond patient care to leadership, management and governance.

In integrated health care systems, physicians help shape the vision of the organization and play a decisive role in carrying it out. Hospital management also has its role, but it differs from the past. Instead of leading the charge, hospital boards and top managers serve in a supporting capacity, collaborating with physician leaders in realizing the shared vision of the integrated health care system.

This chapter discusses five important aspects of leadership, management and governance of integrated health care systems:

- The importance of a common vision in moving ahead with physician-hospital integration.

- The leadership and management roles played by physicians.

- The new roles of hospital CEOs and administrators in integrated systems.

- The role of medical group practice administrators and how they can become important players in integrated systems.

- How physicians, hospitals and health plans work together to coordinate the delivery and financing of health care.

The Importance of a Common Vision

This reminds us of The Old Testament proverb, "Where there is no vision, the people perish" (Proverbs 29:18). It may be just about that serious for physicians and hospitals!

When physicians and hospital managers talk about working together or establishing new types of organizational relationships, they are likely to find that they have radically different views of the future of health care, both nationally and in their community. For example, will managed care include discounted fee-for-service plans, or will providers be at risk through capitation? Another factor for which there are likely to be differences is in assessing the possible strategies of competing hospitals and medical groups. The future role of primary care physicians versus specialists, which was discussed in Chapter 4, is almost always a source of conflict.

A group of industry observers describes the need to develop a common vision in this way:

> The importance of having a vision explicitly stated and then gaining consensus about the vision is twofold. First, the very act of arriving at an agreement about the vision creates a powerful bond that can sustain a group through the conflicts inherent in the health care industry today. Second, a vision provides a direction, albeit general, that can guide groups through the incredible ambiguity of today's marketplace (Harris, Hicks and Kelly, 1992, p. 21).

Our experience, as well as the evidence contained in the case studies and our database on 60 other organizations moving toward becoming integrated health care systems, supports this viewpoint. What we have learned is that despite different perspectives, it is possible for physicians, hospital managers and board members to develop a shared vision. As one physician-administrator put it, "If we are going to be successful, everyone needs to be singing from the same song sheet."

Several examples. For example, for the leaders of the Fargo Clinic, the evolution of a vision for the future had its genesis at an annual meeting of the Clinic Club. As the executive administrator of the Fargo Clinic reflected, "This was where we first heard about the possibility of joining with a hospital. It got us thinking." He and several clinic and hospital leaders subsequently visited Virginia Mason in Seattle, Sharp Rees-Stealy in San Diego and the Ramsey Clinic in St. Paul, to see how other physicians and hospitals had come together, and what they had gained from it.

The birth of the Presbyterian Network in Albuquerque took place when 17 primary care physicians met to figure out how to organize themselves and to improve their future prospects. This led to a report to the Presbyterian Healthcare Services board and the appointment of a task force to study matters in more detail. The task force's report became a blueprint leading to the development of the Presbyterian Network.

The Oregon Medical Group got its start when a small group of physicians had a beer after a tennis match. One of the participants recalls, "As doctors are prone to do, we were speculating about the future of health care. We talked about where we as physicians were headed and what we could do to control our own destiny." This led several primary care physicians, representing eight different group practices, to examine different organizational models. In 1988, 24 of these physicians and Sacred Heart Hospital formed an MSO.

The story was the same in Sacramento. In 1984, 25 physicians decided to form the Sac Sierra Medical Group, largely in response to a common vision of where they thought the health care system was headed in the highly competitive Sacramento marketplace dominated by Kaiser Permanente and other managed care companies.

One of the leaders of Geisinger emphasized the importance of a common vision when negotiating with hospitals and physician groups in the service area in terms of a possible collaborative relationship. He said, "We often talk to people who seem to be mainly interested in preserving the status quo. If it is a hospital, they want admissions. If it is a group of physicians, they want to retain their independence yet still be part of our health plan. Our view of the future is that we have to position ourselves to provide quality care to a defined population at the lowest possible cost. If these other groups don't share that vision, we might as well stop talking because nothing is going to happen."

What happens without a common vision? The lack of shared vision has been a contributing factor to the demise of attempts to achieve physician-hospital integration. We were interested in learning about a group of physicians and a hospital in the Midwest that had formed a physician-hospital organization (PHO), only to find out later that the new organization had collapsed. This is an actual case; the names of the community, hospital and physicians have been withheld at the request of the hospital CEO.

A group of 12 physicians (out of 30 on the medical staff) and a 100-bed hospital in a midwestern city of 30,000 attempted to form a multispecialty group practice and a PHO in 1990. The primary motivations for the physicians, mostly specialists, were to retain their referral base of primary care physicians and to capture more ancillary income. The hospital was concerned about the "leakage" of patients to hospitals in surrounding communities; in 1990, 30 percent of the residents of the area were using physicians and hospitals outside the county. The hospital board recognized the need for action, but several members were concerned about a group of physicians gaining power through the formation of a larger group.

What are the lessons learned from this failed effort? First, the objectives of the various parties-at-interest were to improve their financial positions and ability to survive, not to find new ways to meet the needs of patients and payors. Since primary care physicians in the community had full practices, they were not unduly concerned about the problems of the hospital and specialists and had little incentive to participate. There was also substantial distrust between the hospital governing board and physician leaders; this contributed to the failure.

Physicians as Leaders and Managers

We are convinced that physicians have to be involved in leadership and management positions if the efforts at integration are to be successful. Hospital CEOs can facilitate the process, as discussed later in this chapter, but physicians must take the lead. To the best of our knowledge, there are no exceptions to this finding.

When it comes to planning for physician-hospital integration, doctors have to proceed at their own pace, and do it their own way. The CEO of a large multihospital system on the East Coast noted, "One of the lessons we learned was not to try to move physicians as fast as we did." He went on:

There weren't many clouds on the horizon when we started so it was difficult to get physicians interested. If we had to do it over again, we would rely more on physician leadership, and the hospital management team would go with the flow. We wouldn't be building the ark until the storm clouds are visible. There is an economic cost in preparing for a threat that hasn't manifested itself. We should have had physicians more involved in strategic planning. We have traditionally used a board-led, physician-tolerated approach; it hasn't been very effective (The Future of ..., 1992).

Once the new integrated systems are formed, more and more physicians are filling the roles of policy-makers and managers. In most of the case study organizations and in many other integrated systems, physicians occupy the presidency or chair of the system and are represented on most boards. Physicians also serve as managers, rolling up their sleeves and getting involved in the day-to-day business of creating and sustaining an integrated health care system.

Integrated systems incorporate physicians into the management structure in a variety of ways. Many of these organizations employ physician managers on a full or part-time basis. Systems compensate physicians for administrative duties to encourage their active participation in operations. Many physician administrators also continue to practice medicine part-time; they say this earns them credibility with their peers and keeps them in touch with the day-to-day issues facing physicians. (This is discussed further in Chapter 9.)

According to the medical director of the 82-physician Medical Clinic of Sacramento (part of the Mercy Healthcare System, a competitor of Sutter Health), "We need to better train our manager-doctors," meaning the physicians in the group who want to get involved in administration. Right now the group has 10 physicians who have or are earning MBAs and two who are working toward master's degrees in administration (Clements, 1993, p. 8).

Both Kaiser Permanente and Geisinger make use of a partnership arrangement between physician leaders and administrators. At Kaiser Permanente, this has been the pattern since the 1950s. These individuals share the responsibility for running a program or organization. The medical director of the Colorado Permanente Medical Group, said that this approach was not intended to excuse physicians from developing their managerial skills. "We expect them to learn how to become managers, and most of them do it." Another organization also pairs physician-managers with an administrator characterizing this arrangement as "an administrative shadow."

The Role of Hospital CEOs and Administrators

With all of the emphasis on physicians and physician leaders in the integration process, what about hospital CEOs and administrators? What is their role? Based on our experience and the lessons learned from the case studies and other organizations, hospital CEOs often play supportive roles in the integration process. They are facilitators.

To be successful in the role of facilitator, hospital CEOs usually have to earn the trust of the physicians with whom they are working to form a new organization. CEOs need a comprehensive view of the future and a vision of where the hospital fits in relative to physicians, especially primary care doctors. We find that the most successful CEOs have not just tolerated but have welcomed physician participation in the change process.

In interviewing and listening to hospital CEOs who have made progress in the physician-hospital integration process, we are struck by the fact that they talk differently. They readily admit that they don't have all of the answers. They have a broad perspective on the world of health care, and they recognize that the health care system of the future is not going to revolve around hospitals. They talk in terms of health plan premiums, not hospital revenues. These CEOs recognize the needs of physicians, especially the financial issues facing most primary care doctors, and are interested in exploring ways to solve these problems.

Almost without exception, in the process of becoming a more integrated system, hospital administrators and boards have relinquished a significant share of their authority. Physicians in integrated systems are more likely to be members of boards and committees and occupy paid staff positions in the organization. In several cases, physician administrators have replaced members of the management team.

Finally, successful hospital CEOs and boards of integrated systems have come to grips with new priorities for capital budgeting. As noted in Chapter 5, hospitals continue to be an important source of capital for the integration process, especially the financial support of primary care practices and the development of massive new information systems.

Group Practice Administrators as Participants in the Change Process

We discussed the role of hospital CEOs in developing integrated health care systems; what about medical group practice administrators? Where do they fit in? Much depends on the characteristics of the administrators and their position within their organizations. We observed that administrators who work in partnership with their physician leaders usually play a key role in shaping and implementing integrated health care systems. We also have seen administrators remain on the sidelines, unable to contribute to the bigger picture because they are overly focused on operational details. Many resist change and are concerned about job security.

Characteristics of a participant in an integrated system. Based on our interviews with several medical group practice administrators who are now part of the management teams of integrated systems, here are a few of the characteristics we observed:

In several of the groups we had a sense that the practice administrator and physician leader had a partnership relationship. This differed from anything we had seen in the hospital industry in that it was a close long-time relationship built on mutual trust and respect.

We did not detect a "know it all" attitude among the medical group practice administrators we met with. Instead, we observed individuals who had inquiring minds and were constantly seeking new and better ways to do their jobs and to make their organizations successful; they were not threatened by change. The importance of open and frequent communications is also something we observed about administrators in all of the large clinics.

Nearly all of the group administrators of the large clinics are visionaries when it comes to the future of health care and where their organizations fit in; they sense change in the air and welcome it.

In our judgment, medical group practice administrators with these characteristics, combined with the appropriate training, people skills and experience, have the potential to make major contributions as leaders of the new integrated health care systems.

different personalities will be successf Collaborates

A needed resource. Medical group administrators often represent the business interests of the physicians. They are a critical source of technical expertise, knowledgeable about the latest Medicare regulations, health plan contracts and billing practices. However, their responsibilities go beyond technical knowledge. Because of their stature within the organization, they help physician leadership engender overall support for decisions and serve as communicators to the clinic staff.

This role is important as the founders of the Oregon MSO realized in retrospect. Commenting on one of the lessons learned in the integration process, a hospital manager said "We needed more cross-pollination between senior level executives of the hospital and medical group. We should have brought the group practice administrator into the fabric of the hospital organization."

Coordinating Physician-Health System Relationships

Some integrated systems have designed the linkages between physicians and hospitals along more informal lines while others have formalized reporting relationships and the composition of governing boards and committees. Here are examples of how several of the case study systems and others are coordinating the various components of the system:

Presbyterian Healthcare Services (PHS). The formation of the Presbyterian Network evolved along informal lines leading to the formation of a task force, and finally, the creation of the Network of 390 physicians. The Network board, consisting of 11 physicians, is responsible for overseeing overall Network activities, resolving disputes and planning the desirable physician mix. Despite these significant responsibilities, the Presbyterian Network is not a legal entity; it reports to the PHS board. However, one telling indicator that PHS has tied its fortunes to the Network is that the Network board is responsible for strategic planning for Presbyterian's Albuquerque operations.

Carle. A contrasting model of physician-hospital integration is provided by the Carle Clinic where the fortunes of the Carle Foundation Hospital and Carle Clinic are closely tied. Carle Foundation owns all the assets, including those of the clinic and hospital. The board of the foundation consists of six community representatives, five physicians and the foundation CEO. The policy-making body of the Carle Clinic is its board of governors consisting of six physicians. The hospital and clinic share department heads.

In addition to these functions, the foundation and clinic have two standing committees that coordinate strategies and day-to-day operations. A joint policy council focuses on strategic issues and includes the leadership of the Carle Clinic board of governors and the foundation board. A joint administrative group meets weekly to coordinate activities of the clinic, hospital and other Carle Foundation entities.

Fargo Clinic/St. Luke's Hospital. The St. Luke's Association board is the governing body for the hospital and the Fargo Clinic. This overall body is governed by community representatives who hold 12 of the 18 board positions. Five physicians are also on the board, and the president of the association is a physician.

Lloyd Smith, the hospital president, noted that under this new structure there was substantial cross-over between the hospital and clinic. He said, "I am now on the clinic board. Before the merger the hospital was not represented on the clinic's board and the clinic administrator did not attend our board meetings."

Like the examples described earlier, informal groups supplement the formal organization. An administrative coordinating council resolves disputes, assigning responsibilities between the clinic and hospital and exploring options for coordination. In its first four months, the council identified 20 potential areas for consolidation.

Marshfield Clinic/St. Joseph Hospital. Marshfield Clinic and St. Joseph's Hospital (and the hospital's parent, the Ministry Corporation) have achieved a high degree of integration; however, much depends on informal coordination. A joint conference committee involving hospital and clinic managers meets weekly to coordinate activities and decide how to share resources. In addition, Marshfield Clinic's leadership meets monthly with key staff members of the Ministry Corporation. According to the executive director of the Marshfield Clinic, "This monthly meeting is where serious business takes place regarding the future of the two organizations."

Geisinger. Established as a hospital with employed physicians, Geisinger has always had an integrated management structure with an emphasis on physician administrators. When Geisinger reorganized in 1982, it was the first time the system had a separate medical group, the not-for-profit Geisinger Clinic. One of the motivations for this restructuring was to separate the hospital from the physicians for legal and reimbursement reasons.

However, in late 1992, Geisinger again reorganized, this time along regional lines. While retaining the 1982 structure, which included 10 separate corporations, the essence of the 1993 organization was that physician administrators and professional administrators would team up to supervise all aspects of health care, including the health plan, medical services and the hospital within three geographic regions. One of the administrators said, "This structure was designed to eliminate duplicative services (for example, the clinic had its own finance staff), and to devote our energies to focusing on the health status of the people in the region."

All of these examples point to the continuing need for mechanisms, both formal and informal, to coordinate the policies and operations of integrated health care systems. The systems that directly owned or controlled all of the major elements (e.g., Carle, Geisinger) had just as much need to coordinate activities as integrated systems that relied on networking relationships (e.g., Marshfield and the Ministry Corporation and Kaiser Permanente and Saint Joseph Hospital).

Summary

As we reflected on the case studies and the experiences of dozens of other organizations going through the integration process, three leadership characteristics for physicians, hospital CEOs and group practice administrators stand out:

A sense of priorities. In advising others on developing physician-hospital organizations, those who have been through the process offer the same counsel: put the customers (members, patients and employer groups) first, the organization second and personal interests third. This is true for the physicians and hospital executives leading the charge, as well as practicing physicians and employees.

A physician-administrator at the Carle Clinic said that the majority of physicians think "group" rather than in terms of what is best for them individually. Physicians and employees of Marshfield and St. Joseph's Hospital use remote parking lots so that patients can park next to the clinic and hospital. This is a way of sending the message that payors and patients are important and that physicians and clinic staff exist to serve customers.

Communication skills. The authors of a book on integrative health care strategies wrote, "Effective integrators have strong listening skills and are able to understand viewpoints very different from their own and to reconcile diverse opinions" (Charns and Smith Tewksbury, 1993, p. 46). We couldn't agree more. The successful physician leaders and CEOs have been able to cultivate a common vision among disparate perspectives by listening, communicating and taking issues a step at a time in their efforts to build an integrated system. One of the physician leaders offered this piece of advice for prospective physician and hospital leaders: "Communicate, communicate, communicate."

Ability to build trust. This issue is so important that speakers at a conference on physician-hospital integration started referring to it as the "T" word. Trust between physicians and hospitals. Trust between physician leaders and their colleagues. Trust between hospital executives and boards. If you don't have it, you can't build an integrated system.

At MAPI in Billings, the executive director said that without honesty, courage, communication and trust, productive relationships among physicians who are trying to build an organization, and between that group and a hospital, will not happen. "If you don't have these ingredients, especially trust, don't expect to make much progress."

Case study organizations and others confirm that trust is built slowly with small gains building on small gains. It comes from dealing openly and honestly with all parties involved. As one administrator noted, "Relationships are fragile — if you do one thing wrong and it is interpreted as a bad faith action, what you have been trying to build can come crashing down on you. You have to start over, and you have lost a month or two of valuable time."

Chapter 9 reports on what we have observed to be the unique aspects of the corporate cultures of health care organizations seeking integration.

how do you build trust?

CHAPTER 9.
THE CORPORATE CULTURE OF INTEGRATED SYSTEMS

If we fail in our efforts to integrate physicians and our two hospitals, our inability to create a new, workable culture will be the primary reason.
— Physician-administrator of an integrated system

Management writers have defined corporate culture as "the pattern of shared and stable beliefs and values that are developed within a company across time." Others define organizational culture as shared meaning, central values, assumptions and beliefs (Gordon and DiTomaso, 1992, p. 784). How does all of this play out in integrated health care systems?

It is not our purpose to offer a comprehensive analysis of the corporate cultures of integrated health care systems and compare them to traditional physician and hospital organizations. However, we have selected several of the more interesting and unique characteristics of the integrated systems we studied for discussion in this chapter. We also offer additional observations about the cultural characteristics of a number of the large clinics. This chapter concludes with a discussion of the variations in culture among the traditional multispecialty clinics and the newer physician-hospital organizations and multihospital systems as they move toward becoming more fully integrated.

The Decision-Making Process

Hospital and system boards tend to be deliberate in their decision making. Physicians, on the other hand, are more likely to debate issues and make decisions quickly. How do these two approaches to decision making come together in a single organization? The experiences of even the most integrated organizations confirm that there are some lively debates:

Marshfield Clinic. Monthly board of directors and shareholder meetings are a tradition that goes back to the beginning of Marshfield Clinic. (Over 300 of Marshfield's 390 physicians have been with the organization for two years or longer and qualify for shareholder status.)

These meetings, which are usually attended by two-thirds of the shareholders, are video-conferenced to outlying locations so that physicians in regional centers can participate. Issues are discussed and debated, and decisions made.

Physician leaders at Marshfield attribute the strength of the clinic to the involvement of shareholders and directors in decision making. The Chief Financial Officer of Marshfield said, "The conventional wisdom would say that running an organization with a group this large can't work, but it does. Furthermore, when all of our physicians are involved in a decision, they tend to stand behind it."

Fargo Clinic/St. Luke's. One of the physicians involved with the Fargo Clinic board noted that the hospital board was largely composed of community representatives. "They tend to view being a trustee the same as being on a corporate board. They usually go along with management's recommendations, and there is usually little controversy in the decision-making process. They don't like to ruffle each others' feathers."

He went on, "In the case of the clinic board, we are all involved in the health care field, and the success of the organization is critical to our livelihood. We get a lot more feedback from our shareholders (the more than 200 physicians who own stock in the clinic). When they have a complaint or suggestion they tend to be vocal. We accept this as the normal way of doing business "

While the basis existed for a clash of cultures, physicians found that the new structure offered them a voice in the organization. As one physician noted, "The more I thought about having a lay board in an influential position, the less it bothered me. Being physicians, I think we can influence the board's deliberations and decision-making. I think as long as we are doing a good job they will take us seriously."

Carle. Carle Clinic developed a strong culture among its physicians back in the 1950s when it decided to broaden the ownership and management base by moving away from a small group of owners with most other physicians on salary, to one in which employed physicians have a voice in the governance of the organization. This established a decision-making process very different from the more bureaucratic structure of the hospital. According to one of the physicians at Carle Clinic,

In the hospital, if the CEO tells a subordinate to do something, they do it. In the clinic, however, if the CEO tells one of the physicians to do something, he may find himself in an argument. There is constant friction and a tug of war. You have more big egos and hidden agendas. There is more need for consensus building.

The hospital administrator within the Carle system agreed with this assessment noting that in the Carle Foundation, the board and management drive the system, whereas the clinic is more democratic. Nevertheless they have been able to recognize and transcend the different decision-making styles. The hospital CEO notes, "We can agree to do things more quickly and get them done. The hospital doesn't have to worry about physicians getting upset and threatening to take their business elsewhere. This frees us up to think strategically, rather than constantly putting out fires."

The differences between the way hospitals make decisions versus ✳ physician groups came across in many of the organizations. The typical pattern can be summed up by what the hospital administrator in one system told us. "In the hospital it takes us longer to make a decision, but once we make it, we can hold it. Physicians in the clinic can make decisions faster, but they usually have trouble standing by the decision once it is made. They get pressured and sometimes want to back track."

A physician leader associated with the Sacramento Sierra Medical Group tells how difficult it is to reach and stick with a decision:

We — the board and members of Sac Sierra — went through a terribly difficult decision-making process as part of finding a financial partner. At one meeting, which lasted over six hours, the board approved Sutter by a six to five margin. But, no one felt good about it because of the perceived loss of control and our members asked us to re-evaluate the alternatives. We did and came to the same conclusion — we had to have a capital partner and Sutter Health was our best bet. We went back to the members at the next meeting and everyone felt better; we decided to move ahead.

What can organizations do to work within these different management styles and decision-making processes? The first step is to recognize the differences and accept that these differences are unlikely to change. In our judgment, the combination of the two decision-making styles can often work to the advantage of the overall integrated system. The best decisions are made by individuals or groups who hold different perspectives. In integrated systems, where physicians play such critically important roles, both physician leaders and hospital administrators find they have to continually re-sell decisions; this process keeps the organization focused on its goals.

White Coats versus Blue Suits

The last chapter discussed the important role of physicians as managers in integrated health care systems. Many of these physician-managers stay involved in patient care; they wear white coats and devote 20 percent or more of their time to patients, and take weekend call. This practice is part of the corporate culture in their organizations. In other cases, physician-administrators have become full-time managers. Here is how some of the case study organizations approach this issue:

Carle Clinic. Dr. John Pollard, a cardiologist and long-time CEO of Carle Clinic, spends 20 percent of his time caring for patients. He and the medical director are the only exceptions to the rule that physician-administrators spend a minimum of 50 percent of their time on patient care.

One physician-administrator at Carle said, "I am not in this job because of my administrative skills." Although he has an MBA degree, he said, "I am effective because I am a physician and have the respect of my fellow doctors. To do this job well, I have to keep my hand in the practice of medicine."

Marshfield Clinic. Dr. Richard Leer, President of the Marshfield Clinic and a family practice physician, spends 20 percent of his time with patients. "This is part of our culture, and it is something I enjoy doing." There are no physicians who are full-time administrators at Marshfield.

Colorado Permanente Medical Group. The president of CPMG, Dr. Toby Cole, is the only physician who is a full-time administrator. All other physicians who have administrative responsibilities are expected to devote at least half of their time to practicing medicine.

Geisinger. Geisinger has a different corporate culture. Dr. Stuart Heydt, an oral and maxillofacial surgeon and President of the Geisinger Foundation, dropped his medical practice several years ago. "Being the head of this organization is a big job. The board pays me to be CEO, not to practice medicine. Also, I don't have time to keep up with my field."

At the same time, several other physician-administrators at Geisinger devote 10 to 20 percent of their time to their medical practices. The head of the health plan, a board-certified ER physician, said that if he had to give up practicing medicine as a condition of being an administrator, he would not take the administrative job. Other physician-administrators at Geisinger say that they enjoy medicine and believe it is part of maintaining their credibility with other doctors.

In summary, in most of the case study organizations and in many other integrated systems (e.g., Ochsner, Cleveland Clinic) physician-administrators continue to practice medicine. The major reasons: the corporate culture requires it, physicians don't want to give up practicing medicine (they enjoy it) and the widely-held opinion that continuing in practice increases their effectiveness in dealing with their colleagues.

What is the best approach? It is obvious that both approaches — wearing a white coat and practicing part time, or becoming a full-time administrator — work within certain organizations. However, we heard comments from some physicians we interviewed that colleagues who gave up medical practice entirely to become managers had lost their credibility as physicians; they had become part of "management." We suspect this is typical in the majority of organizations where physicians are in key leadership and management roles.

The Culture of Large Clinics

Several of the integrated systems we studied included large and long-established medical clinics. We observed several interesting characteristics that differed from those of other medical groups and hospitals which are just coming together as systems. These included:

Emphasis on fast information transfer. In walking the corridors of the big multispecialty clinics, we were struck by the large number of workers pushing carts filled with medical records and other packets of information. According to our guide at the Marshfield Clinic, there were 30 people assigned to this job, with the goal of transferring documents from one physician to another or from the lab to a physician within 30 minutes. One of these messengers told us she walked eight miles a day!

One person we met called this system "archaic." As discussed in Chapter 10, all of the large integrated systems are investing millions in improving their information systems, which will include instantaneous on-line access to medical records. Perhaps the need for messengers will go the way of the horse and buggy. But, for the time being, the challenge of information transfer is being met with low-tech alternatives.

Informal consultation among physicians; collegial attitudes. In describing what is different about large clinics, the informal, collegial attitudes that characterize these organizations is often cited. When a patient needs to see a specialist, or a primary care doctor needs a consultation, specialists are "down the hall." This facilitates the referral process. Physicians in these clinics believe it adds up to higher quality of care. The attitude is one of collegiality, not competition.

One physician at Geisinger, a dermatologist, said that he frequently consults with oncologists and rheumatologists who are in the same building. "We found a funny lump on the jaw of a patient recently. We weren't sure what it was, and we had an oncologist looking at this man within 20 minutes. The patient was getting concerned, and we were able to allay his fears in a short period of time rather than waiting several days for another appointment."

Does this collegial approach have a downside? After all, additional use of consults with specialists is not without a price. As the manager of the health plan owned by one of the large clinics noted, consults with specialists tend to drive up costs. He said this can happen rather easily in a clinic because the culture is built around the free and easy flow of information, and physicians are quick to consult with their colleagues. At the same time, he noted that the premiums of the clinic-owned HMO were below those of any other health plan in the region. In addition, this climate of trust facilitates informal peer review.

In our view, the advantages of the collegial approach we saw at Marshfield, Carle, Geisinger, Fargo and the Colorado Permanente Medical Group far outweigh any negatives. Patients must agree with our conclusion; increasing numbers of people are using the medical services of these large medical groups.

Balancing quality and cost. When asked what distinguishes the culture of Kaiser Permanente from a less integrated system, the medical director of the Colorado Permanente Medical Group responded that the KP culture is rooted in the belief that there is no inherent conflict between quality and cost. This aspect of the corporate culture is not new — in fact, it was this philosophy that attracted many of the founding physicians to the organization. He notes, "We expect our doctors to think about how to do something right the first time. What might be different (from private practice) is that we have 400 physicians all thinking this way."

The physician leaders of other large medical groups, such as Geisinger and Marshfield, expressed the same viewpoint — the highest quality medicine is also the most cost effective.

A sense of history. We noted at Geisinger that founding physicians and others who played a key role in the formation and subsequent development of the organization are honored and revered. Buildings are named after Drs. Harold Foss and Leonard Bush (the founder and his successor); the primary care outpatient center is named after a beloved nurse-manager, Emma Jean Knapper, who devoted 40 years to the clinic. Pictures and paintings of the founders and physician leaders, and key events in the history of the organization (ground breakings, grand openings of new wings) are prominently displayed in the hallways of the clinic and hospitals.

Carle Clinic, Geisinger, Mayo Clinic, Ochsner, Kaiser Permanente and other clinics distribute histories of the organizations written by their founders. Employees and patients are constantly reminded of the historical precedents of the organization.

Variations in the Corporate Cultures of Integrated Systems

Any description and analysis of the corporate cultures of integrated health care organizations must differentiate between these old, established clinics (e.g., Marshfield, Geisinger and Carle), and physicians operating in traditional practice settings who have attempted to learn to work together in newly formed physician organizations (POs). This latter group would include the Presbyterian Network, Oregon Medical Group and physicians and hospitals or hospital systems that have come together in new ways (e.g., Fargo Clinic/St. Luke's, Sutter Health, UniHealth America). What are some of the common cultural characteristics of each type of situation, and what are the hurdles standing in the way of developing a strong corporate culture?

Large clinics. Well established groups like Fargo, Carle, Marshfield, Geisinger and the Permanente Medical Group have had many years to develop their corporate cultures. As noted above, the common themes running through these groups are strong physician leadership and management, sharing of information on a real-time basis, collegiality, an easy reliance on other physicians in the clinic, broad-based governance and participation in decision making, and commitment to group practice. There is a strong belief in the importance of primary care and inclusion of family practice physicians in the management and governance of the clinics. In all of the large clinics we studied and in many others, there is a conviction that group practice leads to the highest quality of care for patients.

We also noticed differences among these mature clinics. For example, Marshfield and Geisinger tend to be more academic; many physicians are interested in research and teaching. Both organizations subsidize their research programs, and the amounts are substantial. They believe in it.

The Carle Clinic culture tends to be more business oriented. The medical groups we visited in southern California, especially Harriman Jones and Facey (both part of UniHealth America), are geared up to succeed in a capitated environment, and this means more emphasis on practicing cost-effective medicine. The Permanente Group is more accustomed to using physician extenders and to working hand-in-hand with a health plan.

Newly-formed physician groups. The Presbyterian Network, Oregon Medical Group, Sac Sierra Medical Group and MAPI in Billings are relatively new organizations still seeking to establish a corporate identity and common culture. In most of these types of groups, a strong sense of unity has yet to develop. Physicians have limited physical proximity to one another, and they meet infrequently. Primary loyalties usually remain with the former medical practices. Of course, this is one of the problems with physician organizations of this type; they have not yet developed the cohesiveness to see them through tough times.

At the same time, we were impressed that the initial steps have been taken and the long-term outlook for developing productive corporate cultures is promising. For example, the consolidation of practice sites should help physicians in Sac Sierra develop more meaningful interpersonal relationships. The economically-integrated primary care physicians in the Presbyterian Network are beginning to think like a group practice. Along the same lines, one of the MAPI physicians had this to say:

> A few years ago if one of my patients had complained about rude treatment from another physician, I probably wouldn't have done anything about it. Now, I would call the person because his behavior directly affects me because of our association.

Despite the progress and optimism of these newer groups, we think that the road ahead is long. Special efforts to speed up the process will be needed. Several of the organizations recognize this fact and are promoting monthly luncheons, newsletters and other means of building a culture. While these types of efforts will shorten the time needed to develop a meaningful corporate culture, additional efforts will be necessary to insure the kind of cohesiveness needed to keep the group together during difficult times.

Physicians and hospitals or multihospital systems. The corporate cultures developing between physicians and hospital management and boards is also encouraging. We saw the change most clearly at Sutter Health, Fargo Clinic/St. Luke's, Presbyterian and MAPI/Saint Vincent in Billings. Although none of the physicians or administrators involved in these integrated systems would admit that the progress made has been all that impressive, they agree that the first important steps are being taken.

One of the characteristics of these organizations, which we discussed in Chapter 8, is that a large number of physicians are playing key roles in management and governance. This is having an impact, both in terms of the way hospitals operate, and in physicians' attitudes toward the hospital and hospital managers. For the first time physicians feel that they are a part of a hospital and health care system; they no longer see themselves as outsiders. Along with this, the traditional adversarial relationship between physicians and hospital managers is becoming a thing of the past in many integrated systems.

Summary

As the physician quoted in the beginning of this chapter remarked, while building a corporate culture is not easy, failure to do so is not an option for physicians and hospitals determined to create an integrated health care system. New attitudes of learning, respect for different viewpoints, openness to change and emphasis on communication are needed to develop meaningful corporate cultures in integrating health care systems. Those integrated systems that fail to develop a meaningful culture may find their physician groups picked apart by other organizations willing to pay more for primary care physician services.

Looking ahead, we believe that efforts to achieve a meaningful corporate culture will receive assistance from the health care industry's emphasis on continuous quality improvement. As Donald Berwick, MD, one of the country's leaders in quality improvement in health care and author of the book, *Curing Health Care,* said at a conference we attended, "A hospital and physicians seeking continuous quality improvement are part of a learning organization." The achievement of a new culture, one based on learning and participation by all employees, is the product of most successful quality improvement programs.

Similarly, advances in information and telecommunication systems will enhance the ability of integrated systems to come together. As demonstrated by the Marshfield Clinic, immediate communication through video-conferencing, computer linkages and other technology can be expected to be a great help to the newer integrated systems as they move down the path toward a common culture.

The next chapter looks at continuous quality improvement, information systems and other processes organizations have developed in their quest for integration.

CHAPTER 10.
CONNECTING THE PIECES

It is essential that we begin to function as a seamless organization. To do this we have to share clinical and financial data on a timely basis. Our information system will become the central nervous system of our organization.
— Integrated health care system president

This chapter links three subjects — information systems, quality improvement and outcomes measurement. We found that they were inter-connected in the minds of physicians and administrators in the integrated organizations we studied. Part of the justification for the huge effort being devoted to developing information systems is to provide the data needed to measure medical outcomes and to compare the benefits against the costs of certain procedures or clinical pathways. And, quality improvement is the way that physicians and the hospital expect to modify practice patterns and upgrade their systems in order to demonstrate improved medical outcomes.

Information Systems

The integrated health care systems we studied are consistent with the picture painted by Bob Waterman, the author (with Tom Peters) of *In Search of Excellence* and *The Renewal Factor*, when he says, "Renewing companies have a voracious hunger for facts. They see information where others see only data. They love comparisons, rankings, measurements, anything that provides context and removes decision-making from the realm of mere opinion" (Waterman, 1987, p. 8).

Information systems — both clinical and financial — are frequently referred to as the "glue" that holds together successful integrated systems. They include data on the health status of members of the health plan, both inpatient and outpatient medical records, financial information on health plan coverage, patient utilization of the system, physician practice patterns, medical outcomes, patient satisfaction, patient demographics (age, income, family status), treatment protocols and a host of other pieces of information useful for managing patient care and successfully directing the integrated health care system. The information systems include the ability to access data from any point within the integrated health care system, especially primary care physicians' offices. The specific case study examples provided later in this chapter offer additional insights into the types of information being incorporated into the new information systems of the future.

So far, the ability to turn data into useful information in the health care industry has been spotty at best. As one physician writes:

Integrated regional healthcare systems of the future will need far fewer expensive pieces of diagnostic equipment and fewer inpatient facilities than have been supported by the current way of financing medical care services. But the investments that regional systems will have to make in information and communication technologies will be much larger than what the current, fragmented medical marketplace of independent, small medical groups and hospitals has installed to date (Ruffin, 1993, pp. 47-48).

Each of the nine multihospital systems included in Stephen Shortell's research on the integration process have invested between $30 and $85 million in recent years to upgrade their clinical and financial information systems (Shortell [and others], 1993, p. 25). These numbers get one's attention. They are even higher than we found in the case study organizations, but not by much.

Here is a summary of what several of the organizations are doing in terms of their clinical and management information systems:

Presbyterian Healthcare Services. In early 1993, Presbyterian was in the early design stages of what will be a five-year plan to develop a new information system. The process began with a large number of interviews with potential users of the information system to find out what they needed and in what format.

A key to the plan is the consolidation of patient information, including medical records (both inpatient and outpatient), patient identification numbers, insurance eligibility and coverage and patient financial information. The system will link physicians' offices, hospitals and Presbyterian's HMO. The real-time system also will be used for the following: patient accounting and management, scheduling, reporting laboratory and imaging results, electronic payment, billing and claims, marketing, provider directory and referrals database, drug interaction/

EXHIBIT 10-1
Components of Information Systems
Presbyterian Healthcare Services

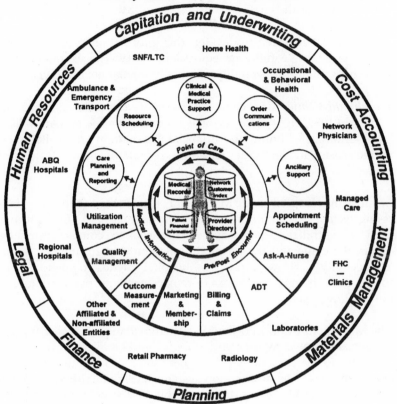

Source: Presbyterian Healthcare Services, Albuquerque,
New Mexico (reprinted with permission).

verification, physician protocols/clinical pathways and utilization management/quality assurance. Exhibit 10-1 shows the relationship of the various components of the Presbyterian information system to patient care, at the center of the circle.

The resources required to develop this information system include an average of 23 to 26 full-time equivalent staff. The estimated cost ranges from $3 million to $6 million annually for the next five years.

Marshfield Clinic. The clinic upgraded its computer systems in 1991. In early 1993, eight of 23 regional sites were on the system, which had 2,400 terminals. Clinical and financial information are available on an on-line basis and provide real-time results of many tests and procedures.

St. Joseph Hospital and Marshfield Clinic have separate data processing systems. The administrator of the hospital said, "In the future we need a centralized data base. We need to connect referring physicians, the clinic and the hospital, and even nursing homes. I call this 'connectivity.'" He went on, "The hospital intends to spend $10 to $12 million over the next two years to replace and improve its database and information system."

The Marshfield Clinic information system will require increasing the size of the mainframe computer, and will involve $4 million for hardware and upgrades to the present system. This figure also includes ongoing operating expenses. The information system staff at Marshfield includes 82 people with 35 to 40 of those directly involved in system development.

The senior associate executive director of Marshfield Clinic said the clinic is talking seriously with the Ministry Corporation (the parent of St. Joseph Hospital) about revamping and connecting the information systems of the two organizations. "We need to be able to connect the 'Tower of Babel.' The new system will include clinical information and the demographic characteristics of patients. It is all part of our ability to measure outcomes." When asked what this would cost, he said, "I don't have a firm estimate, but I know it will be several million dollars over the next few years, and this is on top of what the hospital plans to spend."

Fargo Clinic/St. Luke's Hospital. The hospital CEO said, "Information systems are the key to the future of health care, and this includes our new consolidated organization. We have to be able to integrate the information systems of the clinic and hospital. We are in the process of recruiting a chief information officer in order to help us get this mammoth task accomplished."

Both the clinic and hospital have invested heavily in information systems, but they are not compatible. This means that to take advantage of the opportunities created by the merger, a new integrated information system involving patient data at both the clinic and hospital level must be designed and implemented. The required capital investment is expected to be large — several million dollars annually.

UniHealth America. Paul Teslow, former CEO of UniHealth, said, "I can't say enough about the importance of information systems. Patient records have to be immediately accessible at any point of service within the system. We have spent $50 million on information systems over the past few years" (The Future..., 1992).

A UniHealth staff member noted that information systems in a capitated system need to provide real-time information so operational changes and decisions can be made quickly. He said it is important to be able to constantly compare actual utilization against that projected from actuarial data (similar to budgeted versus actual financial data that executives of most organizations rely on to manage an organization). He also noted that information is important in working with physicians: "They respond much better to data than to anecdotes."

A UniHealth financial manager talked in terms of the need to build an "electronic data interchange." This type of system would include the ability to process claims, prepare reports on patient encounters, determine patient eligibility (e.g., which individuals are eligible for what services, co-payments and deductibles) and a unified medical record. "In addition we want to integrate the records — medical and business — for physicians and hospitals."

Kaiser Permanente/Saint Joseph Hospital. Kaiser Permanente's information system strategies include converting all non-California regions into a common system, improving the clinical database and outcomes analysis and moving toward a fully-automated medical records system. KP typically invests two percent of revenues in enhancing its information system. However, that proportion will be higher over the next few years, mainly because of the effort being devoted to improving the handling of medical records.

The chief information officer for Saint Joseph said that KP and the hospital have linked several areas of their information systems. "Both of us chose the same vendor for our surgery scheduling system. We are currently selecting a common vendor for linking the information systems for the laboratory. Our purpose is to share lab results and to allow physicians to track the status of a patient's lab work."

Other case study organizations. Additional examples of investments in information systems abound. The vice president for medical affairs of Sacred Heart Health System in Eugene said, "The need to revamp our information system is imperative if we are going to be able to integrate physicians and perform well in a managed care environment. We expect to spend around $25 million on this over the next three years."

With hospitals and medical groups over much of northern California, Sutter Health faces a major challenge in linking the various components of the system. One of the top executives said, "The piece we are struggling with is the information system. We are looking at millions of dollars to build this system, but we have to build it in order to manage the care of a large population. We will fail if we don't tie our patient population, medical foundations, hospitals, health plans and other elements together with a sophisticated information system."

Carle is in the process of upgrading its information system with emphasis upon the hospital and improving the compatibility between the clinic and hospital systems. Carle has 75 full-time equivalent staff members in its information systems group, and 45 of these individuals are directly involved with system development.

Information systems — conclusions. What do all these organizations have in common in terms of the investments being made in their information systems?

- *One system for all patient information (ambulatory, inpatient and health plan).* The need for linking information systems and databases for the clinic, hospital and health plan will become even more essential in a capitated environment.

- *Information availability on a real-time basis.* When a patient walks into any one of the many primary care locations or into a hospital that is part of an integrated system, the objective is to have immediate access to the patient's medical records, insurance eligibility and other relevant information. Nearly all of the systems have made progress toward accomplishing this goal.

- *Patient management.* All of the organizations intend to use their new database and information systems to manage patient utilization in a capitated environment and to generate information needed to measure clinical outcomes and improve quality.

Based on what we learned from our interviews with information officers in most of the case study organizations, physician's offices and ambulatory information system development generally lags that of the hospital. Hospitals have more systems available and more vendors than do medical groups. Few vendors are able to offer compatible hospital, clinic and health plan information systems. The major challenge is to upgrade systems on the ambulatory side and to integrate the entire system.

Quality Improvement Initiatives

Our research found that integrated health care systems have incorporated quality improvement into the fabric of the organization. It is an essential component of how they do business.

Presbyterian Healthcare Services got its impetus for quality improvement because of a push from major employers in Albuquerque. One Presbyterian staff person said, "Several years ago when some of the employers in town made inquiries into our system's involvement with quality improvement, it really got our attention."

Presbyterian reports that nine teams have completed CQI projects, and that 35 formal teams are in the process. Another six have self-destructed. It is estimated that there are another 50 teams functioning informally. Processes analyzed by CQI teams include admissions, signage, and pharmacy formulary at the health plan. Studies in five clinical areas were initiated in 1993.

The experiences of four other case study organizations follow:

Carle Clinic. The clinic and hospital spent one year developing vision and values statements, and formed a combined quality council. One of the physician-administrators active in the Carle quality improvement initiative said, "The National Demonstration Project organizations tended to bring physicians into the process later; we think that is a mistake. We find that they are ready to participate."

At the time the case study was prepared, there were between 30 and 50 quality teams working at Carle. All employees had received a three-hour "macro" course, and over 500 staff members, including 90 physicians, had attended one of the three-day training courses.

UniHealth America. UniHealth has an ambitious program called QUEST (Quality Utilizing Excellence, Service and Teamwork). Teams at one of the hospitals were involved in the following projects: patient billing, preoperative patient education, ER waiting times, patient internal transportation, employee back safety, presurgical admission process and rehabilitation patient scheduling. Clinical teams at this hospital were working on projects concerned with oxygen tank utilization, coordinating medical supplies equipment at discharge, antibiotic utilization and DRG 89 (simple pneumonia).

Geisinger. The physician administrator in charge of Geisinger's quality improvement program said, "We have been impressed with what Proctor & Gamble has accomplished. The company has a 3,000-employee paper plant in our area and their staff has been working with us. We have probably learned more from them than anyone else." He said that six teams were working on clinical guidelines, and that there were a large number of informal teams at work.

Geisinger managers expect the payoffs from its continuous quality improvement program to include increased customer loyalty, lower costs, employee buy-in and superior quality. One individual said, "The content of our quality of care may be high, perhaps tops in the region. But, I am not sure our service delivery is nearly as good as it could be. We have to work harder to differentiate Geisinger from other providers."

The CEO of one of the large integrated systems summed it up this way: "We see quality improvement as a way to gain competitive advantage in terms of the services we deliver and improving our cost structure. We are convinced that the highest quality of care is also the most cost effective. Consequently, quality improvement is a core strategy for our organization." Executives of nearly all of the case study organizations would echo this statement.

As noted in the previous chapter, quality improvement initiatives are also likely to impact the corporate cultures of the integrated systems. The process encourages all employees to internalize a sense of responsibility through increased use of teams and task forces, and places more emphasis on measuring the results of various processes.

Outcomes Measurement

The strategic plan of Carle Clinic states that the absence of an "outcomes measurement system" is detrimental to the clinic. "Carle cannot immediately demonstrate to major payors the superiority of the care it can offer patients." Although interest in outcomes measurement was high among the case study organizations, and there was a recognition that this technique will play an increasingly important role, we saw little evidence that solid outcomes measurement systems were in place and producing useful results. Here are some other examples of what we learned when we explored this issue:

Kaiser Permanente and Saint Joseph Hospital. Saint Joseph Hospital participates in MedisGroups (a system mandated by the state) and receives reports on its medical outcomes for selected clinical services (e.g., open heart surgery, pneumonia) as a member of a panel of 550 hospitals nationwide. The hospital has participated in MedisGroups for a decade, and consistently ranks in the top 10 hospitals in most categories. A risk adjusted outcomes program, MediQual, is used to compute outcomes and to make comparisons.

In addition, Kaiser Permanente continuously surveys patients to determine their satisfaction with the system. The response rate is sufficiently high that each physician who sees patients is evaluated at least once a year. One of the physicians at KP, a pediatrician, said that this information is communicated to each doctor, and that it is taken seriously.

UniHealth America. Dennis Strum, UniHealth's Senior Vice President for Corporate Development, said that hospitals focus on hospital outcomes, and "this drives me crazy. Physicians are what sells and what drives the system. Hospitals are incidental; they are like a blunt instrument. We have to have a much broader approach in measuring outcomes." Another UniHealth staff member agreed. "Hospitals deal with episodic care. As we integrate, we need data on both episodic care and encounters in physicians' offices. Our ultimate goal is to keep our population healthy, but when they need our services we have to be able to prove that we are doing an excellent job and achieving top notch results."

Geisinger. The physician-administrator leading Geisinger's quality improvement and outcomes measurement said, "It is part of the responsibility of each formal quality improvement team to develop measurable outcomes. Other than that, we are part of MedisGroups. Their reports show that we stack up OK." Geisinger also has a federally-funded project related to medical outcomes.

Geisinger systematically measures patient satisfaction through the use of surveys. The response rate is sufficiently large to evaluate the performance of each of the network sites. The administrator in charge of this activity said that 70 percent of the patients rated the performance of Geisinger physicians as excellent. "However, this doesn't mean we are satisfied." This individual said that in his opinion, surveys of customer satisfaction were more valuable than financial information systems. "We haven't been giving customer surveys enough attention."

Several other integrated systems report impressive efforts and accomplishments. These include:

Park Nicollet. This organization uses several methods to measure outcomes:

- The clinic has four full-time people who abstract data from the MedisGroups reports for use in analyzing how Park Nicollet compares.

- In-house research attempts to replicate studies in medical literature and apply them to Park Nicollet. The goal is to understand how Park Nicollet compares with national research to improve health care delivery.

- Patients' perceptions of quality are obtained through a 36-question survey that probes various aspects of the patients' functioning after they have received treatment (O'Connor, "Outcomes...", 1993).

Park Nicollet is aggressive in promoting the results of its outcomes measurements. For example, one newspaper advertisement said, "Twenty-five years ago we began recording answers to the following questions. Was the treatment beneficial to the patient? Was the surgery successful? Were there complications? Did the patient feel better? Overall, how effective was the care?" The ads go on to show that Park Nicollet compares favorably with other organizations in the MedisGroups' database.

HealthPartners. In Minnesota, HealthPartners, an organization formed by Group Health (a staff-model HMO with 350 physicians) and MedCenters Health Plans (a large group-model HMO), has teamed with Park Nicollet and the Mayo Clinic to form an institute to develop clinical guidelines and measure medical outcomes. Called the Institute for Clinical Systems Integration, the organization's "mission is to conduct research and studies that improve quality of care, measure medical outcomes and develop appropriate practice guidelines" (HealthPartners, 1993, p. 2).

Scott & White Clinic. This large multispecialty group has formed a center for outcomes studies. In existence since late 1992, the center has been involved in several studies including diabetes, total hip replacement, cataracts, hysterectomies, and mental health screening. Kermit Knudsen, MD, said that the center's mission is to "promulgate understanding and application of measurement of outcomes throughout our integrated health-care system in order to use this information for the continuous improvement of the quality of health-care delivery" (Johnson, 1993, p. 7).

Concerning the relationship between outcomes measurement, continuous quality improvement and strategic planning, Dr. Knudsen said,

> Any strategic planning for health-care organizations must include planning for health-services research, linking the development of practice guidelines or practice protocols together with the measurement of carefully selected outcomes. That information is fed into a continuous quality-improvement process where you have a more or less continuous cycle. If you simply measure outcomes without connecting them to process steps, you have only a half-baked loaf of bread (Johnson, 1993, p. 8).

Some organizations have approached the daunting task of outcomes measurement incrementally. Integrated health care systems, such as Alta Bates, a multihospital system in Northern California, are dissecting and analyzing how they treat patients with a given diagnosis. Through comparisons of alternative approaches, physicians and other care-givers are learning from each other and developing a consensus about the best clinical pathways to follow. Such efforts are the first step toward reducing the variability of medical care and laying the foundation for systematically measuring patient outcomes.

Although we indicated in the first paragraph of this section that the integrated systems we studied were not far along in terms of measuring medical outcomes, we believe these systems have the opportunity to develop meaningful measurements of quality and outcomes. They have the potential to record and monitor all aspects of patient care, and to use the information to improve the care provided. In fact, this may represent one of the major long-term competitive advantages of integrated health care systems.

Connecting the Pieces

Whether it is the "glue that holds the system together," "the central nervous system," or some other description, there is no doubt about the priority integrated providers are placing on the development of systems to link all aspects of their multi-faceted organizations. Sophisticated information systems are the key to this endeavor providing improved communication and immediate access to data and also supporting quality improvement processes and outcomes measurement. These systems will enable providers and health plans to make consistent, accurate, fact-based clinical decisions on a real-time basis. This should contribute to higher quality and lower costs.

As noted earlier in this chapter, substantial dollars and personnel resources are being devoted to this task. At the same time, it was somewhat surprising that each of the systems was doing its own thing, and that the standardized information systems necessary to accomplish the objectives of health care system integration were not available. Nevertheless, the desire to do the job right and the long-term commitment of resources was impressive.

Most of the integrated systems say they are engaging in quality improvement processes and developing their outcomes measurement systems for internal use. They intend to use the data generated to find better, more cost-effective ways to provide care. However, in the health care environment of the future, where payors and patients will be better educated and have access to more meaningful information in selecting among competing health plans, this type of information will also have significant value in marketing and contracting.

All three of the initiatives discussed in this chapter — information systems, quality improvement and medical outcomes measurement — require either a major capital investment or significant time commitments by staff, physicians and senior managers. Furthermore, the implementation of information systems and outcomes measurement have a higher probability of success in large integrated health care systems. If we are correct, small hospitals, solo practice physicians and many single-specialty medical groups will be at a severe competitive disadvantage if they are unable to stay abreast of initiatives under development by integrated systems.

CHAPTER 11.

LESSONS LEARNED

Managing an integrated health care system today is like driving a car with one foot on the brake and the other on the gas pedal. Traditionally we have done everything we could to increase admissions and revenues in the hospital. But, increasingly we have contracts that give us financial rewards for doing less.

— Physician administrator of an integrated
health care system

In this chapter, we have pulled together many of the major lessons learned or insights gained, discussed earlier. We group the lessons learned into four categories: physicians and medical groups, hospitals and health systems, health plans, and general observations.

Physicians and Medical Groups

We lead off with the lessons learned about the role of physicians in the formation of organized medicine.

Unless physicians take the lead in physician-hospital integration, and in developing an integrated health care system, it probably won't happen. We are reluctant to say it can never happen, but we know of no case in which physician-hospital integration has been a major success without strong physician leadership. Even in large health care systems like UniHealth, physicians are the drivers of change at the local level. There is no doubt that in the integrated organizations studied, the role of physicians has dramatically changed:

- More physicians are playing key roles in hospital and health system governing boards and on committees and task forces reporting to the board(s). In one case, Presbyterian in Albuquerque, physicians have been delegated the responsibility for strategic planning for the entire health care system. In another integrated system, physicians are responsible for capital budgeting.

- The role of physicians as leaders of medical groups and organizers of new types of organizations, such as clinics without walls, MSOs and foundations, comes through loud and clear. This was especially noticeable in the merger of the Fargo Clinic and St. Luke's Hospital, in the Marshfield, Geisinger and Carle Clinics and in the two California multihospital systems, UniHealth America and Sutter Health.

- Physicians are participating in quality improvement (CQI/TQM) and in the design of the new, comprehensive information systems. The idea that physicians are not interested in devoting their time and energies to quality improvement is contradicted by the experiences of the 10 organizations studied, and many other integrated systems.

- In the HMOs owned by the integrated systems, physicians serve as medical directors and are usually part of the management team.

To repeat this point, the key insight gained from the experience of the case study organizations and our review of the experience of other integrated health care systems is this: physicians are heavily involved in leadership, and this responsibility is making a big difference in the success of the organization. Hospital CEOs and boards can facilitate this process, but it is physicians who lead.

Primary care is the underlying strength of the integrated delivery system. Prior to performing the research leading up to the preparation of this book we were strong proponents of the importance of primary care physicians and their growing role in the delivery of health care. In other professional services, such as accounting and consulting, individuals who generate new business and take care of clients receive the biggest financial rewards. Health care is the only field of professional services with which we are familiar in which the individuals who bring in the clients and refer them to someone else are not handsomely rewarded. In the health care industry the group of doctors who direct the system — in the fields of family practice, pediatrics, internal medicine and obstetrics/gynecology — have consistently been at the low end of the totem pole in terms of earnings and prestige. But, the pendulum is swinging fast in the direction of primary care.

The experiences of the 10 organizations and of many other integrated systems hammers home the growing importance of primary care. It is interesting that in many communities where we consult, this observation would be arguable. However, the case study organizations have long accepted the expanded role of primary care and are building on it. We think we know who is on the right track!

The winning organizations have ways to access capital. The basic financial principles that apply to any business, small or large alike, are also relevant to medical groups, especially primary care practices. A business has to have capital, or access to it, in order to stabilize its operations, including salaries for key professionals, to invest in system improvements and to expand. Given the relatively poor reimbursement for primary care and declining net incomes for many physicians in this group, their ability to borrow from normal business sources, such as commercial banks, is limited. Many physicians also shy away from incurring debt. Further, since most medical groups operate on a cash flow basis, they lack funds to invest in building primary care networks.

As discussed in Chapter 5, there are basically four ways to generate capital for the expansion of primary care — transfers from the earnings of specialists, income from ancillaries (lab, X-ray, pharmacy), health plan profits or loans or other assistance from hospitals and health care systems, many of which are not-for-profit organizations. In every case study and in many other organizations, one or more of these sources is being utilized.

Does this constitute a subsidy of primary care? Some individuals interviewed, usually specialists, often referred to it in these terms. However, other physicians said that they view primary care physicians as being part of the integrated system, along with specialists, hospitals and health plans. To focus on primary care subsidies is to "sub-optimize" the revenues and profits of the system. One physician said, "You don't hear Kaiser Permanente talking about subsidizing primary care. They think in terms of the whole system, and if the system is working, they could care less about whether or not primary care is being subsidized."

If primary care practices were more favorably compensated, it would place an entirely different light on the way organizations proceed with the physician-hospital integration process. First of all, there would be a larger supply of primary care physicians. Secondly, these physicians would be more difficult to organize into integrated systems since they would have sufficient revenues and income to go it alone; they would not be in such dire financial straits. More private money would flow into primary care, and dependency on hospitals as a funding source would diminish. There would be an end to the typical kinds of stories we heard from a hospital executive: "There isn't a day that goes by without a primary care doctor coming into my office and asking the hospital to take over his or her practice." Our review of the health care literature indicates numerous examples similar to this one.

The way the health care payment system works now, an increasing proportion of primary care physicians are simply not making it financially. They are not earning enough to invest in expanding their practices. Even health care reform with its emphasis on cost containment is likely to reward primary care services, but not at sufficient levels to access capital.

Economies of scale by combining solo practice physicians into medical groups are often illusionary. Although newly formed, or merged, medical groups are frequently advised that expected financial benefits from improved economies of scale, primarily from spreading overhead over a larger base of patients, probably won't be significant, hope often abounds. For example, the consultants advising the Fargo Clinic and St. Luke's Hospital told them: "Don't do this merger to save money, do it for strategic reasons." The experts appear to be correct. In our research we saw little evidence of significant economies of scale as the result of combining medical groups into larger practices, or combining groups of physicians with one or more hospitals.

At the same time, we observed several impressive examples of collaboration in the acquisition of expensive equipment and facilities. Cooperation in the ownership of equipment and technology is obviously in the best interests of payors and the public, and we believe it leads to lower health care costs. In our minds, this reinforces the conclusion that integrated delivery systems have the potential to reduce one of the factors driving health care costs — duplication of facilities, equipment, technology and medical services.

While physicians may not be saving on overhead, they are getting more for their money. The overhead rate of physicians in integrated systems does not differ markedly from more traditional practice settings. What differs is the quality of the management services they receive. Physicians are increasingly in need of more sophisticated management to keep up with the complexities of the health care industry, and integrated systems provide this help. Physicians in integrated delivery systems are accessing the management capabilities and business systems that medical group administrators and hospital partners have to offer. However, a word of caution we heard from many who have been through the integration process — hospitals must understand the workings of physician practices and recognize that they are a very different beast than a hospital.

Physicians in integrated systems often trade income security for autonomy. As a physician in the UniHealth system commented, "I am not sure we lost our autonomy by virtue of the relationship with UniHealth; managed care imprisoned us several years ago." Nevertheless, physicians perceive and experience a trade-off between security and autonomy. This can be a tough pill to swallow, especially for older physicians who have run their own businesses for years.

On the other hand, physicians joining integrated systems are gaining income security and prospects for increased earnings. This is especially true for primary care physicians. Physicians in markets dominated by managed care are able to improve their income by as much as 20 to 25 percent by joining a medical foundation and benefiting from a salary structure which rewards primary care physicians. Specialists associated with integrated systems also stand to gain income security, but they must take a longer term perspective in assessing the pay-offs. While there is little doubt that specialist incomes will decline in the short run, they are assured a steady source of referrals in an integrated system. Specialists in some markets are beginning to see this.

Capitation will dramatically change physicians' compensation patterns. Widespread use of capitation, encouraged by health care reform, will have a favorable impact on the revenues and net income of primary care physicians. Those groups that are savvy in terms of managing a group of patients and controlling utilization of hospitals and medical specialists are likely to experience significant financial gains. Physician groups will devise new formulas for compensating physicians which reward efficient utilization and quality outcomes and do away with productivity based incentives presently in use by many medical groups.

Hospitals and Multihospital Systems

We hear a lot about the "new paradigm" when hospitals become cost centers rather than revenue generators. In geographic areas where HMO market penetration is high, such as California and Oregon, this is already the case. Will hospital managers and board members be able to adjust to the possibility of a diminished role in the delivery of health care services?

Hospital CEOs can facilitate the movement toward physician-hospital integration, but they can't force it to happen. Many hospital and health system CEOs have made comments similar to this in conferences and in articles, and the results of the case studies support this finding. As noted earlier, physicians must drive the development of integrated systems.

This does not mean that hospital CEOs should be content to sit back and wait for physicians to take charge of positioning the hospital or health care system for the future. In several of the case studies we learned how CEOs and boards facilitated the process by providing seed money for the early planning and organizational efforts, and by developing mechanisms, such as MSOs and medical foundations, to provide financing for primary care practices. CEOs have supported the development of information systems and provided leadership in the formation and management of health plans.

Most of all, the outstanding health care system leaders we observed in this research were able to make the paradigm shift and not be threatened by it. It is interesting to hear them talk; they no longer sound like hospital administrators. Not once did we hear complaints from a hospital administrator about physician groups taking away ancillary income. Nor did we hear concerns expressed about the "power" of large physician groups and worries about how the hospital could stand up to them. Instead we heard a focus on what is best for customers (patients and payors) and a strong interest in hearing what physicians, especially physician leaders, thought should be done to better position the integrated system for the future.

A pluralistic approach with physicians works best. By pluralistic, we are referring to a variety of programs, including practice support, participation as providers in one or more health plans, help with an IPA and development of a primary care referral network offered by many hospitals and health care systems.

The best strategy for hospitals is to recognize the contributions of the various types of physicians and to find ways to support and encourage all specialties. To be exclusionary, or arbitrary, in terms of which physicians are invited to become a part of a managed care contract or new venture, is to invite disaster. In the future, this may be less important, but it is a critical factor in today's transitional environment.

Hospital investment strategies are changing dramatically. Two of the authors have served as hospital board members, and a significant part of our consulting practice involves economic feasibility studies or strategic planning when we work with hospital boards. Based on our experience, we have confidence that most hospital boards will be able to adjust to the new health care paradigm.

At the same time, we anticipate two or three areas that will prove troublesome for many hospital board members, especially those who have worked hard to become comfortable with the competitive era of the 1980s and early 1990s. These areas of discomfort relate primarily to setting priorities for the investment of hospital assets and for borrowing. The present emphasis on bricks and mortar and new technology will give way to increased investment in information systems, networking, and developing primary care referral networks and health plans.

For example, as noted in Chapter 10, all of the case study organizations and most other integrated systems are investing huge sums of money in comprehensive information systems that link physicians' offices and provide real-time data on clinical, financial, demographic and other factors. While hospitals have traditionally made significant investments in their management information systems and databases, the requirements of the integrated delivery system of the future are an order of magnitude higher. These and other types of investments are much less tangible (although not necessarily less costly) than the types of investments most trustees have become accustomed to, and a period of adjustment will be required. The problem is that the window of opportunity for making these adjustments will be brief.

Managing the transition to a new health care system is one of the most serious dilemmas facing hospital administrators. Such is the consensus of the many administrators we interviewed in connection with the case studies, as well as those we work with on a consulting basis. Most CEOs recognize that they are managing organizations in a schizophrenic environment.

In the short run it is important to maximize revenues through encouraging specialists to admit patients to the hospital and by taking whatever steps are necessary to increase market share. The more patients and the more complex the procedures performed, the higher the revenues and the stronger the bottom line. More is usually better in a fee-for-service world. At the same time, CEOs have to prepare for a capitated payment system that provides strong incentives for hospitals to avoid the use of high technology and to consume less resources. More will not be better in a capitated world. In the period of transition, hospitals have to chart a course with their "feet in both worlds."

The consequences of inaction. Some hospitals may try but will not succeed in making the transition. We believe that the times ahead, especially through the remainder of the 1990s, are especially dangerous for hospitals and multihospital systems. We look for several large and prestigious organizations to be forced into mergers or closure.

Capitation changes the incentive structure so dramatically that hospital utilization is likely to drop as much or more than it did in the 1983 through 1990 period. The financial incentives and clinical pathways of the new health care system will limit inappropriate and unnecessary care, estimated by many physicians to be in the 15 to 30 percent category. Although hospitals typically do not encourage this type of behavior, they have benefited from it, and on a fairly large scale. While increased demand resulting from the aging of the population will mitigate against the downward trend in inpatient utilization, growing demand from the Medicare population is unlikely to offset declines resulting from success in cutting down the amount of inappropriate and unnecessary care.

The consolidation of health plans, and the need for hospitals and physicians to come together to accept risk contracts, means that there will be serious miscalculations and financial disasters. Let's face it, many hospitals are not experienced in dealing in this type of environment, and are not prepared for it. Passing on the risk to providers means just that: there is significant risk and some hospitals will fall victim to it.

Related to this, the networking relationships developed between hospitals, and with physician groups, are becoming more critical. We expect to see hospitals that have been slow to develop networking relationships experience a 30 to 50 percent drop in the number of patients, almost over night. Hospitals that are left out of the loop in terms of being part of heath care delivery systems, or networks, are likely to be viewed as vendors; payors will expect to buy bed capacity "at the margin." (We first heard this concept expounded by Dennis Strum, Senior Vice President for Corporate Development for UniHealth America. We think he is right.)

We are not among those who say "the hospital bed business is dead," or that hospitals will simply become large intensive care units. We have observed the extent of community support for hospitals, especially in smaller communities, and the desire of business and civic leaders to do everything within their power to avoid closing their acute care hospital. We also recognize the additional demands that an aging population is likely to place on most components of the health care delivery system.

At the same time, we recognize that substantial excess capacity remains in the hospital industry, and capitation will lead to a widening of the gap between supply and demand for hospital beds and inpatient services. And, we see major differences in how hospitals and their medical staffs are positioned for the future. Some hospitals are extremely well positioned (e.g., little competition, strong primary care base, solid financial position, demonstrated ability to provide cost-effective care and cooperative relationships with managed care firms), but many others are not. However, we still see many hospitals pursuing the strategies of the 1980s.

Health Plans

As noted in Chapter 6, all but one of the organizations studied owns or controls at least one health plan, usually an HMO, and many other integrated systems also own health plans. Several of the lessons learned with respect to owning or managing a health plan are summarized below.

Ownership of a health plan offers many advantages. As Chapter 6 related, most of the case study organizations have a health plan and most have been successful in growing that health plan. With insurers forcing more of the risk on providers, it makes sense for systems to offer their own plan. Others have found it advantageous to work with existing payors and have strengthened contracting ties with insurers in their market. The approach will depend on the specifics of the market.

Start-up problems can usually be overcome. Several of the health plans have been through periods of heavy losses before they were turned around financially. CarleCare, the HMO owned by the Carle Clinic, made its way out of red ink by tightening underwriting standards. The plan made more money with 68,000 enrollees than it did with 100,000. Similarly, The Greater Marshfield Community Health Plan experienced difficult times until 1986, the year the Marshfield Clinic bought out its two partners.

One of the lessons learned is the need for patience (as well as a source of capital) in getting an HMO up and running. Many of the case study organizations have shown this type of patience, and are now reaping the rewards, both in terms of owning a profitable HMO and having a health plan that is an important source of patients for the hospital and medical group.

It is important to control the physician panel. For most of the integrated systems, the HMO provider panel was dominated by physicians who were either employed by the organization, or who derived nearly all of their revenues from it. They shared in the risks and rewards of the health plan's performance.

Keeping tight control of the non-system provider panel has paid off for many organizations. For example, CarleCare pays out less than 10 percent of the claims to outside providers. While the Security Health Plan provider panel includes 400 physicians and other health professionals who are not part of the Marshfield Clinic, these providers account for only two to three percent of the costs of the plan.

Controlling utilization and costs with an outside panel of providers can be done. We had been skeptical about the ability to manage the utilization patterns of physicians lacking direct financial interest in promoting cost-effective use of the health plan. It is common, even in urban areas, or in places where HMOs have low market penetration, to capitate an IPA but pay individual physicians on a discounted fee-for-service basis with a withhold. In rural areas, participating physicians are often paid on a discounted fee-for-service basis.

Somewhat surprisingly, however, we found that several of the integrated systems were using non-system physicians and controlling utilization and costs. Others have even managed to capitate specialists. How did they do it? Through financial incentives, careful monitoring of utilization and the cooperation of participating primary care physicians.

The physician-owner of a large IPA said that his organization controls utilization through the strength of his data system, careful management, financial incentives and direction of patients to the most cost-effective, high-quality physicians in the panel. He added, "We have several million member months of experience in our database. Data provide us a substantial base of experience for predicting utilization of the various medical specialties by members. What happens to a physician who is an outlier in terms of utilization? "I don't kick them off the panel; they just won't get many patients. They get the message pretty quickly."

General

There are additional lessons learned that cut across physicians, hospitals and health plans; they are important for all elements of the integrated delivery system. These include the importance of developing a "shared vision," the significant role of strategic planning and the necessity of physician involvement in quality improvement.

How does an organization develop a shared vision? Without a shared vision among physicians and hospital leaders, little or no action will take place in terms of developing an integrated health care system. Vision includes a careful and continuing assessment of the health care environment and where it is headed. It often includes retreats involving physician leaders and hospital board members and where individuals who have thought about future trends in the health care industry are invited to lead a discussion. It involves sending physicians and board members to conferences, such as those sponsored by the Estes Park Institute. And, it often includes field visits to organizations that have the reputation of being leaders in their communities.

Based on our experience, it is a easier to talk about the importance of a shared vision of the future and what it takes to be successful under a new health care environment, than it is to make decisions, commit resources and take action. Most of the case study organizations were able to successfully link these steps in the process. The steps required to take action on becoming an integrated health care system are discussed in the next chapter.

Strategic planning is an essential ingredient of success. We were impressed with the seriousness of the strategic planning of several of the organizations studied, and how the results of this process have affected decisions and actions. Among the case study health care systems, we observed major swings in the directions of large organizations as a result of strategic planning. For example:

- *Sutter Health.* Patrick Hays, the CEO, said, "Sutter had no strategic plan in 1980 (in that year Sutter was a two-hospital system in Sacramento). We did not have a common vision of the future. The first thing we did was launch a strategic planning effort. This allowed us to shift from a survival mentality to one of looking at patient needs and opportunities to grow." He went on to say that Sutter has engaged in three additional strategic planning phases since the early 1980s, and each one has led to major decisions about the future of the system.

- *UniHealth America.* In the spring of 1993, UniHealth announced a series of refinements to its strategic plan to facilitate transition from a multihospital system covering the Los Angeles area to a network of Organized Delivery Systems (ODS). An ODS is a network of medical groups, hospitals and other providers designed to provide coordinated care to a defined population in a more limited geographic area, such as Long Beach or Northern Orange County.

- *Sacred Heart Health System, Eugene.* The preparation of a 1990 strategic plan led Sacred Heart to the conclusion that it needed substantial integration of its hospital, physicians and HMO. The plan, referred to as "Mission 2000," focused on what the system could do to control its costs, improve access and enhance quality. One of the results was an increased recognition of the vital role of primary care physicians. Another finding was that in order to achieve meaningful reductions in costs, the system needed to control major elements of the delivery of health care (e.g., hospital, physicians and the health plan).

Quality improvement is a reality. We noted in Chapter 10 that all of the case study organizations considered quality improvement to be an important business strategy. This is not about giving lip service to continuous quality improvement (CQI) or total quality management (TQM) to satisfy the requirements of the Joint Commission on Accreditation of Healthcare Organizations.

At the same time, most of the quality improvement efforts of the case study organizations were in their early stages. Nearly all indicated that these efforts have a direct link with developing clinical pathways leading to outcomes measurement and that they intended to invest the time and energy to make system improvements.

Part C deals with making it happen; getting started in the development of a physician-hospital organization or an integrated delivery system. One of the important lessons learned from the case studies was that developing an integrated system takes a long time, usually several years. But, as one physician leader who has been through this process said, "I feel sorry for the medical groups and hospitals that have to do this on a crash basis. We had the luxury of having several years to get the job done, but that amount of time won't be available in the future."

PART C.
FROM FRAGMENTATION TO INTEGRATED HEALTH CARE

The world of the integrated health care systems we have been describing in Part B is not the world we typically observe in our health care consulting practice. Solo practice physicians and small groups dominate the medical staffs of most hospitals. Suspicion and distrust characterize the relationships between many physicians, hospital administrators and boards.

In larger metropolitan areas, hospitals continue to compete by adding facilities and equipment, developing centers of excellence, and erecting medical office buildings close to the hospital to attract specialists who like to walk across the street to see their patients. We often refer to these initiatives as the "strategies of the 1980s." They worked then, but can they get the job done in the future? We don't think so.

In smaller communities and rural areas, hospitals and physicians have been largely untouched by managed care and remain skeptical that health care reform will affect them. Residents and businesses in these towns are more concerned about keeping their hospital open than they are about health care costs and system reform. Equally important, physicians in these communities are viewed as a valued asset, and people are worried about losing them.

Many physicians long for the "good old days," and say they will "hang it up" before they will accept the changes likely to accompany health care reform. One of the major changes, of course, is physician-hospital integration leading to the development of integrated health care, a frightful thought for many physicians in their fifties or older who have run their own offices for 20 to 30 years. One physician said, "The hassles created by managed care systems, with someone constantly looking over my shoulder, are bad enough. Now you are telling me that in order to survive I have to get in bed with a hospital, and maybe even an HMO. I can't think of anything worse! I'll quit before I'll do that."

Many hospitals are desperately attempting to hang on to their primary care physicians, but are unwilling (or unable) to invest in helping family practice, pediatrics and internal medicine doctors consolidate their practices and recruit new associates. Specialists often resist attempts to encourage and finance the formation of new primary care groups. Since specialists still hold most of the clout in terms of admitting patients to hospitals, and they tend to occupy key offices on the elected medical staff, their voices come across loud and clear to hospital administrators and board members.

Hospital CEOs, who have long enjoyed the prestige and recognition of being key players in their communities, now find their hospitals referred to as a "cost center" rather than a revenue generator. In the new paradigm, use of the hospital is something to be avoided. They hear that physicians, especially those in primary care, will play a bigger role in managing the entire health care system, and they wonder about the future role of the hospital.

Health plan executives note that the pressure is on to shift risks to providers — physicians and hospitals — and wonder where that leaves them. Even more alarming, they see islands of activity in terms of physicians and hospitals getting organized to aggressively pursue risk contracts. One physician leader of a large IPA said,

> We like capitation and want more of it. Furthermore we want to participate in the hospital risk pool; that is where the big bucks are. We know we can manage patients' use of hospitals, and specialists, and that success in controlling utilization of these high-cost resources will dramatically improve our financial position. Bring on the future — we are ready!

Given the background from the 10 case study organizations, supplemented by the experience of many other health care systems that are on the path toward integration, how can we come up with a plan of action? What does all of this experience mean for hospitals? For physicians and medical group practices? For health plans?

Chapter 12 deals with the first steps in putting the pieces together to develop an integrated system. How can physician leaders and hospital administrators know whether or not the time is right for action? Who should come up with the seed money to pay for these services? How should an aspiring organization identify potential physician leaders? How does one avoid offending elected leaders of the medical staff if they don't have the motivation and qualifications to take the lead in setting up a new physician organization (PO)?

Chapter 13 is unlike any other chapter of this book. It tells a story of the process of moving from a medical staff with a large number of solo practice physicians and small single-specialty groups into a physician organization, and then negotiating with a community hospital to form a PHO. The final step is the PHO joining with a health plan partner to provide a financing mechanism. The basis for the story is a composite scenario taken from situations we were involved with prior to writing this book.

Chapter 14 takes the development of physician organizations, PHOs and other partially integrated health care systems a step farther. One of the common characteristics of every integrated system — the case study organizations and all others — is that they are in a constant state of change. Preparing for health care reform is one reason. Trying to become more cost effective and more responsive to customers' needs is another. When these integrated systems experience success, other physicians and hospitals are attracted to them; there is a constant flow of opportunities for joint ventures or other relationships. Using several composite examples from the case studies, and from our experience, this chapter attempts to give a flavor of some of these changes.

The case studies provide a substantial database about the accomplishments of integrated systems in terms of increased market share, more control over payment sources (e.g., ownership of health plans), higher incomes for primary care physicians and impressive overall growth in revenues, number of facilities and the geographic areas served. The case studies also provide a significant amount of information that relates to an assessment of the cost effectiveness of integrated health care systems.

In Chapter 15 we summarize the results of our analysis of the accomplishments, or benefits, reported by the case study organizations and by others. This chapter is intended to be an objective assessment of the benefits achieved from the movement toward integrated health care systems. We conclude by summarizing what we have learned about the adaptability of these organizations.

CHAPTER 12.

BUILDING AN INTEGRATED SYSTEM: WHERE TO BEGIN?

*So it's our choice. We can sit here and talk some more about
the philosophy of integrated systems and the future of medicine
— or we can stick our necks out a little bit and do something.*
— Pediatrician and PHO task force member

Much of this book has summarized and analyzed the experiences of several large and successful health care systems that are moving down the road toward increased integration. This chapter goes back to square one; the lower left corner of our matrix diagram in Chapter 1 (see Exhibit 1-2). What about the typical medical staff and hospital that have yet to take a meaningful first step toward becoming an integrated health care system?

Once a group of physicians and one or more hospital managers decide that forming an integrated system makes sense, the next logical question is, "How should we proceed?" The questions that most often come up in getting started include:

- What are we trying to achieve?

- Whom should be included in the initial discussions?

- Which physicians or medical groups should take the lead?

- What hospital and health plans should be part of the organization?

- What obstacles will be encountered?

- What goals and strategies should we consider?

- What are the next steps?

These questions are closely related and have to be considered as a group; the relationships are shown in Exhibit 12-1. For example, the choice of hospital relates to the physicians and medical groups that are clustered around the facility and with which health plans they contract.

EXHIBIT 12-1
Getting Started

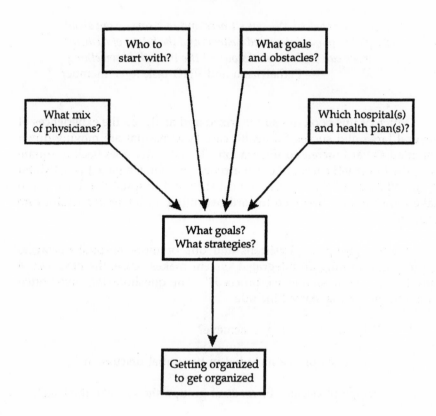

Where to Begin?

Integrated health care systems have come out of a large number of strikingly different origins; the combinations are almost infinite. For example, among organizations studied we saw examples of integrated systems being formed by:

- Multispecialty groups networking with a multihospital system (Marshfield/Ministry Corporation).

- Hospitals merging with multispecialty groups (Fargo Clinic/St. Luke's Hospital and Billings Clinic/Deaconess Medical Center in Billings).

- Multihospital systems acquiring the assets of multispecialty medical groups (Sutter Health and UniHealth America)

- Primary care physicians forming group practices without walls and developing special relationships with a hospital (MAPI/Saint Vincent Hospital; Sac Sierra/Sutter Health; Premier Medical Group/Rose Medical Center in Denver).

- Primary care physicians forming an MSO as a joint venture with a hospital (Oregon Medical Group/Sacred Heart).

- Primary care physicians initiating discussions with a hospital, followed by participation of a broad base of physicians in forming a network relationship (Presbyterian Network).

- Large HMOs contracting for hospital services (Kaiser Permanente/ Saint Joseph Hospital in Denver).

This is far from a complete list of possibilities. Here are several others:

- A group of private practice physicians, seeking first a hospital and then a health plan partner to join with them in forming an integrated system.

- A hospital encouraging two primary care groups to merge and form some type of PHO with the hospital.

- Hospitals bringing together numerous primary care physicians from solo and small practices and either employing them or forming a group for managed care contracting.

- Hospitals taking the lead in organizing a select panel of physicians, both primary care and specialists, from within their medical staff, largely for the purpose of managed care contracting.

- An insurer hand-picking a core multispecialty panel of physicians and then seeking to expand the core.

- A physician-owned IPA selecting several hospitals for inpatient services and contracting with numerous health plans.

- Insurers purchasing primary care practices and contracting with a single hospital in an effort to control the financing and delivery of care in a market.

It is obvious from the examples cited above that there is no single formula for getting started on the road toward becoming an integrated system. However, after observing several attempts at physician-hospital integration, it is equally obvious that some combinations work better than others.

Multispecialty groups — the quickest road to integration. The easiest place to begin to build an integrated system is with a successful multispecialty group practice. The size of such groups depends on the market. We work in communities where a 15-physician multispecialty group is dominant. In the Los Angeles area, UniHealth America is building portions of its integrated system around medical groups with 60 and 80 full-time equivalent physicians (Facey and Harriman Jones Medical Groups).

If the goal is to build a fully integrated organization around a multispecialty medical group, the most difficult-to-assemble component is already in place. Reaching the point of a smoothly functioning group of physicians takes more work, time and energy than forging any of the other required alliances (see example in next chapter).

In terms of their relationships with hospitals and health plans, successful multispecialty groups will have even more leverage in the future than at any time in the past. They can provide the basis for jump-starting an integrated system. Therefore, when multispecialty groups with a strong primary care base already exist, they will experience an even greater competitive advantage in terms of their bargaining position with hospitals and health plans, and the speed at which they can develop into integrated health care systems.

From the other side, where these types of clinics exist, they are part of the external threat we discussed in Chapter 8. We saw it in Billings where MAPI was formed largely as a competitive response to the 95-physician Billings Clinic. Sac Sierra was formed because of the need to develop a Kaiser-competitive delivery and contracting system in Sacramento. The Lovelace Clinic in Albuquerque was the catalyst for the development of the Presbyterian Network. And, we have seen the same pattern in numerous other markets.

A more common scenario — a fragmented medical staff. Despite the relative ease of starting with a successful multispecialty group, most integrated systems will not be based on this kind of building block; there simply are not enough large multispecialty groups in existence. Therefore, the most common building block for a physician organization (PO) is likely to be a core group of physicians who are currently clustered around a hospital and who make up the medical staff of the institution.

Once a small group of physicians decide to explore the organization of an integrated system, the next logical question is, "Whom do we talk to first?" In most cases the answer may be to identify as many well-regarded and not overly cautious primary care physicians as possible and begin with them.

Should the core group of physicians be limited to primary care doctors? This may well be the majority point of view, but we believe that the answer depends on local circumstances. Factors to consider would include the strength, leadership and business background and motivations of available primary care physicians; the availability of one or more large primary care practices to serve as a leadership force; the relationship between the hospital and its medical staff; and the nature of the external threat that is spurring interest in forming a new entity. It can also depend on the willingness of specialists to work with primary care physicians and a hospital to achieve some form of integration (this is what happened at Presbyterian in Albuquerque).

Merging primary care groups to form a building block. In Charlotte, North Carolina, an effective PHO began with a joint initiative between two internal medicine groups (30 physicians in total). In several other areas of the country, initiatives are currently underway to form physician organizations as the initial step toward developing an integrated system. (This is the trend we discussed in Chapter 1 referring to the horizontal movement across the bottom of Exhibit 1-2). The concept is that if physicians can unite, they can be more effective in dealing with hospitals and health plans.

However, many physician-led efforts have and will continue to experience serious problems in assembling this basic building block. Although it may be one of the best investment opportunities they will ever encounter, few physicians are likely to commit the capital required to get an independent physician organization off the ground. And, selecting physicians for a core group based on their willingness to invest is likely to lead to a poorly balanced group in terms of the mix of specialties. Those physicians who are needed the most — primary care physicians — are the ones typically experiencing the most financial stress and are the least likely to have financial resources available.

If integrated systems are to be built upon the base of a physician organization, it will usually be because the group organized itself quickly and at low cost, had heavy primary care involvement and quickly added a partner with deep pockets — usually a hospital or health plan. It is also conceivable that other financial partners could assist in the formation of independent physician organizations. For example, management companies like PhyCor or Caremark might serve this function.

Hospitals and health plans as the initiators. We suspect that the future will bring more integrated system start-ups that begin with an alliance between a health plan and a hospital. Obviously, these two partners cannot form a PHO by themselves. For this reason, the next steps in this option do not differ significantly from those a hospital would take on its own in forming an integrated system. The hospital-health plan alliance would immediately be followed by the formation of a PHO taken from within the hospital's medical staff and/or a core of the health plan's physician panel.

Alternatively, the hospital and health plan could immediately initiate discussions with a multispecialty group. TRIAD, a three-way joint venture among Saint Joseph Hospital, Accord Medical Centers (multispecialty group practice) and Rocky Mountain Healthcare

Corporation (the parent of Blue Cross/Blue Shield of Colorado) in Denver in the mid 1980s, was such an organization. TRIAD was unsuccessful and has since been disbanded. The organizational approach worked reasonably well; the reasons for TRIAD's failure lay in its cost structure, business strategies, execution and timing.

Specialists alone. In Chapter 8 we briefly described the case of a failed effort to integrate physicians and a hospital. The leadership in this initiative came from specialists with little or no primary care participation; in fact, primary care doctors in the community had full practices and said they were too busy to participate. Besides, the motivations behind the effort — to increase referrals to specialists and keep inpatient hospital admissions from leaving the community — were of little interest to primary care physicians.

When our specialist friends ask, "How long do I have to wait for primary care physicians to get on board?" our answer is, "However long it takes." Specialists who fail to bring their primary care referral sources (and their basis for success in a capitated system) with them are asking for trouble.

Which Physicians Should Take the Lead?

Most capitated health plans require a 40/60 or 50/50 ratio of primary care physicians to specialists; this compares with 20 to 25 percent primary care doctors on the medical staffs of most large acute care hospitals. This primary care pool often includes a number of doctors who practice part-time and/or have very limited tolerance for group initiatives.

How then is a competitive, balanced physician group that will function well under capitation to be formed from the members of the traditional hospital medical staff? This question must be addressed regardless of whether the initial organizing group consists of physicians, physicians and a hospital, physicians and a health plan, or physicians, a hospital and a health plan.

Four approaches have been used in moving toward a desired mix of specialties in a physician group:

- Include only primary care physicians in the core group; this was the approach used by the Oregon Medical Group.

- Organize the group in two phases. Start with primary care physicians, and then let these doctors pick the specialists who will be invited to join. This was the approach originally visualized for the Premier Medical Group in Denver.

- Organize with a core group of specialists and work toward becoming a balanced group by adding primary care physicians. Most of the large clinics included as case studies used this approach.

- Organize by letting all physicians on the medical staff join, but refer patients to a select group within the broad panel. Lutheran General Health Care System in Park Ridge, Illinois is an example.

The choice of approach can determine the speed with which an organization can be formed, the degree of support from the medical staff during the formative period and the ultimate effectiveness of the group.

Organizing with primary care physicians. This is the approach used by many physician-hospital organizations. Primary care physicians are recruited into a network or an MSO. As Chapter 3 describes, they are offered inducements, such as practice support services, recruiting help (e.g., salary subsidies for new physicians) and access to managed care contracts. A hospital may provide management services to the practices, and guarantee to return the physicians a fixed percentage of their net revenues.

Relying solely on primary physicians can lead to difficulties in that such an arrangement may not be financially viable for the primary care physician or the hospital. As the Sac Sierra case study demonstrates, it is difficult to produce a favorable bottom line or stable incomes for primary care physicians without consolidating practice locations, capturing more ancillary revenues, getting financial help from specialists or operating more efficiently. Meanwhile, if the hospital simply subsidizes this physician organization year after year, both the hospital and the physicians risk accusations of inurement, and fraud and abuse.

When the PHO contracts to provide medical services on a capitated basis, it often negotiates with specialists to purchase their services on a discounted fee-for-service basis. This is basically a "make or buy" decision. If the PHO can buy services from specialists at an attractive price, it does so. If the volume of cases gets high enough, and the asking salary for specialists low enough, the PHO may hire a specialist (for example, a general surgeon or orthopedist) to provide these services.

From the specialist's perspective, this approach produces uncertainty as well as reduced income. For example, we interviewed several private practice specialists who had been providers of services for Kaiser Permanente in Denver. As the HMO grew, it "internalized" more and more of the specialty services it purchased. One specialist told us, "I knew it was coming, but you never fully appreciate the economic impacts of these kinds of decisions until they hit."

Developing the physician organization in two phases. A second option is to organize primary care physicians first, then follow, within a reasonable period of time, by adding specialists on a selective basis. The medical director of a hospital smiled when we asked him how the hospital-sponsored primary care group would decide which specialists to take into the group or who would receive the patient referrals from the primary group. "The primary care doctors have been waiting for years to make these kinds of decisions; they are looking forward to it."

However, this approach sounds better in theory than it works in practice. It is our observation that many specialists become agitated (an understatement) at the thought of this approach. In Eugene, specialists were extremely upset over the decision of the Oregon Medical Group to add four surgeons. Several specialists went directly to the board of trustees of Sacred Heart, and were successful in stirring up enough controversy that Oregon Medical Group and the MSO backed off from the decision.

We have observed similar patterns in other communities. At Presbyterian in Albuquerque they refer to this as the problem of the "innies" and "outies." Many specialists would rather that all specialists be left out rather than having the hospital sponsor a primary care organization that favors one specialist or single-specialty group over another.

Starting with a specialty-oriented core group, then growing to a balanced organization. In a sense this was the approach of several of the large multispecialty clinics (Carle, Fargo, Marshfield, Ochsner and Geisinger). As reported in Chapter 4, building the base of primary care physicians has been handled gracefully by these organizations. Of course, they have had a decade or more to make the transition.

Numerous PHOs currently being formed are using this approach; it has the advantage of including strong physician leaders who are specialists. We think this approach can work if the specialists have the appropriate motivations — helping build an integrated health care system that meets the needs of patients and payors. The case studies illustrate that there are specialists who embrace this approach; they put the needs of customers and the organization ahead of their own interests.

Given the pure numbers of specialists on the medical staffs of most hospitals and their stronger financial positions, we think that building a physician organization (which will eventually become a PHO and then an integrated health care system) around specialists can work. The key, of course, is finding the right physician leaders.

Letting anyone join but utilizing only cost-effective physicians. Numerous organizations have been formed with physician panels that are large and out of balance with respect to the mix of specialties. In part, the theory behind this approach is that it is easier to include all physicians who want to participate than to go through the hassles of leaving some doctors out of the panel.

The process of reducing the number of specialists on the provider panel can be accomplished in a number of ways: economic criteria, such as cost-effectiveness and utilization data can be used to qualify participants; some organizations simply wait for attrition (i.e., retirement or relocation) to reduce the numbers.

Most physician groups that have been formed in this manner have yet to reduce their size and improve the balance of their physician panels; therefore, this approach is largely untested. Among the case study organizations, the Lane IPA in Eugene and the Capital IPA in Sacramento are examples of large physician panels.

Which Hospital and Health Plan?

Once the physician group is organized, which hospital should be approached? Is one hospital enough? How does the newly-formed physician group decide on the best approach to health plans? These and other closely related issues are addressed below.

Since health care integration initiatives are often organized by a hospital or by a group of physicians who practice at the facility, the choice of a preferred hospital partner is the first choice to be made. In these cases, the hospital usually plays a major role in initiating the development and financing of the new organization. Among the case studies, MAPI is the best example of a newly organized physician group aligning itself with a hospital.

Once the initial physician and hospital partners are identified, what about choosing a health plan partner? Or, as discussed in Chapter 6, would it be better to start an HMO? In managed care markets that are already highly competitive, it may be more feasible to purchase an interest in an existing plan. Sutter Health, for example, purchased 50 percent of Omni Health Plan in Stockton rather than starting its own HMO.

In other parts of the country where managed care has yet to gain a large share of the market, several physician-owned health plans have survived. These plans typically include physicians as owners and pay on a discounted fee-for-service basis; several of these plans operate under the name "Physicians Health Plan." These types of organizations have the opportunity to form stronger links with physicians, thus improving their ability to deal with hospitals.

When the starting point is a physician-health plan organization, the health plan is the logical source of start-up capital. In most of these cases, the expectation is that the physician-health plan organization will increase in numbers of subscribers, and the hospital will decline in profitability and financial strength, so that the hospital can be added to the integrated system later under more favorable terms.

Generally speaking, we believe that it will be easier to choose an existing organization as a partner — physician groups, hospitals and health plans — than to delay adding one leg of the stool. If existing organizations are compatible, committed and can move ahead rapidly, it is better to build a strong partnership and move ahead. Unfortunately, this often is not the case. At least one of the needed parties may be trapped with a mind set, a bureaucracy or a consensus-based decision-making process. Therefore, if progress is to be achieved, at least one of the three legs of the stool will need to be built from the ground up.

Exhibit 12-2 offers a checklist of considerations in choosing a physician, hospital or health plan partner.

EXHIBIT 12-2. Choosing Integration Partners — A Checklist of General Considerations

Considerations in Choosing **Physician** Partners	Considerations in Choosing **Hospital** Partners	Considerations in Choosing **Health Plan** Partners
Understanding of and commitment to the integration process.	Understanding of and commitment to the integration process.	Understanding of and commitment to the integration process.
Compatibility (e.g., in goals, culture, experiences).	Compatibility (e.g., in goals, culture, experiences).	Compatibility (e.g., in goals, culture, experiences).
Likelihood of building trust.	Likelihood of building trust.	Likelihood of building trust.
Ability to make decisions and act expeditiously.	Ability to make decisions and act expeditiously.	Ability to make decisions and act expeditiously.
Market and financial strength.	Market and financial strength.	Market and financial strength.
Projected ability to attract new primary care physicians and/or merge in other existing groups.	Projected ability to lower overhead and cost structure.	Capability to provide suitable management information systems as soon as possible.
Quality of leadership. Projected ability to modify behavior as practice issues evolve.	Capability and willingness to bear organizational costs, provide capital and serve as focal point for partnership.	Willingness to invest substantial capital in systems and marketing and yet share later savings with other two partners.

Developing a Strategic Plan

Concurrent with moving ahead with the activities discussed above, someone in the core group needs to be identifying and researching the issues the new organization is about to face.

Initial identification of issues. The organizers need to begin to quickly envision a preliminary business plan. For example, the initial questions should include:

- Who are our competitors? What are their strengths and weaknesses? What will they likely do in the future based on their current plans? How will competitors' plans change in response to this integration initiative?

- What is the business environment facing the new organization (e.g., employers' receptivity and objectives, regulatory reactions, over served and under served areas)?

- How will we stack up as a competitor once we form the new system? Our strengths and weaknesses?

- What will be the reaction of those who are left out (physicians, hospitals, health plans)?

- What are the critical success factors for the new organization?

- What are the biggest obstacles in forming the organization (from the perspective of physicians, hospitals and health plan)? What are each group's "must haves" in the upcoming negotiations?

- What distinct and sustaining competencies and advantages do we have?

In some cases, this step can be carried out informally. In others, a more formal feasibility assessment or preliminary evaluation should be carried out, followed by a "go/no go" decision as to whether to proceed.

Common vision. The issues may change as different partners are considered or rejected. As soon as possible, however, the various parties must agree on a common vision of the future of health care in the community, goals of the new organization, major obstacles to be overcome and key milestones down the road after the organization is in place.

The shared vision needs to be stated over and over, in opening statements at subsequent organizing meetings, in assumptions for financial projections, and as preambles to discussions about organizational design and legal structure. As one physician-leader of a newly organized PHO told us, "Whenever we reach an impasse, we find it useful to go back to the basics — what are we trying to accomplish, and why? Who are our customers and what are their needs? When we do this, we can usually set aside our parochial interests and get back on track."

This common vision usually includes a preliminary concept of the form of the new organization. For example, will this start out as a loosely organized PHO involving private practice physicians, plus a hospital and a health plan with certain defined areas for joint decision-making? Or will it be a fully integrated system with physicians, hospitals and health plans under common management equally at risk?

Preliminary strategies. The issues discussed above are reflected in a preliminary strategic plan that lays out assumptions that can serve as a basis for the negotiations which are about to begin. The plan answers these types of questions:

- What business locations will we have initially? What will we need in five years?

- What type of health plan(s) will we offer?

- Will we participate in health plans owned by other organizations and practice medicine at other hospitals?

- What are our first marketing priorities?

Getting Organized to Get Organized

Once the questions listed above are answered on a preliminary basis, the actual process of organizing an integrated health care system can begin. We can now "get organized to get organized." The next steps often include:

- Establishing decision-making and communication protocols within each medical group, hospital and health plan.

- Selecting an integration management task force or committee.

- Selecting an integration facilitation team.

- Agreeing on a process to negotiate the details of the new physician organization and PHO.

Establishing decision-making and communication protocols within each organization. Each organization needs to set up a decision-making team that will monitor progress and make key decisions with respect to building the new system. The team will also be responsible for communication within its organization and for deciding who needs to participate in, or approve, its decisions. For a medical group, this may be the executive committee and top administrator. The hospital's team might include the CEO, the chief operating officer, the vice president for medical affairs, the vice president for planning and the chief financial officer (CFO). The health plan might include a regional senior vice president, a senior financial executive, the local plan manager and the head of marketing for this region. Each team will need back-up assistance — including legal counsel, financial analysis (including sophisticated financial modeling), human resources/benefits consultation, and accounting.

The integration management group. In essence, this group functions as the board of directors of the about-to-be-formed organization, making decisions at each milestone about how the new organization will take shape. Decisions are not usually by vote of each member, but rather by the joint acquiescence of each party. The senior person present — hospital CEO, senior physician — speaks for his/her organization.

Selecting a facilitation team. In rare cases, the integration management group facilitates its own deliberations and makes decisions without the help of a third party. More commonly, an outside individual or consulting team is selected by the participating organizations to provide third-party analysis of the issues from all perspectives and to facilitate the integration process. The consulting team's client is the new organization, not the various participants. The consulting team usually includes individuals with legal, financial and group process skills.

Agreeing on an integration process. Discussions are ready to proceed. Whew! The next step is to agree on an orderly process and a schedule for identifying key concerns, analyzing options and making decisions.

Chapter 13 uses a different approach to communicate how a physician organization (PO), then a physician-hospital organization (PHO) and eventually, an integrated health care system, might be put together. We describe the various steps taken by a hypothetical group of physicians, a hospital and a health plan as they work their way through the process. This "story" is based on a combination of actual situations in which we participated, and it is intended to convey some of the complexities and challenges involved in building an integrated system from scratch.

CHAPTER 13.

NEGOTIATING THE INTEGRATED SYSTEM

The secret is in keeping the pressure on. We want to move as fast as we can through each phase in the negotiations.

If this is meant to happen, we will find ways to get through the rough spots. But if we slow down, the whole idea can die of its own weight.

— Merger and PHO attorney

In this chapter we continue to step back from the large, integrated systems that were the subject of Part B of this book and get down to the basics. How does a fragmented medical community, characterized by many solo practitioners and small single-specialty groups and a not-for-profit community hospital, start to build an integrated health care system from scratch?

Chapter 12 discussed the initial planning needed for the development of a physician organization (PO) and a physician-hospital organization (PHO). Chapter 13 focuses on implementation by describing the experiences of a hypothetical group of physicians, a hospital and a health plan as they work to put the pieces together. As noted in the previous chapter, our example represents a composite based on our experience. All of the conversations, problems and successes actually did occur.

In this composite example, a 300-bed community hospital (called St. Alexius) is the initiator of discussions about forming an integrated system. The external threat — the purchase of several primary care physician practices by a competing hospital — is serious, but it has not struck fear into the hearts of physicians in the community. There are 500 physicians on the medical staff of St. Alexius, and the hospital is located in a suburb of a metro area of 400,000 residents. At the time the physicians and hospital began talking about forming a PHO, the group had a rating of 6 (out of 100 possible points) on the integration index described in Chapter 1.

The Negotiation Framework

Moving beyond a rating of 6 does not take place overnight. We are convinced that there are no short cuts in the negotiations necessary to develop an integrated system. It is not possible, for example, to form a successful integrated system by transplanting the structure, financial terms and legal documents from another system. Not only is each circumstance different, but the negotiating process itself — considering the options and making the choices — is essential in establishing working relationships, understanding each partner's perspective and developing the trust needed to hold an integrated system together over the long haul.

Deciding on the pace of negotiations and development — when to move ahead quickly and when to slow down — is one of several instances in which effective merger negotiations are as much art as science. Negotiations need to begin from a firm agenda which includes the identification of issues, key decision points and target dates. Once negotiations begin and complex issues unfold, this schedule may be changed, often as many as 10 times over two or three months. But, each time a new schedule is established, the negotiators keep the pressure on to make progress and maintain momentum.

The integration process is usually managed by an outside facilitator. This is in part because prior experience in negotiating these new arrangements is helpful at every step along the way. More important, however, is the facilitator's role in managing the sporadic bursts of mistrust. Mistrust can be well placed, or it can be a holdover from prior times. In successful negotiations, time and time again the leaders sort through the sources of mistrust and provide updated, accurate information as the basis for resuming the process of integration.

Forming the Physician Organization — The First Step

A primary care physician said, "I'm not interested in having some hospital, or some specialist for that matter, tell me how to run my practice. Besides, if we wait long enough, we can name our deal. They need us a lot more than we need them."

"I've felt the same way in the past, Jeff, but I think now is the time," said another physician. "If we wait much longer, everyone else will be organized. As many problems as we've had with our hospital (St. Alexius), I still don't think we want the guys across town stealing all of our patients."

This was the third meeting of the primary care physicians task force at St. Alexius and the first where nearly everyone showed up. The first two meetings had been organized by the hospital and the agendas had been heavy on presentations by physicians, lawyers and consultants who had been involved in developing integrated systems in other communities. Now that the hospital was offering to underwrite the front-end costs of developing a physician organization and then a PHO, interest picked up.

At the prior two meetings, St. Alexius' CEO had made a strong case for action. Indeed, the facts made for a strong case. When the hospital across town had bought several practices and located primary care clinics in the major growth corridors, the St. Alexius medical staff had bristled. However, they blocked a proposal for a similar action by St. Alexius. Now, however, the competing hospital and its physician group had entered a long-term contract with three major employers for their exclusive business. The discounts involved were large, and the new contract was the talk of the town.

"If we can't buy practices, then let us join with you," said the St. Alexius CEO. "If we become partners, we should be able to regain the momentum. We can take back our lost market share."

There was some interest among the primary care doctors, but there was also plenty of suspicion. Now, at this third meeting, the physicians were meeting by themselves, and resentments that had been building for years were coming to the surface.

By the end of the meeting, the following issues had emerged:

Reasons to Be Interested in a PHO

- Practice support (e.g., help in choosing computer systems) could be made available.
- Economies of scale appear possible (joint purchasing of malpractice insurance and health insurance for employees, joint purchasing of supplies, etc.)
- Without us, the hospital will founder. Whom will that help?
- Integrated systems are the way of the future. We can sit back and let someone offer us a contract to join one later, or we can step forward and take a seat at the table in deciding how our system takes shape.

Reasons to be Skeptical

- Hospital management thinks it knows a lot more about how to run a medical practice that it really does.

- Economies of scale aren't our problem; low revenues and loss of patients are our problem. Mal-practice premiums are more of an issue for specialists than for primary care.

- The hospital has paid lip service to primary care physicians for years.

- We're tired of specialists' Porsches and their big egos. Now is our time, and we're not going to get co-opted.

While there was no shortage of skepticism, the primary care physicians decided to move ahead with further discussions. They withheld making any firm commitment, however, until the options were clarified.

They also approved the use of a consulting team as facilitators, but only after voicing objections that they had not had a say in the selection process. The team, which was a cooperative effort between a law firm and a management consulting organization, had gained trust. It had worked on several similar assignments and had expertise in health care, antitrust law, and in strategic planning, organizational design, financial modeling and facilitating mergers. Still, it was only after a private meeting with the team leaders that the primary care physicians became convinced that the consulting team was not in the hip pocket of the hospital.

The hospital leaders' caucus. The president of the medical staff was an orthopedist and was a member of the hospital's board. Referring to the primary care task force, he said, "It's one thing to have the task force work on recruiting more family practice physicians and going after managed care contracts. But I don't know how we got to the point that they set themselves up as the vehicle for forming a PHO."

"Officially they aren't the vehicle for forming a PHO, Charlie," said the hospital CEO. "On the other hand, I'm going to make very certain that they have what they need in order to feel comfortable in participating. They are critically important to the success of both the specialists and this hospital."

"I think most of the medical staff is going to understand that. However, a lot of loyal doctors are going to question moving forward with only part of the medical staff."

The chief of surgery interrupted, "Don't forget, the strength of St. Alexius is our reputation. We have the strong specialties, we have the referrals from the small towns in our service area, and we have the most physicians. Let us help form this new venture. Don't put us on the sidelines by relying on a primary care group."

Although he had wanted to form a primary care group before bringing in specialists, the CEO had also decided that the hospital board would not be able to take the heat from the medical staff (three-quarters were specialists). Therefore, the CEO reluctantly agreed that the hospital would support the formation of a new PHO task force with "broad specialty representation." "But," he said, "I expect the new organization to be designed in such a way that it has inducements for primary care physicians to participate. We can't afford to lose them."

Pre-meetings were held with key members of the medical staff, and with the heads of large medical groups whose participation was badly needed and/or would be influential in terms of attracting other potential participants. Pre-meetings were also held with primary care physicians to bolster their support for the revised plan.

The first PHO task force meeting. "The purpose of the physician's organization is so that you can speak with one voice to the hospital and in the PHO. It's a way for everyone involved to be assured that this will be a physician-driven organization. This is in the hospital's interest as well as yours." The facilitator was describing the role of the new organization the 80-physician task force was about to form.

As the first step in the process, the facilitator laid out the tasks that needed to be accomplished in establishing the physician organization. The initial schedule is shown in Exhibit 13-1.

During the second task force meeting two weeks later, the general picture of the physician organization and the PHO was discussed in further detail. At the end of the meeting, an executive committee of the physician task force was formed. This eight-person committee would serve as the decision-making group for the task force and all physicians in future negotiations with the hospital.

EXHIBIT 13-1
Physician's Organization and Physician Hospital Organization Development Schedule

EXHIBIT 13-1 Continued
Physician's Organization and Physician Hospital Organization Development Schedule

■ Task Force
● Executive Committee

	June			July			Aug			Sept	
	1	15	30	1	15	31	1	15	31	1	15	30
6. PHO Legal Structure												
Organizational form and powers					●●		■■	●●				
Ownership								●●				
Affiliation agreement								■■				
Articles of incorporation									●			
Legal documents reviewed										■		
Legal documents executed											■	
7. PHO Governance												
Board structure and powers								■				
Board election								●				■
8. PHO Business Plan												
Financial structure							■					
Action plan								■■■				
Revenue sources, budget								■■■				
Staffing		●						●●●				
9. Communications												
Medical staff update								■				
Medical staff full briefing									●			
Marketing strategy discussion								■				
Names selection (PO and PHO)											■	
Meetings with medical groups and hospital staffs								●●				
Public announcement												●

Source: BBC, Inc.

Nobody underestimated the time commitment required from the eight members of the executive committee. For the next three months, the committee would meet weekly with hospital management in the role of the overall integration committee, usually a second time each week with one another as the physicians' decision-making representatives and informally other times with various members of the medical staff.

PO legal structure and governance. "I'm convinced that this committee will not mean anything unless physicians trust us to negotiate for them," said the chairman of the executive committee, a gastroenterologist. The key issues to be resolved at this June 22 meeting were:

1. Organizational form

   For-profit, not-for-profit, or taxable not-for-profit

   Shares allocations and basis

2. Physician organization powers

   Areas of action on behalf of members

   Ability to negotiate managed care contracts on behalf of members

   Policy on individual participation in managed care contract negotiated on behalf of PO

3. Governance

   Board structure

   Board powers (and alternatively, the designation of decisions that will require shareholder approval)

Meeting with hospital management over its next two meetings, the executive committee made three decisions:

(1) Even though most of the organization's activities would be taxable, a not-for-profit structure would be used. This was done to allow for the possibility that the organization might later be merged with the not-for-profit hospital.

(2) The physician organization would have strong "single signature" negotiating powers. A member would have to

accept all contracts negotiated by the PO or leave the PO. This decision was made only after a long debate between those who wanted to retain more autonomy and those who wanted the new organization to have strong negotiating powers.

"Why should I approve what we negotiate in advance," argued one side. "If this organization is as effective as we think it can be, then I will want to take all of these contracts." The other side countered, "If you are not committed in advance, then we don't have the same bargaining position. Besides, why should you be able to pick off our best contracts and kiss off our weaker ones?"

(3) Primary care physicians, who constituted an estimated 30 percent of the projected membership of the PO, would be guaranteed a minimum of half of the seats on the board.

"I'm convinced that this is the only way we are going to begin to reassure them that this will not be a hospital and specialist-dominated organization," said the hospital CEO.

Financial structure and business plan. The facilitator said, "You want to set the entry fee high enough that members will take this organization seriously. There is also another argument for a higher number: over and over again I see this type of organization struggle because it is undercapitalized."

"I don't disagree with you, but I'm telling you, you won't be able to bring in most family practice physicians at that price," said the committee's one family practitioner.

The executive committee reached a middle-of-the-road settlement on the capitalization structure — neither as high as the consultant had recommended nor as low as the family practice physician felt comfortable with. In another gesture to primary care, the committee agreed that family practice physicians, pediatricians and internists could spread their initial contributions over four years.

"Selling" the PO. "I'm still skeptical," said the leader of the premier cardiology group in the area. "I like what we can do in managed care, but I guess I'm not ready to give up much autonomy."

"We will be back to you about these issues," said the executive committee chairman. The formation of the PO was at a critical point.

There was one week left before the August general medical staff briefing on the PHO project, and here was a key group — the cardiologists — unwilling to play. Fortunately, because they had been pre-processing the issues with key members of the medical staff, the executive committee was aware that there were pockets of opposition. There was time to make adjustments before the medical staff meeting.

Once back in a closed meeting, the chairman said, "We have to have the cardiologists for managed care, but do we really need to water down the whole concept just to get them to go along?" The answer was "no." The executive committee, working with hospital management, agreed to create a new category they called "PO Contractor". The physician organization would offer to contract with additional non-members needed to fulfill its managed care commitments. Contractors would not have a vote on the board or a say in PO or PHO decisions.

The meeting with the general members went well. The PO was presented as a new organization that was open to voluntary participation. Resistance was minimal since there were opportunities for both total refusal to participate and for being included later as a PO Contractor. After thinking further about the long-term implications of not being involved, the cardiology group decided to join as full members of the PO.

Forming the PHO

The physician organization had been fleshed out and was ready to begin. The task immediately ahead was to do the same for the PHO.

PHO legal structure, governance and finances. "The idea is 50/50, right? This is the way we are going to approach managed care contracting, and we're going to be in this together," said the hospital CEO. Other key issues to be resolved included the following:

- What is the desired form and function of the PHO?

- Do legal constraints (e.g., constraints resulting from inurement, Medicare fraud and abuse restrictions, Stark bill, antitrust legislation and administrative interpretations) limit the choices of structure?

- Given all of the above, what is the structure that will best meet the needs of the PO and the hospital?

- How should the financial structure be set up?

- How should the board be structured?

- If the board is to be 50/50 hospital and PO members, what mechanisms are provided for resolving conflict?

The organization was intended to be owned and controlled 50/50 by the PO and the hospital. It was agreed that the organization would need to be able to engage in any or all of the following activities:

- Negotiating with a managed care plan to provide hospital and physician services on a bundled price basis (i.e., single signature risk contracting.)

- Owning or being a partner in a health plan.

- Going "at risk" in terms of managing care for a specific population for a capitated fee.

- Entering into agreements with other PHOs or integrated systems to form regional, statewide or national networks.

- Negotiating with an insurer to purchase malpractice, errors and omissions and other forms of insurance at a better price.

- Negotiating with vendors for quantity discounts on the purchase of supplies and services.

- Negotiating with a health plan or third-party administrator to purchase health insurance for employees of all participating organizations.

- Providing certain services that might otherwise be organized by the hospital (e.g., physician recruitment and outreach into nearby communities).

The agreed-upon financial structure called for revenues left over after expenses to be distributed to the two shareholders, the PO and the hospital, on a 50/50 basis. However, it was anticipated that the PHO would be initially capitalized by the hospital.

It was apparent to all that, while integrated systems are increasingly seen as the preferred form of health care delivery by public policy makers, today's legal system does not yet recognize the value of these types of organizational arrangements. Representative Stark's legislation imposed major constraints on the ability of medical groups to collectively own and manage diagnostic equipment. Administrative interpretations of Medicare fraud and abuse law differed among the Internal Revenue Service, the Office of the Inspector General of the Justice Department, the state attorney general's office, and the Health Care Financing Administration (HCFA). In the eyes of some, this placed constraints on the ability of the PHO to channel excess funds to the PO or its physician shareholders. There was also concern, from an antitrust perspective, that the PO would grow so large that it could be construed as having the ability to exert monopoly power in its negotiations with health plans.

Nevertheless, these concerns were worked through, and the following was agreed to:

- 50/50 ownership of the PHO by the PO and a subsidiary of the holding company that controlled the hospital.

- For the time being no attempt would be made to jointly own diagnostic equipment or other ancillaries; however, the PHO could be involved in the management of ancillaries.

- Half of the board members would be elected by the PO, with a requirement that half of these be primary care physicians, and half would be elected by the hospital-related subsidiary.

- No "easy-out" methods for resolving conflicts on the 50/50 board would be included in the agreement.

- There would be no plans for distributing excess revenues. For the time being, the organization would accumulate reserve funds and build its financial base.

Financial issues and the business plan. Since no major asset purchases were envisioned and the physicians were to remain in their individual private practices, the financial issues were disposed of quickly. A business plan was developed, showing anticipated actions, revenues, expenses, accumulation of reserves and staffing. An action plan identified who was expected to do what, when, and with what resources.

Approvals. As it turned out, the August meeting with the whole medical staff was the turning point for negotiations with the hospital.

Once an overwhelming majority of physicians, including informal opinion leaders, indicated support, it was clear that the PHO was going to be formed. From this point on, approvals were relatively easy. Documents were executed by physicians and the requisite hospital boards in late November, four months after the date negotiations began and only one month behind the initial schedule.

Communication. A communication plan was developed and implemented. Physicians were nominated for positions on the PO and the PHO boards. A coordinated campaign was developed to inform the support staff within the medical groups and the hospital of the new organization. Immediately thereafter, a public communications and marketing campaign was initiated.

By forming the physician organization and PHO, the physicians and St. Alexius moved along the integration index from a rating of 6 to 14 on a scale of 100. Progress, but also indicative that the group had a long way to go before becoming an integrated health care system.

Negotiating the Managed Care Partnership

"The answer used to be obvious," said the hospital CFO. "No hospital in its right mind would have started its own managed care plan. Look at what happened to AMI and Humana when they tried to get into the health plan business back in the 1980s. But that was before PHOs and managed competition. Now I'm not so sure."

It was September, one month after the medical staff meeting, and it seemed increasingly obvious that the PHO would become a reality. Therefore, the integration management group (the PO executive committee plus hospital senior management) had gravitated toward acting more like the board of the new organization. They were discussing what they knew to be the next big challenge: either choosing a managed care partner or building a health plan from the ground up.

Options assessment. After three meetings and a substantial amount of staff work, the group considered three options.

Option 1: Negotiate with Carecorp. Of the existing local managed care plans, Carecorp had the second highest market share. After brief preliminary discussions, the group had rejected the concept of negotiating with the current market leader. The market leader health plan was already tied to a broad-based network of physicians and hospitals. The market leader liked the concept of entering a partnership with a closely-knit PHO, one with the potential to actually manage care, and to get out of the current adversarial relationship between health plans and providers. However, it was clear that too much would have to be sacrificed; negotiating with the PHO would have meant forgoing the larger provider base that served the entire metro area. The more exclusive arrangement with the PHO would probably mean giving up some market share, at least in the short run. The reality was that the large HMO was locked into its current network.

Carecorp was a different story. While it had significant market share, it had far less to lose by changing its provider network. Furthermore, Carecorp's national leadership was convinced that being part of integrated systems would be the company's future.

From the PHO's perspective, the pros for negotiating with Carecorp were:

- The ability to start out with a sizable membership base.

- Carecorp management's enthusiasm for integrated systems.

- Carecorp's existing marketing staff and relationships with employers.

- The company's expertise in managed care and its management information system.

The cons were:

- The likely terms. Carecorp was not likely to offer as large a partnership share as other plans and might even negotiate tougher on the dollars per member per month paid for physician and hospital services.

- An "adequate" local reputation. Carecorp had been in the market with an "adversarial" health plan long enough to develop some negative perceptions with physicians and patients. Physicians reported numerous instances of what they considered to be unresponsive behavior.

Option 2: Bring in another national health plan partner. Several large national insurers had expressed interest in working with the PHO. One approached the hospital, saying, "We're coming to this market anyway. What better way than to come with a new partner like you?"

The pros of Option 2 were:

- The PHO brought more value added to its partner and thus presumably could negotiate more favorable terms.

- There would be opportunities to link up with other sister plans in nearby markets.

- The major negative factor was that this would be a start-up health plan. Even though the plan had considerable potential in the long run, physicians and the hospital would receive fewer benefits in terms of new patients in the short run.

Option 3: Start a health plan. This option was similar to Option 2, but there were differences.

The pros were:

- PHO in control of its own destiny.

- Flexibility in choosing future alliances. The fact that the new plan would not be tied to any national network had its strengths as well as weaknesses. The strongest plans in two neighboring communities were also unaffiliated. It might be possible to ally with them in a regional network.

- Use of the hospital as a marketing identity. Surveys showed that the hospital had an excellent reputation, better than any existing managed care plan or any other hospital or insurer. Why not build off of the hospital's reputation?

On the negative side, start-up costs would be higher than for any of the other alternatives. Meanwhile, the PHO was severely handi-capped in its ability to provide capital. The initial capitalization had not been large enough to begin to contemplate something as aggres-sive and capital intensive as a PHO-owned managed care plan. There was concern about alienating other managed care companies who were existing customers. The absence of significant managed care expertise in the PHO was also a negative.

After asking the hospital's chief financial officer (CFO) to prepare preliminary income and expense projections under Option 3 to serve as a basis for comparison, the PHO management group decided to enter negotiations with Carecorp.

The first meeting with Carecorp. The PHO executive committee chairman was reflecting on the first meeting. "I'm not sure I will ever speak the same language as those guys. Furthermore, I don't think I ever want to."

On the surface, the meeting had gone well. Each side had listed its goals and concerns, the major steps in negotiating had been identified and a schedule had been set for future meetings.

Key goals and concerns listed by each side were:

Carecorp	**PHO Executive Committee**
Goals	Goals
Profitability.	A quality plan that achieves an excellent reputation in the marketplace.
"Gain sharing" financial incentives, by which everyone benefits as the cost of care is reduced. "Let's become a third generation health plan!"	"We want managed care that saves dollars by managing care, as opposed to saving dollars by extracting discounts from providers."
Ability to recoup the costs of adjusting the existing provider network and re-marketing the plan.	
Commitment from physicians to use a gatekeeper model.	
Concerns	Concerns
"Will the hospital be able to withstand the demands for new equipment and services of specialists and by physicians outside the plan and actually begin to reduce costs aggressively?"	"Do you really understand us and our jobs?"
"We need assurance that the PHO will expand rapidly and soon serve multiple locations. We also need a voice in where the new sites are located."	"They are willing, in fact eager, for us to buy shares in the plan. But the price is going to be way too high."

The match was far from perfect. However, the discussion of goals and concerns was cordial, and it appeared that there were no insurmountable obstacles. But in the back of the PHO group's minds — both hospital executives and physicians — was a lingering doubt that the Carecorp people would make good partners. "They were too quick with the dollars and too slow with everything else."

The consultant looked at the hospital CFO and the family practice representative on the executive committee nodding at one another and thought to himself, "The insurance team is just who we thought they would be. The amazing thing is to watch you two, who were at each other's throats a month ago, now on the same side."

The negotiation schedule. Following the meeting, a schedule of future meetings was prepared, taking into account the work that needed to proceed in the interim. The PHO-Carecorp negotiations schedule is shown in Exhibit 13-3. Unlike the PO and PHO negotiations, where several activities were coordinated simultaneously, negotiations with the health plan were sequential and deliberate. A general, "big picture" agreement had to be reached before either side was convinced that it should share confidential data. A preliminary design of the financial flows and legal responsibilities was prepared and approved before it was agreed to prepare any final documents.

EXHIBIT 13-3. PHO-Health Plan Negotiation Schedule

Issue/Task	Date
1. Preliminary Assessment	
• Objectives and concerns of the parties	Oct 5
• Potential structure for sharing control and risk	Oct 5
• Negotiation schedule	Oct 5
• Letter of intent	Oct 11
• Site visit to another plan by PHO representatives	Nov 2
2. Preliminary Financial Analysis	
• Plan history and financial performance	Nov 16
• Financial projections	Nov 16
• Preliminary financial design of partnership	Dec 7
3. Preliminary Legal Analysis	
• Legal issues and choices	Nov 30
• Preliminary legal design	Dec 7
4. Final legal and financial documents	
• Documents review	Jan 18
• Closing	Jan 31

Financial negotiations. "We want to be partners, but to us that means equal risk," stated the Carecorp executive. There was no effective way for the PHO to provide sufficient capital to buy a partnership in the plan. Instead, a risk sharing arrangement was negotiated.

The PHO entered a long-term agreement to provide services to a capitated plan established by Carecorp. The PHO also agreed to provide "most favored nation" pricing to the plan. This gave Carecorp protection against any competing plan's being able to negotiate a more favorable arrangement.

In return, the PHO, while not a legal partner in the plan, was able to negotiate a share of the potential profits. It was agreed that either the PHO would become a limited partner in the local health plan, or that some other mechanism would be found to share long-term profits. Long-term profits were defined as those profits that might be realized after Carecorp had received a reasonable rate of return on its initial investment.

Legal arrangements. The insurance executive said it, but everyone agreed, "It is in everyone's interest to have physicians and the hospital at the table in managing costs." The PHO assumed full responsibility and risk for managing the physician and hospital cost components of the plan. In addition, the PHO obtained two seats on the advisory committee that established overall strategies and pricing for the plan.

Summary

As laborious and painful as the steps described in this chapter were, St. Alexius and its physicians increased their level of integration, as measured by the integration index, from 6 to 21 on a scale of 100. While much had been accomplished, many challenges lay ahead.

As we state in Chapter 1 and elsewhere, the more completely integrated the health care system, the better. But, it is not often that physicians and a hospital can go from a fragmented, traditional structure to an integrated system in a single leap. How far and fast physicians and hospital managers can push toward building a fully integrated system will depend on how integrated the system is to begin with and the strength of the external threat.

Putting the pieces of an integrated health care system together takes time. Old relationships slowly dissolve and new ones come into play. Developing these new kinds of organizational structures presents constant challenges in finding better ways to meet customer needs. But, every step forward leads the organization along the integration pathway toward controlling costs and improving the quality of care.

One of the safe generalizations about integrated health care systems is that they are always in a state of change. In every case study organization, we sensed dissatisfaction with the way things were being done and a desire to find new and better approaches to achieving the objectives of the organization. This is the subject of Chapter 14.

CHAPTER 14.
A CONTINUOUS STATE
OF CHANGE

*No one realizes just how fragile this thing still is ... despite
how far we've come, we still have a long way to go.*
— Physician leader of a "model" integrated system

Regardless of where they stood on the integration index, each of the case study organizations was gearing up for change. None of the physician leaders and CEOs of integrated systems would say that they were satisfied with what had been accomplished. In every case, the planned changes would lead to a higher degree of integration.

Here are four examples:

- Sutter Health is continuing its discussions with other Northern California acute care hospitals and medical groups interested in becoming part of the system. It is integrating the Sac Sierra Medical Group into the Sutter Medical Foundation and assisting many primary care physicians relocate to three suburban sites. It is marketing Omni Health Plan (the HMO it jointly owns with a Stockton hospital) and pushing to be better positioned for risk contracting and health care reform.

- UniHealth America is emphasizing its presence in a limited number of sub-areas within the greater Los Angeles area. A key part of this strategy involves expanding the presence of three medical groups that have joined UniHealth (Facey, Harriman Jones and Bellflower) in the San Fernando Valley, Long Beach and northern Orange County.

- MAPI is considering alternative organizational structures that will strengthen the ties among physicians, provide access to capital and bring the group into a tighter relationship with Saint Vincent Hospital.

- Kaiser Permanente's Colorado Region is continuing to evaluate how it can become more cost effective and how it can compete with a large IPA-model HMO. Saint Joseph Hospital is seeking ways to strengthen its relationships with three physician groups and to improve its geographic coverage of the Denver area.

We could present similar summaries for each of the case study organizations; they are all in the process of evolving into stronger, more integrated systems. They are in a constant state of change, and everyone we talked to expects this to continue. Existing enclaves, barriers and bureaucracies are coming down. Functions within organizations are becoming more integrated. Information is passing from one part of an organization to another more rapidly. Systems are becoming more cost effective.

In Chapter 13 we described the formation of a physician organization (PO) which led to establishing a PHO. This was followed by adding a health plan partner. Even with the tremendous changes that occurred with this composite example, the new entity was far from a fully-integrated health care system. In fact, it scored only a 21 on our integration index.

In this chapter we present two additional composite descriptions of physicians and hospitals taking the next steps toward achieving a higher degree of integration. The first example relates to two internal medicine groups that merged and then added additional physicians, both primary care and specialists, to move toward becoming a multispecialty clinic. Referring back to the integration matrix in Chapter 1 (Exhibit 1-2), this composite represents moving horizontally along the axis toward a greater degree of physician-to-physician integration.

The second composite involves the merger of a multispecialty clinic and an acute care hospital advancing along the vertical axis. One of the case studies — Fargo Clinic/St. Luke's Hospital — formed part of the basis for this composite. However, information on the mergers of other clinics and hospitals was also incorporated.

Achieving More Complete Physician Integration

Three leaders from two large internal medicine groups were having breakfast. "Somebody has to break out. This will never happen if we just go to task force meetings," said the president of the Boyd Medical Group. (He was referring to a task force of primary care physicians, mostly solo practitioners, that had been meeting monthly since the first of the year.) The head of the Johnson Clinic said, "You're right. There are too many doctors and too many agendas to agree on anything."

Breaking away. "What we ought to do is move ahead as fast as we can. We'll see who follows," said the president of Boyd. After further discussion, the two groups agreed on a plan: they would merge and negotiate as a single entity with the hospital. The merged group and hospital would form a PHO that other primary care doctors could join later if they so desired.

The idea began to pick up momentum. The two groups, both founded in the years following World War II, had always respected one another. Several physicians in one group were social friends with physicians in the other. However, there were differences to overcome, particularly in management style and culture. Still, the more they thought about the possible combined entity, the more they began to refer to it informally as "the Dream Team."

Merger talks. The two groups engaged a legal/financial team to assist in effecting the merger. They soon found that some issues could be dealt with quickly and others were much more complex and time consuming. Merging their strategies was easy; on a combined basis the offices of the two groups provided better geographic coverage of the metro area, and they were in a better position to bid on managed care contracts. Combining call schedules would ease everyone's work load; this was embraced by all physicians in both practices.

It was obvious that two offices adjacent to a suburban hospital should be consolidated, and that money could be saved by combining medical records, management information systems, billing and related services. Even the question of who would be the administrator of the combined group proved less difficult than originally expected.

The tough issues boiled down to these four:

- Physician compensation formulas.
- Merging assets.
- Merging benefits.
- Naming the merged group.

The Boyd Medical Group had long been on a "production formula," whereas the Johnson Clinic paid partners equally. To make matters worse, the average production (defined as charges less contractual allowances, with a partial credit for ancillary income) was far higher in the Boyd group. On a per physician basis, the Boyd Medical Group was billing 30 percent above the MGMA national median for internal medicine groups. The Johnson Clinic, on the other hand, was 15 percent below the median.

For a while, these differences appeared to represent an insurmountable obstacle. "It's going to be hard to get anyone to sign on the dotted line if he or she is going to lose money," observed Boyd's leading producer. On closer inspection, however, it was possible to craft a compensation system that did not result in a loss of income for any of the signers. The steps in designing the new formula were:

- Prepare standalone financial projections for the two groups, including projections of production and income for each physician.

- Prepare combined financial projections, including income estimates for each physician.

- Discuss compensation philosophies with physicians in both groups and probe for areas of compromise.

- Using the projection models, test alternative approaches, looking for one that met acceptable philosophical objectives while not producing drops in incomes for any physician.

Sound impossible? Finding an acceptable compensation formula was made easier by the fact that the financial model for the combined group indicated that the merged entity was going to be five to 10 percent more profitable than the predecessor clinics operating on their own.

The merging of assets was made more difficult by the fact that each group occupied a combination of owned and leased space. In this case, the simplest approach proved to be to have the hospital purchase all owned space and lease it back to the new organization. The office furniture, fixtures and equipment of the two practices and the other assets (e.g., cash, bank deposits and accounts receivable) were valued by a third party.

The only politically acceptable solution to the merging of benefits proved to be the adoption of the most generous aspects of each medical group's plan. However, without closing an office (a controversial issue), the dollars could not have been made available to fund the new, richer plan.

Agreeing on a name for the new group was the toughest problem. Neither Dr. Boyd nor Dr. Johnson was alive, but both groups were strongly attached to the names of these beloved founding physicians. Finally, market research was conducted to help identify a new, acceptable name.

Both the announcement of the Boyd-Johnson merger and the planned affiliation with a local hospital, came as something of a shock to other physicians and residents of the community. Several members of a primary care task force were indignant: "Here we were all going to do something together. But the Johnson and Boyd people think they're special." These independent physicians were also threatened. "If the hospital does this for these two groups, what happens to us? Are we going to be left out in the cold?"

One hospital executive's first reaction was one of surprise and almost defensiveness: "This is not what we had in mind. What will the other task force members think?" The CEO, however, saw the Boyd-Johnson merger as a tremendous opportunity: "The leaders of the Boyd and Johnson medical groups are willing to take the heat for actually doing something. What's more, they are not saying that the two of them will be the ultimate group. We can add primary care docs step by step and form something that really makes sense. Ultimately we will need 100 physicians in this group. But the Boyd-Johnson merger is an excellent building block."

The merger went forward and, simultaneously, negotiations began to form a PHO with the hospital. The group, which started out with 30 internal medicine physicians, soon added additional internists plus existing OB/Gyn, family practice and pediatrics practices. Within three years, it was projected that this would be a 100 physician multispecialty group with a strong primary care orientation.

The hospital continued to support its broader IPA-model physician contracting group for managed care as well. However, the handwriting was on the wall — the group of the future was to be the combination of the hospital and the Boyd-Johnson multispecialty group.

Integrating a Multispecialty Group, a Hospital and a Health Plan

"We've never seen eye to eye, and there is no reason to think that we ever will. They are too slow at everything, and they don't know the first thing about a medical practice." The administrator of the 120-physician Dalton Clinic was not particularly fond of the idea of having the hospital next door as a strategic partner.

On the other hand, she did not have a better option. The two allied hospitals across town had formed a loosely-knit 100-physician MSO and had begun to aggressively discount to major employers in the area. The new organization was already taking patients away from both the Dalton Clinic and the Ridgeway Hospital next door.

The Dalton Clinic's competitive advantage was that it was already far more integrated than the PHO would ever be. It was more cost effective, it could control quality, and it had an outstanding reputation in the community. Still, the only way to stay ahead of the competition was to take the next step. The ideal answer was for the clinic and the hospital to merge and then develop their own capitated health plan.

Vision and strategy. Early meetings between the clinic and hospital focused on establishing a common vision and strategy for the merged entity. To both group's surprise, this went smoothly. "You both had pretty much the same concept of what the future would bring and how to respond, but you didn't know it," observed the consultant retained to facilitate the merger.

The statement of future strategies for the new organization included the following:

- The two organizations agreed that they would either bring in a health plan partner or start their own plan.

- Four dispersed primary care sites were to be developed in the metro area. Two of these sites were to be in the other hospitals' back yards.

- Outreach plans included buying, starting or establishing strong relationships with existing practices in seven small communities in the service area.

- The merged organization would invest in a new information system capable of integrating the data produced by the hospital, the clinic and eventually the health plan.

The two parties decided to move farther along in the negotiating process before deciding whether to start a health plan.

Financial, legal and organizational structure. It was clear to both parties that the clinic was negotiating from a position of strength. The clinic had more options than the hospital. It was equally clear, however, that negotiating this partnership would be in the best long-term interests of the clinic.

How would the clinic use its negotiating strength? The answer depended heavily on the clinic shareholders' attitudes toward risk and control. Substantial capital had to be invested in developing an HMO, new primary care sites, information systems, and marketing. The physicians in the clinic wanted to minimize their personal investment; therefore, the hospital would need to bear more of the risk and would, in return, seek more control. Physicians might receive salary guarantees for a period of time, for example, but have a limited role on the board of the new organization. After numerous meetings during which the pros and cons of the new governance arrangement were aired, the physicians decided to go along.

Other key design objectives — the desire to continue to have the hospital eligible for tax-exempt financing, to have a community board for the hospital and to avoid legal prohibitions — were viewed as beneficial by both parties. The physicians recognized that some of these limits were necessary in order for the new organization to make capital available to build the integrated system.

The resulting preferred structure was a foundation that served as the majority owner of both the hospital and health plan. The professional corporation remained under separate ownership by the physicians; however, the foundation owned all the plant and equipment. Physicians had a majority of the seats on the board of the health plan, 20 percent of seats on the board of the hospital and 20 percent representation on the foundation board.

Other key steps in developing the integrated system. The leaders of the merger process found themselves being stretched repeatedly from very big picture issues to day-to-day matters, such as staffing plans and employee communications. The other key issues included merging benefits plans, and communicating with individual physicians, their staff and people in the community.

In this case merging benefits plans inevitably meant reducing the benefits of the physicians and the former clinic employees. There was no way to justify the increase in benefits plan costs that would have been required to bring hospital and health plan employees up to the benefits levels that had been maintained in the clinic.

High priority was given to developing the staffing plan for the new entities and quickly engaging employees in discussions regarding potential new responsibilities. Still, the process took too long and there was a price to pay. The major problem was disagreement on who would be the CEO of the foundation. The issue was too hot to resolve early in the negotiating process. Meanwhile, how could other positions in the new organization be sorted out if there were no CEO to establish the framework and start the sorting process?

Soon after the merger, the board of the new system decided that it had to start an HMO. The new physician-administrator said, "Although we haven't seen much managed care in our area yet, we know it's coming. We have to have our own financing mechanism. I don't know of a single example of an integrated system that isn't looking to do this. We don't want to become a vendor of physician and hospital services for several other health plans."

Following a feasibility study, the foundation board approved $5 million in capital for the HMO and began developing the first products to be offered by the fall. Once the foundation had recovered its initial capital investment, the multispecialty group and hospital would share equally in the profits of the health plan. The physician-administrator added, "We have to give high priority to developing a Medicare risk product. We have a lot of our patients on Medicare, and we need to find a better, more cost-effective approach to meeting their needs. Now that we have control of all of the resources — physicians, hospital and other services like home health care — I think we can do it."

After the Deal is Done

The arduous process of bringing physicians, hospitals and health plans together doesn't stop when the legal documents are signed. After the negotiations, the hard work of becoming a unified organization really begins. As one physician-administrator told us, "This is an extremely difficult and sometimes brutal process. People are hurt; careers suffer. But, we have to keep our eye on our original objectives — providing higher quality health care at a more reasonable cost."

We have often noticed that leaders of merged organizations do not appear to be having much fun. We have also observed considerable turnover in upper management in months immediately following a merger. And, we often ask ourselves, does there have to be a management failure in order to set in motion those forces necessary to create a management success?

One would hope the answer to the last question is "no." In fact, several of our case study organizations provide evidence to this effect. For example, many of the large multispecialty clinics have had the same administrator and/or medical director for years, and sometimes decades. On the other hand, newer organizations, such as Sac Sierra, Premier Medical Group in Denver and others, have undergone management changes after a much shorter time. In fact, there are a number of cases where it has taken a management change to re-establish the confidence of physicians and board members. In some situations, the seeds of failure have been sown during the negotiation process. In other cases, difficulties have surfaced during the transition. We were told, "Some people can make the adjustment to this new way of thinking, and others cannot. Change in leadership is inevitable."

Many of the case study organizations and other organizations that have made successful transitions appear to have several common traits that ease the process of molding an effective integrated team. Here are a few:

Visualizing success. Not surprisingly, leaders who make the transition in leadership are those who fought for it to be created in the first place. In cases in which the medical group or hospital administrators have been ambivalent about the advisability of proceeding, or dragged their feet, it is a foregone conclusion that they will not survive.

Reaching out to all elements of the new organization. Leaders who move quickly to demonstrate concern and understanding for parts of the organization he or she has not been associated with in the past are able to earn the trust and respect of the entire integrated system. These leaders often build new management teams through a combination of personnel from all the organizations involved. For example, the new management team that evolved from the merger of Fargo Clinic and St. Luke's included representatives of both the clinic and hospital.

One technique leaders of integrated systems use is to immediately assign key staff to one or more of the organizations they did not work for previously and mix in some outsiders to help forge new relationships. They consciously build new teams and alliances that cross functional areas. This is one of the key factors in the success of UniHealth America, Geisinger, and Kaiser Permanente (shifting people between the Permanente Medical Group and the Kaiser Foundation Health Plan).

Managing communication. Physician administrators and others in integrated systems talk constantly about the importance of communication. Effective communication is especially important in the early stages of development of an integrated system. We are aware of a number of organizations that developed communication plans to keep employees of the various entities informed throughout the merger process.

Successful integrated systems carry this approach forward into the new organization. For example, one group established an emergency "rumor control" plan. As potentially damaging rumors surfaced within the new integrated system, a centralized response team pulled in appropriate managers to immediately address the issues behind the rumors.

Those involved in forming new organizations have commented on the importance of quickly developing new types of indices and reports (e.g., financial, market share, lives covered under capitated contracts) that convey a picture of the progress of the organization toward meeting its objectives and sharing them with all the component organizations.

The Integrated Health Care System of Tomorrow

One of the biggest challenges faced by most integrating systems is to make the transition from the traditional model, in which the majority of patients are on Medicare or discounted fee-for-service plans, to a system where most payment is received on a capitated basis. This is the problem we referred to earlier as driving a car with one foot on the gas pedal and the other on the brake. But, this transition will be made, albeit painfully in many cases, as integrated systems move into the future.

In our view, the integrated health care system of the future will:

- Work harder to find out what customers want.

- Further redefine the relationship between physician extender, primary care doctor and specialist. This will include resolving the issue of the role of primary care physicians as a gate keeper or in performing more diagnosis and treatment themselves and determining the scope of service of mid-level practitioners.

- Continue to improve its geographic coverage of service areas.

- Identify new ways to bridge the gap between physician administrators and physician practitioners.

- Complete the transition to fully integrated information systems, including electronic medical records and outcomes measurement capabilities.

- Invent still more gradients of care between acute inpatient care and outpatient visits.

- Expand the system's role in the spectrum of care to include mental health, rehabilitation and long-term care.

- Deliver demonstrably higher levels of quality at lower costs.

- Assume responsibility for the health status of health plan enrollees.

The good news, as has been stated so often, is that integrated health care systems have the power to change. As skills are developed, experience accumulates and information technology and systems advance, and physicians, hospitals and health plans engaged in integrated systems are positioned to make significant advancements in providing high-quality, cost-effective care.

CHAPTER 15.

THE BENEFITS AND POTENTIAL OF INTEGRATED HEALTH CARE

Our health care system is a fragmented mess. We are all over the landscape. We have unhappy employers and patients. We really have to take a careful look at what we are and the way we do things.
— CEO of a large integrated system

What are the benefits from the time, investment and "brain damage" associated with physician-hospital integration? Do the benefits outweigh the costs? Or, in response to the question raised by a physician: "Where is the carrot?"

Seven useful criteria for evaluating the benefits versus the costs of integrated health care systems, and whether or not they are in the public interest, are:

(1) *Physicians and medical group performance.* Will integrated systems be able to recruit and retain good physicians? Are physicians who participate in integrated systems better off in terms of the number of patients, income security and ability to practice quality medicine than their counterparts in solo practice or other types of group practice settings?

(2) *Hospital performance.* Have hospitals in integrated systems out-performed those in non-integrated situations? Are they stronger financially? Are they better able to serve community needs, or is it too early to tell?

(3) *Cost effectiveness.* Are integrated systems more cost effective and competitive than other forms of health care delivery?

(4) *Employer and consumer satisfaction.* Are accessibility, service, cost and quality to employers and individuals better when integrated health care systems are financing and delivering the care?

(5) *Quality.* How does the quality of care (as measured by risk-adjusted outcomes) provided by integrated health care systems compare with that provided by physicians and hospitals organized in more traditional settings?

(6) *Positioning for health care reform and changes in local markets.* How well have integrated systems positioned themselves for the health care payment system of the future? Will they be able to effectively compete in their markets, especially those dominated by managed care?

(7) *Adaptability and innovation.* How well can integrated systems respond to further change, particularly when it is unanticipated? Are the incentives in place to continue to adopt new approaches to cost-effective, quality care that health care customers may seek?

Physician and Medical Group Performance

The group with the most to gain or lose through physician-hospital integration and the development of integrated health care systems is physicians. Issues relating directly to physicians include the number and types of patients served, compensation, lifestyle (especially hours worked, and weekend and evening on-call requirements) and preserving clinical autonomy and independence.

Primary care physicians. Given the national shortage of primary care physicians, there is not much concern about the supply of patients for these doctors. The real issues have to do with the ability of primary care physicians to practice in settings where they can be adequately compensated, enjoy a reasonable quality of life, and be free to practice high-quality medicine at an affordable price.

Based on the case studies, we believe that the earnings, fringe benefits and the quality of life are substantially better when primary care physicians choose to be part of an integrated system. This was especially noteworthy for physicians in the four large clinics and Kaiser Permanente where primary care physicians typically earn $100,000 to $120,000 annually, plus fringe benefits. Primary care doctors in these organizations also had less restrictive on-call schedules than their private practice counterparts.

There is little question that integrated health care systems enjoy a substantial advantage when it comes to recruiting and retaining primary care physicians. They are well positioned to capitalize on the trend toward primary care doctors seeking group practice opportunities. Integrated systems offer a practice free of heavy buy-in requirements and can offer most physicians a full practice almost immediately.

On balance, we believe that primary care physicians stand to gain in an integrated health care system. Some individual physicians may see themselves as giving up a degree of independence in return for a more secure income and better practice environment. Nearly all accept the trade-off.

Specialists. In the larger clinics like Marshfield and Geisinger, most specialists are not maximizing their short-term earnings. They are investing in primary care network development and the establishment of a health plan with the anticipation of securing a long-term supply of patients or of being successful in a managed care environment. Most specialists in these organizations believe they are securing their long-term financial potential by taking home less now.

Physician leaders in all of the case study organizations believe that specialists' earnings will decline. As one physician said, "specialists' gross and net incomes will cascade downward in the future." However, the impacts of health care reform, changes in compensation, and the growing surplus of physicians in most specialty areas are not likely to affect specialists in integrated health care systems as severely as doctors in solo or small group practices. In other words, the adjustment will be less traumatic for specialists in integrated organizations.

Medical groups as a whole. There is a generalized concern that in joining an integrated system, medical groups will lose autonomy. In some integrated systems that have been formed to date, this concern has proven valid. The hospital/physician/health plan relationship remains cumbersome, and decision making is still more difficult than it needs to be. However, for those integrated systems that are further along, change continues, and one of the main directions of change is the ceding of greater and greater decision-making latitude to physicians and medical groups. Meanwhile, physician influence and leadership continues to gain ground.

In the first generation of integrated systems, loss of physician autonomy may be a concern. Later generations of integrated health care systems, however, may look more like a physician takeover than a merger. Physicians in existing large multispecialty medical groups may want to look less to the threat of losing autonomy and more to the potential of controlling the entire system.

Performance of Hospitals and Multihospital Systems

The usual indicators of success for hospitals are trends in admissions, patient days, revenues, market share, profitability and overall financial strength (borrowing power and the balance sheet). We recognize that under the new paradigm, these indicators will be less meaningful. In a future dominated by managed care and capitation, the ability to provide high-quality hospital services to a defined population at the lowest cost will be the defining measure of success. But, at the time this book was prepared, capitation was not the most predominant financing mechanism in most parts of the country.

Admissions and patient days. Our review of the trend in hospital admissions — both inpatient and outpatient — among the more fully integrated case study organizations indicates that they have out-performed competing organizations in their regions. The growth in admissions could usually be attributed to an increase in the number of patients served by the physician group of the integrated system, and the growth of membership in system-owned health plans.

Over a five-year period, inpatient days for nearly all of the case study hospitals either grew more rapidly, or decreased less, than competing hospitals. Nearly all of the hospitals included in this study were able to reduce their average lengths of stay during this period. One that did not, Geisinger Medical Center, experienced a substantial increase in its case mix index over the 1988 through 1992 period (patients were sicker).

Market share. The ability to build a primary care distribution network and achieve market recognition has meant that hospitals that are part of integrated systems have almost always gained market share in their respective communities and service areas. For example, one case study hospital increased its market share from 48 to 60 percent in five years.

Profitability. Since all of the case study hospitals were not-for-profit organizations, the more accurate term would be "surplus of revenues over expenses" rather than profitability. But, whatever the choice of terms, nearly all of the hospitals we studied have experienced either steady growth or stability in earnings over the past five years. This is especially impressive given the fact that in several of the integrated systems, most of the ancillary income from laboratory, radiology and the pharmacy goes to the medical group.

On a national basis, the average US acute care hospital is earning two to three percent on operating revenues and slightly more when the impact of contributions and other income sources are considered. As a group, the case study hospitals were at least twice as profitable as acute care hospitals in general.

Impact on the financial condition of hospitals. Although the investment required to move ahead with the development of an integrated health care system is often high, the overall financial condition of most of the hospitals in the case study organizations improved substantially during recent years (e.g., current ratios were higher, net worth as a percent of assets increased, debt service coverage ratios were strong, borrowing capacity was higher).

Our overall conclusion is that despite the need to invest in primary care networks, health plans, information systems and more physician managers, nearly all of the hospitals and multihospital systems studied improved their competitive positions by virtue of being part of integrated health care systems. These hospitals have also improved their financial performance and strengthened their balance sheets.

Cost-effectiveness of Integrated Health Care

Based on our research and analysis, we conclude that integrated health care systems are significantly more cost effective than are physicians, hospitals and health plans functioning in the traditional, fragmented model. We arrived at this conclusion by examining the performance of integrated systems against a number of factors relating to the cost effectiveness of health care.

We have been analyzing the forces driving health care costs for several years, and have stated our findings in a previous book — *The Crisis in Health Care: Costs, Choices and Strategies* — and in numerous articles and speeches. Most of the factors driving health costs, and their relationship to one another, are shown in Exhibit 15-1. The factors at the top of Exhibit 15-1 are the primary forces driving demand for health care services. The resources used to provide medical services are noted at the bottom of the exhibit. Pricing, or the payment system, influences both demand and resources utilized.

Duplication of facilities and services. One of the lessons learned is that in integrated systems, internal competition between physicians and hospitals is either severely curtailed or eliminated. Since duplication of equipment and services tends to stimulate demand and also lead to higher expenses (in other words, it impacts both demand and resources utilized — see Exhibit 15-1), it is an important driver of health care costs.

A desire to eliminate duplication of expensive equipment and services was one of the major factors motivating the merger of Fargo Clinic and St. Luke's Hospital. Marshfield Clinic and St. Joseph's Hospital have avoided duplication, as have Carle Clinic and the Carle Foundation Hospital. Geisinger's organizational structure reduces the chances of duplication occurring. Kaiser Permanente does not duplicate the services offered by area hospitals; in fact, in 1985 KP reversed an earlier decision to build its own hospital because of substantial excess inpatient bed capacity in the Denver marketplace.

The Oregon Medical Group and Sacred Heart Health System in Eugene do not duplicate facilities or services. Physicians in the Presbyterian Network do not compete with Presbyterian's hospitals.

We estimate that reductions in the amount of duplication we have seen in the case study organizations saves payors as much as 10 percent on their medical bills.

Inappropriate and unnecessary care. Based on our research, we believe that integrated systems have less incentive to provide inappropriate and unnecessary care. In large clinics, the connection between productivity (dollars billed) and physician compensation is often less direct than in more traditional practice settings.

In Los Angeles, the Harriman Jones and Facey Medical Groups, both part of UniHealth America, receive most of their revenues from capitated contracts. There is no financial incentive to provide inappropriate or unnecessary care under this type of payment system. Many of the Sutter Health physicians and medical foundations also operate in capitated environments with no incentive for doing more procedures.

EXHIBIT 15-1
Conceptual Model, Factors Impacting Health Care Costs

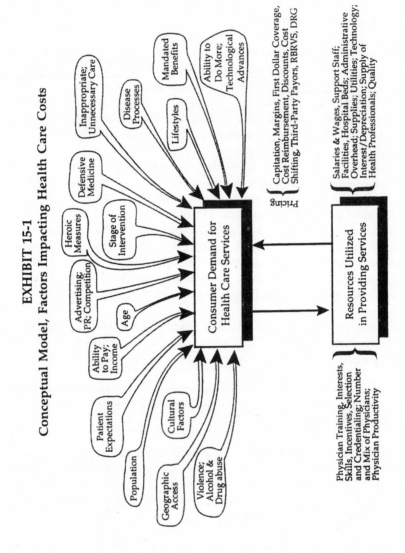

Our experience is that nearly all physicians and hospital administrators will readily admit to the huge amount of inappropriate and unnecessary care in the health care system. However, it always takes place in someone else's hospital or in another medical practice! We believe inappropriate and unnecessary care occurs in integrated systems but with much less frequency. If we are correct, the cost advantage for these types of provider groups is impressive — perhaps as high as 15 to 20 percent of total costs.

Less reliance on specialists. The evidence is overwhelming that health care systems — and countries — that make greater use of primary care physicians and physician extenders provide more cost-effective health care than those with a high proportion of specialists. One of the lessons learned from the 10 organizations studied is that nearly all have made major investments in adding primary care physicians. Organizations such as Carle Clinic and Kaiser Permanente have made effective use of physician assistants, nurse practitioners and nurse midwives to augment primary care services. At the same time, all are careful in terms of adding specialists.

While for many of the organizations studied, the motivation for primary care initiatives (outreach and an increased base of primary care doctors) was to develop a stronger referral system, this strategy also improves the ability of integrated systems to provide health care services at a lower cost.

Lower administrative overhead. The administrative expenses associated with the US health care system — physicians, hospitals and health plans — are huge. One study estimated that these costs range from 19 to 24 percent (Woolhandler and Himmelstein, 1991, p. 1253).

Even though we agree that reducing overhead through combining functions is not, in itself, a sufficient reason to develop an integrated system, we also believe that the potential exists for cutting administrative expenses. For example, the Geisinger Health Plan has half the staff of the typical HMO with comparable membership. Furthermore, a payment system relying on capitation is less complex than the claims processing associated with traditional experience-rated PPO or indemnity insurance plans.

Hospital utilization. Although many of the case study hospitals reported excess bed capacity, utilization rates were typically higher than regional or national averages. In several of the cases, hospitals were actually experiencing periods when there was a shortage of bed capacity.

In terms of efficiently using hospital resources, Kaiser Permanente reports that its ratio of hospital beds per million population is 1,130 in northern California, less than half the 2,641 for other hospitals in the area. Hospital occupancy rates for Kaiser Permanente average 74 percent versus 65 percent for all other hospitals in the region (Caulfield, 1993).

Rate increases of system-owned HMOs. The Geisinger Health Plan has been able to keep its annual premium increases to 8.6 percent per year since 1985, and this is on a low base to begin with. This compared with an average of 11.7 percent for all HMOs in the country from 1986 to 1992. An article in The New York Times said that this plan "has the lowest rates in Pennsylvania" (Eckholm, 1993). At the same time, the health plan was profitable and payments to physicians and hospitals were higher than those of Medicare, Medicaid and other managed care plans.

In Albuquerque, Presbyterian's HMO, Health Plus, has not had a rate increase over the past five years. The HMO earned a significant profit in 1992 and paid participating physicians a considerable "withhold."

Savings on malpractice premiums. In the case studies, the evidence of savings in malpractice expenses was most pronounced at Carle Clinic, MAPI and Marshfield Clinic. In each of these cases, the reduction in malpractice premiums was in the 25 to 50 percent category. In one case the savings occurred because of self insurance; in a second case the savings were realized through group purchasing. In another situation, the malpractice insurance company is a wholly-owned subsidiary.

The second component of this issue is defensive medicine — the performance of tests and procedures primarily to avoid malpractice claims. We don't have hard evidence on this point, but we believe that physicians practicing in large clinics and in groups associated with integrated systems are less likely to allow worries about malpractice suits push them into practicing defensive medicine. This relates to our earlier point on inappropriate and unnecessary care.

It is generally agreed that the combination of high malpractice premiums and defensive medicine add significantly to health care costs. The integrated systems have been able to reduce costs in both of these categories.

Spreading overhead expenses over a larger base. This factor, which might be called "economies of scale," is important in terms of driving down hospital costs per patient day or discharge. Saint Joseph Hospital has been the lowest cost hospital in the Denver Area for 10 years. A major contributor: higher-than-average utilization, largely because of the hospital's unique relationship with Kaiser Permanente. Overhead expenses are spread over a larger base of patients. As a trustee of Saint Joseph Hospital in Denver said, "Our relationship with Kaiser Permanente allows us to utilize our investment in fixed assets more efficiently. This is in the public interest."

Several other hospitals included among the case studies were busy; occupancy rates were significantly above regional averages. All of these hospitals benefit from being able to spread their fixed administrative expenses over a relatively large base of patients.

The issue of price versus cost-effectiveness. As noted in the Marshfield and Carle case studies, both of the organizations are considered to be "pricey" by many people in their service areas. According to clinic officials, if a payor or patient looked only at charges per encounter, this would be their natural conclusion.

However, Marshfield and Carle physicians and administrators argue that if they were judged on the basis of their ability to provide care for a defined population over time (capitation), the results would show that they are cost-effective providers of care. This is because of their emphasis on primary care, their ability to control utilization of higher-cost specialists and hospitals, less duplication of equipment, and a lower incidence of inappropriate and unnecessary care. Their allegation is supported by the experience of the Geisinger Health Plan and Health Plus in Albuquerque (discussed earlier).

We believe that the evidence supports the view that integrated health care systems are significantly more cost effective than traditional fragmented medical groups and hospitals. The trend toward the formation and growth of integrated systems bodes well for limiting future rates of increase in health care costs.

Employers and Consumers

It is our conclusion, largely based on the experience of the case study organizations, that an increasing number of consumers and employers are attracted to the type of care provided by integrated systems. Employers want lower costs and fewer employee complaints. Consumers are voting with their feet by signing up with health plans that contract with integrated systems and by using the medical groups and physicians of these organizations.

Many employers and health plans prefer to deal with a single entity rather than developing multiple contracts with a number of physicians and hospitals. This was one of the major reasons leading to the formation of the Sacramento Sierra Medical Group, MAPI and the Oregon Medical Group.

What about the loss of freedom of choice? It is true that those individuals who place a high value on maintaining traditional relationships with their personal physician(s) are less likely to be attracted to integrated systems. But, again, the situation is not static; many integrated systems have an emphasis on the patient's "personal physician" that does not differ from traditional private practice. The evidence points to a long-term, steady shift toward more patients using these types of organizations. Many integrated systems systematically survey patients and employers, and the results are impressive.

One of the characteristics of medical groups operating in a capitated environment is that they provide extended hours, usually in the form of urgent care centers attached to a clinic. This earns favor with subscribers and accomplishes two important objectives: it keeps patients away from higher-cost hospital emergency rooms, and it provides needed medical services to patients, thus reducing the pressures on clinic physicians during regular working hours.

We have previously concluded that employers and patients receive more health care services for their dollars with integrated systems. In terms of the important issue of accessibility, integrated systems have an excellent track record of attracting and retaining primary care physicians and of opening practice sites in areas convenient to consumers. This is a fundamental element of the strategies of all of the integrated systems. Also, several of the integrated systems devote substantial resources to providing consulting clinics (sending specialists to patients) in outlying communities.

Quality of Care

Physicians and managers of integrated systems say that they provide high quality, coordinated care to patients. Based on our consulting experience, independent physicians and smaller hospitals argue just as vehemently that they provide very high quality care. In fact, we have never been to a community hospital, whether it had six beds or 600, that didn't claim to provide the highest quality of care in the area! And, every community believes that its physicians are the best.

Proponents of integrated systems rely on a number of arguments to make their point relative to the quality of care delivered:

- Presence of a "seamless" delivery system for their patients which offers better coordination among primary care physicians and specialists, among different specialists and sub-specialists, and between physicians and a hospital. For example, the common medical record helps assure continuity of patient care.

- Ability to institute standards of care and to measure the performance of physicians and hospitals in terms of how well they meet these standards. This is sometimes referred to as "clinical pathways."

- Less inappropriate and unnecessary care. This is the point made earlier in discussing the cost effectiveness of integrated systems. Doing too much may be just as harmful as doing too little.

- Higher volume of patients and procedures. Most studies of health care quality show that physicians and hospitals performing a higher volume of certain procedures, such as cardiovascular surgery, experience better medical outcomes.

- Commitment to continuous quality improvement, especially in clinical applications, is an increasingly important factor.

- Most integrated systems claim they are well positioned, and have a sufficient volume of patients, to be able to monitor and report medical outcomes in a statistically valid way. As noted in Chapter 10, integrated systems are investing millions of dollars to be able to better manage care and improve quality.

Coordination of care. This is a major differentiating factor among the large clinics studied; they take pride in offering a coordinated approach to patient care. The rapid communication of patient records among physicians and the informal ability to consult with specialists, all contribute to higher quality.

Development and implementation of clinical standards. Kaiser Permanente was the best example of an integrated system that has implemented clinical standards in a number of areas, such as the management of prostate cancer. Many of the other organizations, such as Geisinger and Marshfield, had task forces working on the development of clinical standards.

Quality improvement. As noted in Chapter 10, nearly all of the integrated systems studied were well into the implementation of quality improvement programs (continuous quality improvement or total quality management). Furthermore, physicians and clinical processes were nearly always an important component of these efforts.

None of the integrated systems we studied has taken the position that continuous quality improvement should be limited to administrative procedures and processes; all are focusing on improving clinical processes.

Outcomes measurement. Even though this is an important area for the future, the evidence collected from case study participants relative to their ability to demonstrate superior medical outcomes was not impressive (see Chapter 10). Although there was almost uniform recognition of the importance of outcomes measurement, few of the organizations had systems in place to adequately measure clinical outcomes.

An exception is Saint Joseph Hospital in Denver. Saint Joseph is one of the hospitals participating in the MedisGroups benchmarking program, and was in the top four among 100 hospitals in terms of successful outcomes with cardiovascular surgery programs, and in the top 10 (out of 550 hospitals) in several other clinical areas (e.g., congestive heart failure). Hospital leaders attribute much of their success to the presence of the Colorado Permanente Medical Group physicians on the medical staff of the hospital.

Many of the case study organizations (e.g., Kaiser Permanente, Carle, Geisinger) emphasize patient surveys as part of the process of measuring outcomes and patient satisfaction. Several integrated systems perform these types of surveys on a continuous basis, and achieve a sufficiently large response to measure the performance of individual physicians. One manager at Geisinger said, "I think these surveys are more important than all of the financial information we collect."

On an overall basis, it is clear that integrated systems provide high quality care. These organized systems include many of the most prestigious medical group practices in the country. At the same time, until outcomes measurement systems become more refined and widely applied, it is difficult to support a broad statement about the quality superiority of these organizations compared with physicians and hospitals functioning in more traditional settings.

Positioning for Health Care Reform and Managed Care Growth

At the time the research for this book was conducted there was considerable interest and planning in anticipation of state and federal health care reform. This interest included recognition of the importance of being able to participate in capitated contracts, and the need to provide coverage within large geographic areas. Streamlining the cost structure was also viewed as important; investment in information systems was part of this thrust. There was also evidence of rapid change in many markets (e.g., growth in HMO enrollment; mergers of physician groups and hospitals), and all of the integrated systems studied were concerned about maintaining or improving their competitive positions.

Geographic coverage. The success of integrated systems in establishing their regional networks was one of the most impressive aspects of the case study organizations. There were no exceptions to the statement that integrated systems have invested large sums in solidifying their geographic coverage. In the case of the large multispecialty clinics, this has meant the establishment of networks of primary care practice sites. For Sutter Health and UniHealth America, both multihospital systems, it has meant the acquisition of physician group practices in strategically important geographic areas within northern and southern California respectively.

Emphasis on primary care. All of the case study organizations had anticipated the message that primary care is the driving force for the health care delivery systems of the future. As discussed in Chapter 4, this has manifested itself in an increase in the proportion of primary care physicians in the integrated organizations and emphasis on controlling the geographic distribution of primary care practices. Most of the large integrated systems have moved beyond allowing primary care physicians to practice wherever they please, and have increasingly taken control of this aspect of the delivery of health care.

Capitation. Preparation for capitation takes several forms. First, all but one of the case study organizations owns or is developing an HMO. This means that with the progression of health care reform, these systems already will have a significant base of patients enrolled in capitated plans.

The experience gained by the integrated systems in managing capitated contracts, either their own plans or those owned by others, is invaluable. Physicians and managers of integrated systems either know, or are learning, how to allocate dollars among primary care physicians, specialists, hospitals, ancillary services and administrative expenses. One hospital CEO told us, "This is the biggest payoff from starting an HMO."

Finally, the term "single signature contacting" is widely used among physicians and hospital managers in integrated systems positioning themselves for capitation. There is a belief that physician and hospital services will be bundled; health plans will not separately contract with specialists for their services.

Administrative streamlining. The integrated systems studied are taking steps to further improve their cost effectiveness through streamlining their administrative structures. One of the changes has involved more physicians in high-level management or governance positions. Several case study organizations had emphasized a flat organizational structure and the elimination of large numbers of middle management positions. (Integrated systems are not unique in having taken these kinds of actions.) Implementation of quality improvement programs, with an emphasis on empowering lower-level employees, has further facilitated the streamlining process.

In summary, there can be little question but that integrated health care systems are in the driver's seat when it comes to positioning themselves for success under health care reform and the growth of managed care. They are taking, or have taken, the steps necessary to be part of the health care system of the future.

Adaptability, Innovation and Learning

Dr. David Lawrence, Chairman and CEO of Kaiser Permanente and the author of the Foreword of this book, said, "The power of an integrated health care system — its unique advantage, if you will — lies in its potential to create an environment that supports innovation and learning . . . Only through continuous learning, innovation, and experimentation can we understand how best to enhance the effectiveness of care, its availability and cost (Kaiser Permanente, *Environment...*, 1993, p. 1).

It comes as no secret that health care is undergoing revolutionary change. Meanwhile, try as we might, the authors of this book and the thousands of others who try to help health care providers anticipate and prepare for change will not succeed in predicting the health care system of the future and how physicians and hospitals should respond to these changes. The organizations that will fare best are those who can continue to adjust, not only to the changes that are accurately predicted, but to those that will inevitably come by surprise.

As we indicated in the Preface of this book, integrated systems impress us most by the adaptability they have demonstrated and by their apparent ability to continue to change more rapidly than their competitors. This ability of integrated systems to learn and change stems from several characteristics:

New lines of communication. Try as they will, physicians and hospitals in traditional health care environments will never be able to replicate the ease and frequency of communication typical of an integrated system. They will never have management information systems that share as much data on patients, utilization and practice patterns or costs. Physicians will not talk with one another as quickly and frequently. Medical group practice and hospital administrators will not work together as well as their counterparts in integrated systems. Even increasingly common technology, such as voice mail, will never be used as effectively as it can be in an integrated system.

Common vision, shared goals and economic integration. A common vision of the future leading to shared goals, a tighter corporate culture, and consistent financial incentives equals success. Not only will those physicians and hospitals operating in traditional health care environments never have the same reasons to communicate with one another, they will not experience the same degree of shared economic and financial interests and the common commitment to providing high-quality, cost-effective care. Equally important, when one element of an integrated system experiences an opportunity or a need to change, the other components are far more likely to be interested in its success.

Mobility of resources. Once a critical issue requiring change has been identified, the integrated system can mobilize and deploy human resources and dollars wherever it needs them and on a timely basis. It can shift people and dollars in terms of space (e.g., from one part of the service area to another) and among functions (e.g., between investments in equipment, physician recruitment or in even public relations and image building). This can be accomplished without going through a painful process of negotiations; the primary objective is to invest resources in a way that accomplishes the objectives of the integrated system and meets the needs of customers.

The Future of Integrated Health Care

Is integrated health care the wave of the future? The evidence leads us to conclude that the answer is "yes." Not only do integrated systems function better today, they are better suited to the health care environment of tomorrow. And, they appear to learn from their experience and be more adaptable to both anticipated change and surprises.

But, for most communities, how achievable is integrated health care? The evidence suggests that it is difficult for physicians and hospitals to attain even a small degree of integration. This book has focused on those health care systems that have already achieved a significant degree of integration. By and large, these integrated systems look like tomorrow's winners. However, it has been a struggle for each of the integrated systems to get where it is today, and every single organization we studied identifies a need for further change.

In Chapter 11, we have noted a number of lessons learned from the first generation of integrated systems. We have learned, for example, not to put the cart before the horse. For example, hospital administrators can't drive the change; they can facilitate the process, but physicians must lead. It doesn't pay to invest in a managed care plan without physician involvement, leadership and support. We have learned to take integration as far as we can today in a local situation, but not to expect to accomplish full integration in a single step. We have found that developing an integrated health care system requires significant investment, both personal and financial, under conditions of great uncertainty. Not every physician, medical group or hospital board is willing to make the decisions and devote the energy to developing an integrated health care system.

While it is clear that achieving success in integrated health care is no easy matter, the goal appears to be worth it. The potential benefits outweigh the costs, especially the costs of doing nothing.

APPENDIX A.
INTEGRATION CHECKLIST

The purpose of this checklist is to estimate the extent of integration of a health care system. The relative weights of responses are shown in parentheses.

(1) **Are physicians in leadership positions within the organization?**

- ☐ One or two physicians on hospital or system board; physicians functioning in traditional manner (e. g., leading medical staff). (0)
- ☐ System has paid medical staff director (or VP for medical affairs); job is at least half time. (3)
- ☐ Significant physician representation on the system board. (6)
- ☐ Physicians hold key executive positions. (9)
- ☐ Physicians involved in management of HMO, contracting entities, and overall leadership of the organization. (12)

(2) **Do organizational structures facilitate common management and coordination?**

- ☐ Hospital, medical staff and health plan management and governance independent; no coordination. (0)
- ☐ Hospital management and some physician leaders meet regularly to coordinate activities. (1)
- ☐ Joint strategic planning by physicians and hospital. (3)
- ☐ Physicians and hospital coordinated through corporate structure (i.e. some form of PHO). (6)
- ☐ Physician-hospital organization and health plan coordinated through corporate structure. (9)
- ☐ Hospital, physicians and health plan all part of the same organizational structure. (12)

(3) To what extent are primary care physicians economically integrated?

☐ Primary care physicians on medical staff are independent practitioners. (0)

☐ Physicians belong to IPA for contracting purposes; system assists with access to managed care contracts or administrative support. (1)

☐ High proportion of primary care physicians are organized into physician organization or clinic without walls; no control over locations of practices. (2)

☐ High proportion of physicians belong to MSO which has financial support of hospital; some control over practice locations. (4)

☐ Physicians are economically integrated with health system; system controls practice locations and administrative support; may retain professional corporations. (6)

☐ All primary care physicians are part of single PC that contracts exclusively with system or are employees of the hospital or system. (8)

(4) To what extent do primary care offices provide geographic coverage of the service area?

☐ No influence over geographical distribution of primary care practices; poorly located. (0)

☐ No direct control over location of primary care practices, but the system has reasonable geographic coverage. (3)

☐ System has the ability to direct where primary care physicians practice. (7)

☐ System has excellent coverage of service area through a number of conveniently located primary care branches. (10)

(5) Are the hospital(s) and the number and type of specialists sized for the needs of the service area?

☐ Significant over-supply of hospital beds within the system. (0)

☐ Significant over-supply of most medical specialists within the system. (0)

☐ Plan exists for sizing the hospital and medical staff to match the needs of the area. (4)

☐ System has ability to maintain appropriate balance in hospital capacity and supply of specialists. (8)

(6) To what degree are physicians themselves integrated?

☐ Medical staff is fragmented with many solo practitioners and small groups. (0)

☐ Some members of medical staff have formed physician organization to negotiate with hospital and health plans. (2)

☐ Medical staff includes a few single-specialty groups and/or one or two large multispecialty groups. (4)

☐ Two or three primary care and multispecialty group practices provide 50 to 75 percent of referrals to hospital. (6)

☐ Single medical group accounts for at least 75 percent of hospital admissions. (8)

(7) Does the system own a financing mechanism, and/or have the ability to enter into single signature risk contacting?

☐ No ownership interest in an HMO; physicians and hospital contract independently. (0)

☐ Own interest in an HMO but it represents small portion of revenues; physicians and hospital contract independently. (2)

☐ No ownership interest in an HMO, but hospital and physicians organized for single signature risk contracting. (4)

☐ Own an HMO (small) and hospital and physicians organized for single signature risk contracting. (6)

☐ Owned HMO represents large proportion of system revenues (more than 30 percent) and positioned for single signature risk contracting. (8)

☐ Single HMO accounts for 100 percent of revenues of system. (10)

(8) Are the financial incentives aligned?

☐ Physicians and hospital focus on full or discounted fee-for-service patients; health plan incentives opposite of those of providers. (0)

☐ Payor mix includes both fee-for-service and capitation, but physicians and hospital are concentrating on maximizing earnings through generating more revenues. (3)

☐ Fee-for-service and capitation revenues roughly equal, but physicians and hospital have made commitment to operate as if in a capitated environment. (6)

☐ Majority of patients on capitated basis and physicians and hospitals operate to maximize earnings with capitation. (9)

☐ All patients on capitated basis. (12)

(9) Are real-time communications systems and a common data base for physicians and hospital available?

☐ No common communications systems or data base, either manual or computerized. (0)

☐ Have manual communications system (e.g., couriers) and a limited data base. (2)

☐ Hospital and physicians have their own computerized information systems, and are working to interconnect them. (4)

☐ Committed to the development of interconnected information system and common data base; in process of implementation. (6)

☐ Have interconnected information system and common data base for hospital, physicians and health plan(s). (8)

(10) Does the system have the ability to access capital and shift financial resources where they are needed?

☐ Capital resources are limited. (0)

☐ Capital available but no mechanisms exist for shifting financial resources within the system. (3)

☐ Capital available and MSO or other mechanism allows for some transfer of financial resources. (6)

☐ Significant capital available and medical foundation or other mechanism exists for transferring financial resources within the system. (9)

☐ Significant capital available; no constraints on transferring financial resources within the system. (12)

BIBLIOGRAPHY

Anders, George. "McDonald's Methods Come to Medicine as Chains Acquire Physicians' Practices" *The Wall Street Journal*. August 24, 1993, pp. B1, B4.

Arbitman, Deborah B. and King, Paul H., CPA. "Affiliated Practices Can Boost Patient Referrals" *Healthcare Financial Management*. August 1990, article reprint.

Becker, B. Frederick and McManis, Gerald L. "Market Memo: Mastering the Art of Hospital-Physician Collaboration" *Health Care Strategic Management*. December 1992, pp. 1, 15-21.

Benvenuto, John, MD, Stark, Michael J., DO and Radoccia, Richard. "From 12 Solo Practices to a Hospital-based LMSG in 100 Easy Steps" *MGM Journal*. July/August 1991, pp. 84-91.

Bohlmann, Robert, FACMGA, Reich, Janet, Korenchuk, Keith M., JD, MPH, Rowland, Robert, McCarthy, Gerald J., MD, Barnett, Albert E., MD, Floyd, Morris L., Holz-Bergmann, Betty, Goldberg, David M., Caillouet, Phil, PhD, Hulse, Chuck, FACMGA, Keckley, Paul H., PhD, Schryver, Darrell, L., DPA. *Integration Issues in Physician-Hospital Affiliations*. Englewood, CO: Medical Group Management Association, 1993.

Borzo, Greg. "Market Memo: Closer Ties With Physicians Skirt Safe Harbors Fears" *Health Care Strategic Management*. November 1992, pp. 1, 19-22.

Breisch, Sandra and Johnsson, Julie. "Hospitals are Gobbling Up Practices, Should You Sell?" *American Medical News*. September 27, 1993, pp. 15, 17.

Burda, David. "For Insurer's Sake, Mullikin Stops Short of Full Integration" *Modern Healthcare*. October 19, 1992, p. 42.

Carpenter, Russell B. and Peters, Gerald R. "Joint Ventures in the Next Decade: Four Approaches" *Healthcare Forum Journal*. January/February 1990, pp. 43-46.

Carpenter, Russell B. "Collaboration 301" Sisters of Providence Leadership Retreat. San Diego, CA, April 1, 1992.

Caulfield, Walter, H., MD. Letter to Ira Magaziner, Senior Policy Advisor, regarding Kaiser Foundation Hospital Inpatient Utilization Statistics. April 16, 1993.

Cerne, Frank. "Balancing Complex Choices" *Hospitals & Health Networks.* June 20, 1993, pp. 28-30.

Charns, Martin P. and Smith Tewksbury, Laura J. *Collaborating Management in Health Care: Implementing the Integrative Organization.* San Francisco: Jossey-Bass, Inc., Publishers, 1993.

Clarke, Richard L., FHFMA. "AMA's Todd Pushes for Reform -- Cautiously" *Healthcare Financial Management.* May 1993, pp. 20, 23-24.

Clarke, Richard L., FHFMA. "Viewpoint" *Healthcare Financial Management.* May 1993, p. 12.

Cleaveland, Clifton R., MD, FACP. "Gloom in the Trenches" *Health Management Quarterly.* First Quarter 1993, pp. 12-16.

Clements, Bill. "Foundation Model: Best for Both Worlds" *AMA News.* April 12, 1993, pp. 6-8.

Coddington, Dean C. and Moore, Keith D. *Market-Driven Strategies in Health Care.* San Francisco, CA: Jossey-Bass Inc., Publishers, 1987.

Coddington, Dean C., Keen, David J., Moore, Keith D. and Clarke, Richard L. *The Crisis in Health Care: Costs, Choices and Strategies.* San Francisco, CA: Jossey-Bass Inc., Publishers, 1990.

Coile, Russell, C., Jr. "Merger Model, Quaternary Care and Practice Assessment" *Healthcare Forum Journal.* January/February 1992, pp. 65-66.

Copeland, William M., FACHE. "Recruiting Physicians: Avoiding the Legal Minefield" *Hospital and Health Services Administration.* Summer 1992, pp. 269-282.

Davidson, Richard J. "Letter to the Editor, Health Care for the Future" *Harvard Business Review*. March-April 1993, pp. 139-142.

de Lafuente, Dela. "Doctors' Orders: Integrate" *Modern Healthcare*. May 3, 1993, pp. 25-26, 31-32.

Eckholm, Erik. "Doctors Say They Can Save Lives and Still Save Money" *The New York Times*. March 18, 1993.

Enthoven, Alain C. "The History and Principles of Managed Competition" *Health Affairs*. Supplement 1993, pp. 24-48.

Findlay, Steven. "Networks of Care May Serve as a Model for Health Reform" *Business & Health*. February 1993, pp. 27-31.

Fine, Allan. "Building Physician-Hospital Integration for Managed Care" Quorum Executive Forum on Physician and Hospital Integration. Keystone Resort, CO, June 28-29, 1993.

Flower, Joe. "Getting Paid to Keep People Healthy" *Healthcare Forum Journal*. March/April 1993, pp. 51-53.

Forster, Robert J., MD. "Putting Together a 'Group Practice Without Walls'" *The Internist*. October, 1988, pp. 12-15.

Gaucher, Ellen J. and Coffey, Richard J. *Total Quality in Healthcare: From Theory to Practice*. San Francisco, CA: Jossey-Bass, Inc., Publishers, 1993.

Goldfarb, Bruce. "Corporate Healthcare Mergers" *Medical World News*. February 1993, pp. 26-28, 31-32, 34.

Goldsmith, Jeff. "Driving the Nitroglycerin Truck" *Healthcare Forum Journal*. March/April 1993, pp. 36-38, 40, 44.

Goldsmith, Jeff. "Hospital/Physician Relationships: A Constraint to Health Reform" *Health Affairs*. Fall 1993, pp. 160-169.

Gordon, George G. and DiTomaso, Nancy. "Predicting Corporate Performance From Organizational Culture" *Journal of Management Studies*. November 1992, pp. 783-795.

Grant, Peter N., JD, PhD, Hanlon III, William B. and Margulis, Marc, CFA, ASA. "National Office of the Internal Revenue Service Approves Tax-Exemption for Medical Group Practices in Integrated Delivery System Context: The IRS Issues a Tax Exemption to the Friendly Hills HealthCare Foundation" *Tax Exemption for Physician Organizations.* February 10, 1993.

Grant, Peter N., JD, PhD. "Dramatic Developments in IPA, Medical Group Practice, and HMO-Hospital-Medical Group Relations in California" *California Physician.* September 1991, pp. 32-38.

Grant, Peter N., JD, PhD. "Looking Before You Leap -- Alternative Models for Integrated Delivery Systems" The First Annual Symposium on Integrated Healthcare: A Summit Meeting for Innovators. Aspen, CO, March 29-30, 1993.

Greene, Jay. "Systems Scurry to Find 'Partners' for Networks" *Modern Healthcare.* June 28, 1993, pp. 58, 62.

Harris, Charles, PhD, Hicks, Lanis L., PhD and Kelly, Bruce J., CMC. "Physician-hospital Networking: Avoiding a Shotgun Wedding" *Health Care Management Review.* Fall 1992, pp. 17-27.

HealthPartners. *News Release: Questions and Answers.* March, 1993.

Holoweiko, Mark. "How Megaclinics are Building Competitive Clout" *Medical Economics.* April 20, 1992, pp. 98, 100-101, 104, 107, 111-112, 114-115.

Hudson, Terese. "Flexibility and Teamwork are Keys to Success in Worcester System" *Hospitals & Health Networks.* June 5, 1993, pp. 29, 32.

Hudson, Terese. "The Race to Integrate: Who Will be the Leaders?" *Hospitals & Health Networks.* June 5, 1993, pp. 25-27.

Hudson, Terese. "Three Major Models" *Hospitals & Health Networks.* June 20, 1993, pp. 31-34.

James, Cal. "Critical Success Factors for MSOs" Quorum Executive Forum on Physician and Hospital Integration. Keystone Resort, CO, June 29, 1993.

Jamplis, Robert, MD. "Palo Alto Medical Foundation: The Sutter Connection" The First Annual Symposium on Integrated Healthcare: A Summit Meeting for Innovators. Aspen, CO, March 29, 1993.

Johnson, Donald E.L. "Scott & White Measures 'Quality of Health' in Outcomes Studies" *Health Care Strategic Management.* March 1993, pp. 7-9.

Johnsson, Julie. "Hospitals Binge on Practice Buy-outs" *American Medical News.* September 13, 1993, pp. 1,7.

Kaiser Permanente. *Environment for Innovation: 1992 Annual Report.* Oakland, CA: Kaiser Permanente, 1993.

Kaiser Permanente. *Lessons From the Permanente Medical Groups: Examples of Cost-Effectiveness in a Prepaid Group Practice Model.* Oakland, CA: Kaiser Permanente, 1993.

Kenkel, Paul J. "Filling up Beds No Longer the Name of the System Game" *Modern Healthcare.* September 13, 1993, pp. 39-41, 44, 46, 48.

Korenchuk, Keith, JD, MPH. "Direct Contracting: The Future of Health Care?" *MGM Journal.* March/April 1993, pp. 15-20.

Korenchuk, Keith, JD, MPH. *Transforming the Delivery of Health Care: Mergers, Acquisitions and Physician-Hospital Organizations.* Englewood, CO: Medical Group Management Association, 1992.

Koska, Mary T. "Hospitals and Medical Staffs: The Concept of Planning Takes on New Meaning" *Hospitals.* October 20, 1992, pp. 22-24, 26-28, 30.

Lewin-VHI, Inc.: Atlas, Robert, Kennell, David, Sockel, David and Lewin, Lawrence. *Managed Care: Does It Work?* Lewin-VHI, Inc. January 27, 1993.

Ludden, John M., MD. "Doctors as Employees" *Health Management Quarterly.* First Quarter 1993, pp. 7-11.

MacKelvie, Charles F. "Fraud, Abuse, and Inurement" *Topics in Health Care Financing.* Spring, 1990, pp. 49-57.

Mandell, William J., DO, JD. "Sometimes We're Our Own Worst Enemies" *Physician EXECUTIVE*. September-October 1992, pp. 45-48.

Mason, Scott. "Physician Linkages Through Integrated Decision Making" The Future of Integrated Healthcare Systems Conference. Reston, VA, November 4, 1992.

McKell, Douglas C. "Management Service Organizations Can Provide Transition for Integration" *Report on Physician Trends*. March 1993, pp. 7-8.

McManis, Gerald L. and Stewart, Jerrie A. "Hospital-Physician Alliances: Building an Integrated Medical Delivery System" *Healthcare Executive*. March/April 1992, pp. 18-21.

McManis, Gerald L. and Stewart, Jerrie A. "The Integrator of Care: A Coordinated Health Care System" *Health Care Strategic Management*. February 1993, pp. 1, 17-19.

Meyer, Paul G. and Tucker, Stephen L., FACHE. "Incorporating an Understanding of Independent Practice Physician Culture into Hospital Structure and Operations" *Hospital and Health Services Administration*. Winter 1992, pp. 465-476.

Montague, Jim. "Straight Talk" *Hospitals & Health Networks*. July 5, 1993, pp. 22-27.

Nemes, Judith. "Hospital-owned Practices Acquire Borrowing Power" *Modern Healthcare*. March 2, 1992, p. 50.

O'Connor, J. Paul. "A Multispecialty Group Practice Response" *MGM Journal*. March/April 1993, pp. 38-42, 78.

O'Connor, J. Paul. "Outcomes Measurement: Employer Expectations, Implementation and Potentials" 11th Annual CRAHCA Conference, The Future of Medical Group Practice: Strategies and Alliances for Surviving Change. Denver, CO, March 4-5, 1993.

Ottensmeyer, David J., MD. "Governance of the Integrated Health Care System: A New Governance Issue for Group Practice" *Group Practice Journal*. January/February 1993, pp. 12-16.

Ottensmeyer, David J., MD. "Integration, The Next Strategy" The First Annual Symposium on Integrated Healthcare: A Summit Meeting for Innovators. Aspen, CO, March 29-30, 1993.

Pallarito, Karen. "Rochester Health Plan Studied as a Model for National Reform" *Modern Healthcare.* May 4, 1992, pp. 28-29.

Pasternak, Derick P., MD. "Integrated Healthcare Systems Evolution of Governance and Management" Quorum Executive Forum on Physician and Hospital Integration. Keystone Resort, CO, June 29, 1993.

Peters, Gerald R., JD. "Fixing the Quick Fixes to Physician Relations" *Healthcare Financial Management.* November 1991, article reprint.

Peters, Gerald R., JD. "Integrated Delivery Can Ally Physicians and Hospitals Plans" *Healthcare Financial Management.* December 1991, pp. 20-22, 24, 26, 28, 30, 32.

Philbin, Patrick W. "Transition to a New Future" *Hospitals.* March 5, 1993, pp. 20-23.

Premier Hospitals Alliance, Inc. "Hospital's Most Wanted: The Primary Care Physician" *Premier Exchange.* Westchester, IL: Premier Hospitals Alliance, Inc., May 1993, p. 5.

Premier Hospitals Alliance, Inc. *Premier Exchange.* Westchester, IL: Premier Hospitals Alliance, Inc., May 1993.

Quorum Executive Forum on Physician and Hospital Integration. Keystone Resort, CO, June 28-29, 1993.

Reich, Janet, RN, MSHSA. *Hospital/Physician Organizations: Models for Consideration.* Reich Consulting: Flagstaff, AZ. February 1992.

Reich, Janet, RN, MSHSA. "Recognizing and Overcoming Barriers: Physician/Hospital Relationship Building" *MGM Journal.* July/August 1991, pp. 69, 71-72.

Reinertsen, James L., MD. "Transforming a Group Practice: A Progress Report on Application of Continuous Quality Improvement" *Group Practice Journal.* January/February 1991, pp. 9-10, 12-14.

Reinhardt, Uwe E. "Reorganizing the Financial Flows in U.S. Health Care" *Health Affairs.* Supplement 1993, pp. 172-193.

Report on Physician Trends. March 1993.

Ruffins, Marshall, MD. "Medical Informatics" *Healthcare Forum Journal.* March/April 1993, pp. 47-50.

Saalwaechter, John J., MD, MBA, FACPE. "MSO -- The New Kid on the Block?" *Physician EXECUTIVE.* July-August 1992, pp. 50-51.

"Sharp Healthcare: Six Years After the Foundation" *Integrated Healthcare Report.* August 1992, pp. 8-9.

Shortell, Stephen M., Anderson, David A., Gillies, Robin R., Mitchell, John B. and Morgan, Karen L. "The Holographic Organization" *Healthcare Forum Journal.* March/April 1993, pp. 20-26.

Shortell, Stephen, M. "Developing Effective Culture Vital to Hospital Strategy" *Modern Healthcare.* July 30, 1990, p. 38.

Slomski, Anita J. "Practice Sales to Hospitals: Who Gets the Best Deal?" *Medical Economics.* February 22, 1993, pp. 136-140, 143-144, 146.

Smith, Jennifer, L. "Hospital IS Integration and Health Reform" *Health Systems Review.* July/August 1993, pp. 36-38.

Sollins, Howard L. "Purchasing Physician Practices: Legal and Regulatory Concerns" *Healthcare Financial Management.* January 1988, pp. 56-64.

Sommers, Paul A., PhD. "A Natural Partnership, Physician and Hospital: The Ramsey Clinic Model" *Group Practice Journal.* March/April 1989, pp. 34-39, 42, 46, 48-50, 52-53.

Sommers, Paul A., PhD. "Longitudinal Analyses of a Physician-Hospital Collaboration That Works: The Ramsey Model" Submitted to the *Journal of the American Medical Association* for Publication Consideration, March 25, 1993.

Starr, Paul and Welman, Walter A. "Bridge to Compromise: Competition under a Budget" *Health Affairs.* Supplement 1993, pp. 7-23.

Stromberg, Ross E., Esq. "Regulatory Issues: Catching Up With The Innovators" The First Annual Symposium on Integrated Healthcare: A Summit Meeting for Innovators. Aspen, CO, March 29, 1993.

"The Fallon Foundation" *Integrated Healthcare Report.* November 1992, pp. 13-14.

The Future of Integrated Healthcare Systems Conference. Reston, VA, November 4-5, 1992.

The Governance Committee. *The Grand Alliance: Vertical Integration Strategies for Physicians and Health Systems.* Washington, DC: The Advisory Board Company., 1993.

Truitt, Leigh, MD. *The Fourth Generation: A New Way of Contracting for Health Care Services.* Denver, CO: Colorado MSO, Inc., 1993.

Unland, James. "Group Practices and Hospital Affiliation of Medical Practices" *Health Care Strategic Management.* March 1993, pp. 15-19.

"Virginia Mason Clinic: A Veteran of Integrated Healthcare" *Integrated Healthcare Report.* November 1992, pp. 12-13.

Waterman, Robert H., Jr. *The Renewal Factor: How the Best Get and Keep the Competitive Edge.* New York City, NY: Bantam Books, 1987.

Woolhandler, Steffie, MD, MPH and Himmelstein, David U., MD. "The Deteriorating Administrative Efficiency of the U.S. Health Care System" *The New England Journal of Medicine.* May 2, 1991, pp. 1253-1258.

Woolhandler, Steffie, MD, MPH, Himmelstein, David U., MD and Lewontin, James P. "Administrative Costs in U.S. Hospitals" *The New England Journal of Medicine.* August 5, 1993, pp. 400-403.

INDEX

C

H

Harriman Jones Medical Group, 35, 66, 130, 166, 199, 215
Hays, Patrick, 56, 90, 157
Health care reform, 15, 19, 61, 159, 199, 223-224
Health care system, 2, 5
Health maintenance organizations (HMOs), 11, 17-18, 35-36, 42-43, 61, 63-64, 71, 87-101, 147, 154-156, 165
    —   see also health plans, independent practice associations and specific HMOs by name
HealthPartners, 143
Health plans, 18, 31, 35, 61, 87-101, 151-152, 154-156, 160, 168-169
    — Benefits, 93-96
    — Controlling utilization, 91, 97, 100, 155-156
    — Enrollment trends, 89
    — Ownership of, 88-96, 154
    — Profitability, 92-96
    — Source of funding, 84, 173
    — Start up costs, 73, 80-81, 93, 154
    — Success of, 92
    — Which health plan to affiliate with, 172-174
        see also health maintenance organizations and independent practice associations
Health Plus, 35, 91-92, 218-219
Healthcare Financial Management, 74
Healthcare Financial Management Association, 15
Heydt, Stuart, MD, 106, 126-127
HMOs see health maintenance organizations
Horizontal integration, 1
Hospital administrators, 117, 149-150, 160, 207
    — Leadership characteristics, 121-122
    — Role of, 117, 151
Hospitals, 150-154, 166, 168-169, 213-214
    — Capacity, 8, 12
    — Checklist on partners, 174
    — Source of capital/financial strength, 83-84, 149, 151, 168-169
    — Utilization; indicators of volume, 153, 217-218
    — Which hospital to affiliate with, 172-174
Hub and spoke system, 64, 97
Humana, 90

I

Incentives, alignment of, 12
Income distribution see physician incomes
Income guarantees see under physician incomes
Independent practice association (IPA), 2, 5, 9, 38, 68-69, 72, 81, 88, 91, 94, 99-101, 151, 155, 166
Information systems, 13, 25, 34, 46, 94, 117, 132-139, 147, 151-152, 172, 225
    — Clinical and financial information, 133-139
    — Cost, 73, 80, 134, 136
    — Functions, 133-139

W